global

pre-intermediate teacher's book

Frances Watkins & Lindsay Clandfield

This book was used to create scripts for YouTube channel:

Adi Sensei

Macmillan Education
Between Towns Road, Oxford OX4 3PP
A division of Macmillan Publishers Limited
Companies and representatives throughout the world

ISBN 9780230033146

First published 2010

Designed by eMC Design Limited
Cover design by Barbara Mercer

These materials may contain links to third party websites. We have no
control over, and are not responsible for, the contents of such third party
websites. Please use care when accessing them.

Teacher's Resource CD
The authors and publishers would like to thank the following for
permission to reproduce their photographic material:

iStock/LuisPortugal; iStock/Kkgas; iStock/gibson ff; iStock/fpm;
iStock/Pertunisas; iStock/idrutu; iStock/Cloki; iStock/tacojim.

Printed and bound in Hong Kong

2014 2013 2012 2011 2010
10 9 8 7 6 5 4 3 2 1

Contents

Coursebook contents map

EV - Extend your vocabulary   P - Pronunciation

Course overview

Components for the learner

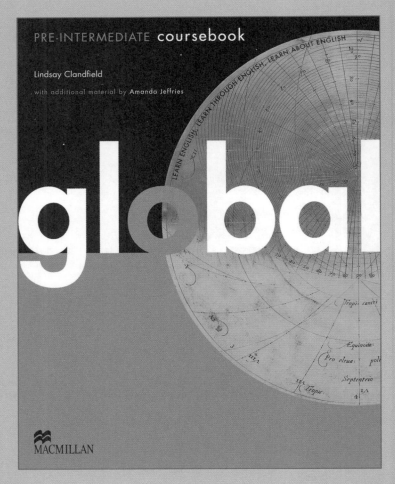

Coursebook
see pages viii-xiii

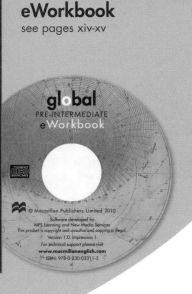

eWorkbook
see pages xiv-xv

Components for the teacher

Teacher's book &
Teacher's Resource CD
see page xvi

Class Audio CDs
see page xvii

Global Website
see page xvii

Global Digital
See pages xviii-xix

Coursebook: lessons 1 and 2 of a unit

Unit structure

Each unit is divided in six two-page lessons. The first four lessons are the core part of the unit. The last two lessons include additional material (e.g. Study skills, Review). In this unit, the first two lessons are about Art, the next two spreads are about Music.

Headings

Clear headings throughout the book show what you are teaching at each stage of the lesson.

Unit 3 Art & Music

Part 1

Vocabulary & Speaking
Works of art

Reading
Discovered!

Speaking
Art

Vocabulary and Speaking

1 Match the words to the pictures a–h.

cave art	old manuscript	painting
photograph	sculpture	self-portrait
sketch	statue	

2 Work in pairs and describe the pictures. Use the words in exercise 1 and the useful phrases to help you.

Useful phrases

* This picture shows …
* I think this is a picture of …
* It looks as if + clause …
* This is from + time / place …
* I (really) like / don't like this picture …

Reading

1 🔊 1.33 Read and listen to *Discovered!* on page 31 and match each text to a picture. There are four pictures that you do not need.

2 Read the texts again and complete the sentences with one or more words.

1 The *Venus de Milo* is a statue of _____.
2 The *Venus de Milo* is now in _____.
3 Some Mexican workers discovered a sculpture while they were installing _____.
4 The sculpture is now in _____.
5 The couple from Milwaukee thought their Van Gogh painting was _____.
6 *Vase with Flowers* sold for _____.
7 The man found the Declaration of Independence while he was shopping at _____.
8 The manuscript was inside a _____.

Extend your vocabulary – *discover*

Words in the same family:
discover – verb
discovery – noun
discovered – adjective
undiscovered – adjective

Complete the sentences with the correct form of *discover*.
1 The archaeologists made an important _____ near the town castle.
2 We only want to _____ the truth.
3 News flash: Picasso sketches _____ in church basement.
4 The painting was _____ until the dealer noticed it on the wall.

Speaking

Work in pairs and choose **one** of the tasks below.

A Tell your partner about an object that is important in your family. Use these questions to help you prepare.
* What is the object?
* How old is it?
* Where did it come from?
* Why is it important to you?

B Ask each other these questions.
* Do you like art?
  What kind of art do you like?
* Do you have any art in your house?
  What is it? Who is it by?
* Have you ever been to an art gallery?
  Which one?

Discovered!
True stories of how valuable works of art were found in unexpected places

In a field
In 1820 a Greek peasant named Yorgos was working in his field on the island of Milos when he found several blocks of stone. Under the stones were four statues: three figures of the God Hermes and one of Aphrodite, the goddess of love. Three weeks later a group of French archaeologists arrived by ship. They bought the Aphrodite and took it to France. The king, Louis XVIII, called it *Venus de Milo* and gave it to the Louvre. It is now one of the most famous works of art in the world.

Under a street
On February 21, 1978, workers were putting down electrical cables on a busy street corner in Mexico City when they discovered a huge sculpture of the Aztec moon goddess Coyolxauhqui. It was more than four hundred years old and is now in the Museum of the Great Temple in Mexico.

On a wall
A man and his wife from Milwaukee, US, asked an art dealer to look at a painting they had in their home. While he was walking through the house, the dealer saw a different painting. The couple thought this was a reproduction of a Vincent Van Gogh, but it was in fact the original. On March 10, 1991, the painting *Vase with Flowers* sold for $1.4 million.

At a market
A man from Philadelphia was shopping at a flea market when he saw a wooden picture frame he liked. He paid $4 for it. When he got home he took the old picture out of the frame and found an old document behind it. It was a copy from 1776 of the American Declaration of Independence. The copy sold for $2.4 million in New York in 1991.

Glossary
archaeologist (noun) – a person who studies ancient societies
dealer (noun) – a person who sells a particular product
flea market (noun) – a market where old things are sold at low prices
peasant (noun) – a poor person who works on another person's farm
reproduction (noun) – a copy of something

Art Unit 3 — 31

Contents sidebar

Content is summarised on every spread so you can see at a glance what the lesson is about.

Balance of skills

Each lesson has a balance of skills work and language work.

Texts and Topics

Topics and texts are chosen to appeal to the learners' intellectual curiosity. Texts are authentic, with information about the real world. Attractive and stylish design makes the text more attractive and motivating to read.

Grammar explanations

Short grammar explanations are provided on the page, with a **cross reference** to further explanation and **practice** at the back of the book.

Texts

Texts are either **information rich** or excerpts from **literary texts**, modern and classic, with background information about the book and the author provided to give students **extra cultural information**. All the literary texts are also on the class audio, so students can read and listen to them.

Grammar practice

Grammar practice is **highly contextualised** and **meaningful**, often in texts that provide **additional information** about the topic of the lesson. Many grammar practice exercises are designed in a similar way to the reading texts.

Short writing tasks

Some lessons end with a short writing task to give students the opportunity to **develop fluency** in writing as well as speaking.

UNIT 3 **Art & Music**

Part 2

Speaking
Retelling stories

Grammar
Past simple & past continuous

Vocabulary
Furniture & furnishings

Reading
The Picture of Dorian Gray

Pronunciation
Past simple regular verbs

Writing
A scene from a short story

Speaking

1 Work in pairs. Tell each other what you remember about the works of art from page 31. Use the phrases below to help you.

A Greek peasant was working in his field when …

In 1978 a group of Mexican workers were putting down electrical cables when …

One day an art dealer went to visit a man and his wife in Milwaukee. While he was walking through the house …

A man from Philadelphia was shopping at a flea market when …

2 Check your answers in the texts.

Grammar

1 Write the past simple form of the verbs in the box. All the verbs are in the text on page 31.

arrive   ask   buy   discover   find
get   pay   see   sell   take

2 Put the verbs into two groups, regular and irregular verbs.

*Three weeks later a group of French archaeologists **arrived** by ship.*
*Yorgos **was working** in his field.*
*While he **was walking** through the house, the dealer **saw** a different painting.*

- use the past simple to talk about completed actions in the past
- use the past continuous to talk about an action in progress in the past
- the past continuous is common with a simple past action when one action interrupts the other

G Grammar focus – explanation & more practice of past tenses on page 136

Vocabulary

1 Which of these things can you see in the picture on page 33?

armchair   carpet   coffee table
curtains   lamp   mirror   shelf
sofa   wall   window

2 Which things do you have in your house? Where are they?

3 Complete the texts with the past simple or past continuous form of the verbs in brackets.

In a hole in the ground

In 1978 workers _____ (dig) behind an old casino in Dawson City, Yukon when they _____ (discover) more than 500 films from 1903 to 1929. The films _____ (be) in perfect condition because of the cold temperatures.

In an attic

In 1990 Barbara Testa, a librarian, _____ (find) 665 pages of an old book while she _____ (look) through a trunk in her attic. The book _____ (be) the original manuscript of the great American novel *Huckleberry Finn* by Mark Twain.

As a bicycle rack

Every day employees of the God's House Tower Museum in Southampton, UK _____ (put) their bicycles against a black rock in the basement. In 2000 two Egyptologists _____ (visit) the museum. They _____ (examine) other items when they _____ (see) the black rock. They _____ (identify) it as a 2,700-year old statue of the Egyptian King Taharqa.

Reading

1 🔊 1.34 Read and listen to an extract from the book *The Picture of Dorian Gray*. What was happening?

2 Work in pairs. Choose two of these questions and then discuss them.

- Have you read this book? Would you like to?
- Dorian makes a wish by saying: 'I wish that I could always be young. I wish that picture could grow old instead of me.' Would you make the same wish as Dorian? Why?
- Do you think people are too concerned with being young in today's society?
- 'Your personality is written on your face.' What does this quote mean? Do you agree with it?

Pronunciation

1 🔊 1.35 Listen to some sentences from the text. Tick (✔) the verbs that have an extra syllable in the past tense.

1 decide – decided _____
2 walk – walked _____
3 stop – stopped _____
4 look – looked _____
5 open – opened _____
6 remember – remembered _____

2 Practise saying the verbs and the past tense forms.

3 How do you pronounce the past tense of these verbs?

asked   discovered   hated   finished
listened   loved   needed   started
wanted   worked

The Picture of Dorian Gray

Dorian decided to go to bed and went slowly towards his bedroom. He walked along the hall and through the library. Basil's portrait of Dorian was on a wall in the library. Suddenly Dorian stopped and looked at the portrait. He was surprised. The painting looked different. The face in the painting had changed. Yes, it had changed! Quickly, Dorian opened the curtains. Sunlight came into the room. Dorian looked closely at the picture and saw that the face was different. It looked unkind and cruel. A huge mirror hung on another wall. Dorian looked in the mirror at his own face. He saw a beautiful young man. He had not changed. What was happening to the picture?

Suddenly Dorian remembered the day that Basil finished the picture. Dorian remembered his wish. He remembered his own words.

'I wish that I could always be young. I wish that picture could grow old instead of me. I would give anything and everything for this to happen. I would give my soul!'

Why did the face in the picture look cruel and unkind? Was his wish coming true? Was the picture changing?

The Picture of Dorian Gray (1890) is one of Oscar Wilde's most famous novels. The main themes are the purpose of art and the obsession with youth and beauty.

Glossary

cruel (adjective) – causing pain to people
huge (adjective) – extremely large
soul (noun) – the spiritual part of a person
wit (noun) – the ability to use words in a clever way that makes people laugh

Writing

1 Read the opening sentences from four short stories.

Mark was sitting in the most comfortable armchair when he heard the strange noise again.

I was happy when I received the sculpture, but I didn't know its secret.

As she was looking at the photograph, she was certain she saw the eyes move.

It was the most beautiful painting, and the most dangerous.

2 Choose one of the sentences and continue the story. Write two or three more sentences.

3 Work in pairs. Swap your stories and add another sentence to your partner's story. Then return the story to your partner.

Oscar Wilde (1854–1900)

Oscar Wilde was an Irish writer of plays, poetry and novels. He was famous for his wit and commentary on the society of Victorian London.

Coursebook: lessons 3 and 4 of a unit

Speaking

A wide variety of speaking tasks are presented in the book. Support is given in the form of vocabulary (useful language) and constructions (useful phrases).

Many speaking tasks include an element of choice (students can choose from different tasks or questions). This gives the teacher and students flexibility and can be used in mixed ability classes.

Vocabulary

Vocabulary is presented in a meaningful context with clear visual support and opportunities for students to begin using the language right away.

UNIT 3 Art & Music

Part 3

Speaking
Describing pictures

Vocabulary
Audio & video

Listening & Writing
The history of sound recording

Grammar
Used to

Pronunciation
Used to

Speaking

1 Look at pictures a and b. Make some notes on the differences between them. Use the useful language and phrases to help you.

Useful language
- classical music
- conductor
- guitarist
- play
- concert hall
- drummer
- orchestra
- rock group

Useful phrases
- This looks like …
- The picture on the right / left shows …
- Maybe / perhaps it's in …

2 Work in pairs and describe the differences between the pictures.

3 Work in pairs and ask each other these questions.
- What kind of music do you like?
- Where do you usually listen to music? At home, at work, on the bus etc?
- Do you listen to music while you are working or studying? What kind of music?

Vocabulary

1 Rearrange the letters to make the correct words.

yapl   wirend   staf wadfror

pots   saupe   cejet

2 1.36 Listen and check your answers. Then repeat the words.

3 Match the words to the pictures on page 35.
audio cassette ___
CD ___
DVD player ___
headphones ___
MP3 player ___
record ___
record player ___
video cassette ___
Do you have any of these things at home?

4 1.37 Complete the instructions with the words in the box. Then listen and check your answers.

button   down   off   on   plug   up   watch

Right, to use this DVD player, first you ___ it in here. To turn it ___, just press this ___. Now press eject and put the disc in the tray. Close the tray and press play to ___ the film. To turn ___ the volume, use this button. If it's too loud, turn ___ the volume with this button. And, to turn it ___, press here.

5 Work in pairs. Make a similar set of instructions for a CD or MP3 player.

Listening and Writing

1 You are going to hear a lecture about the history of sound recording. Before you listen, list the words from vocabulary exercise 3 in order from oldest to newest.

2 1.38 Listen to the lecture and check your answers.

3 Listen again and complete the notes.

History of sound recording

The first: Thomas Edison in ___.
Edison predicts sound recordings for office dictation, speaking ___, education, talking ___ and music.
1900s: people play ___ on ___ players.
1920s: first films with sound – called ___
___; Philips introduces audio cassette.
1963: first ___ opens in Los Angeles.
1970s–1980s: VHS video, cassette walkman and ___ – ends era of the record.
Early 1990s: DVD
1990s: first digital music player sold in ___.
2001: Apple iPod, a popular ___, appears.
Current music devices can store ___ songs, video and ___.

Extend your vocabulary – saying and writing decades

In English we can use the phrase *the nineties* to describe the years from 1990 to 1999.
I was at university in the nineties.
In informal writing we can write *the 90s*.
The years 2000 to 2010 are sometimes called *the noughties*.
Complete the sentences with the correct decades.
1 I don't like music from ___ (1980–1989).
2 I was born in ___ (1960–1969).
3 I was at school in ___ (1970–1989).

Grammar

People used to listen to music on vinyl discs.
Vinyl records used to be popular.
They didn't use to have CDs.

- use *used to* to talk about regular actions in the past which don't happen now
- use *used to* to talk about situations in the past which aren't true now
- the negative of *used to* is *didn't use to*

1 Look at the picture below and rewrite the sentences with *used to*.
In those days families were bigger.
In those days families used to be bigger.
1 Most women were housewives.
2 People didn't have lots of things.
3 Most families didn't have a television.
4 Some families had a radio in the living room.

2 Make questions with *did* and *use to*. Add two more questions.
1 What music ___ you ___ listen to?
2 Where ___ you ___ go to school?
3 ___ you ___ have long hair?

3 Work in pairs and ask each other the questions.

G Grammar focus – explanation & more practice of *used to* on page 136

Pronunciation

1 1.39 Listen and repeat these sentences. Pay attention to the stressed words.
My brother used to play the guitar.
I didn't use to listen to classical music.
In connected speech, *used to* is pronounced /ˈjuːstə/.

2 Underline the stressed words in grammar exercise 1.

3 1.40 Listen and check your answers. Then repeat the sentences.

Unit 3 Music   Music Unit 3

Extend your vocabulary

Regular *Extend your vocabulary* boxes draw on language in the unit and help students gain a deeper word knowledge. Word families, easily confused words and different ways of expressing concepts are covered in these sections throughout the book.

Pronunciation

A focus on sounds, stress and intonation are included at regular intervals in *Global*. Pronunciation is integrated into the language points of the lesson. The aim is for students to achieve international intelligibility.

Listening

Every lesson has a reading or listening text. Listening texts are supported by different tasks for gist and specific listening. The listening texts in *Global* include a variety of genres, including lectures and presentations as well as interviews and dialogues.

Developing critical thinking

Reading tasks and discussion questions for texts encourage reflection and critical thinking.

Literary texts

Short extracts from modern literature are also included, as secondary texts, with information about the author and the book.

UNIT 3

Art & Music

Part 4

Vocabulary
Feelings

Listening
Music in film & TV

Speaking & Reading
High Fidelity

Vocabulary

1 Match the words in bold to the words in the box with similar meanings.

I was feeling **cheerful** today because …
… makes me feel very **calm**.
Last week I was **miserable** because …
I'm **frightened** of …
… makes me **sleepy**.
I'm always **anxious** when …

| angry | bored | excited | happy |
| relaxed | sad | scared | tense | tired |

2 Complete the sentences in exercise 1 so they are true for you.

3 🔊 1.41 Listen to four short pieces of music. How do they make you feel?

4 Imagine one of the short pieces of music is part of a scene from a film. Listen again and answer the questions.
- Where is the scene?
- Who is in the scene?
- How do they feel?
- What is happening?

5 Work in pairs and tell each other about the scene you imagined.

Listening

1 🔊 1.42 Listen to the composer Andy Price talking about how he uses music in films and TV programmes. Tick (✔) the feelings he mentions.

| angry | calm | excited | happy |
| sad | safe | scared | tense |

2 Listen again and choose the correct answers.

Music used to be / has always been an important part of film and television.

If you want an audience to feel scared / angry then use violins, played very quickly and on a high note.

Gentle music on a guitar, piano or violin is good for love scenes / death scenes.

Choral music (people singing) can make an audience feel tense / sad.

When the character of Robin Hood appears in the programme you can hear trumpets / guitars.

The orchestra used to play / usually plays in front of a large screen showing the film.

3 Work in pairs and compare your answers.

Andy Price is a composer for theatre, film, television and advertisements. His work includes the music to the BBC programmes *Robin Hood*, *Score* and *The Six Wives of Henry VIII*. He has won many awards for his work.

Extend your vocabulary – Using *just*

You can use *just* in spoken English in different ways.
For emphasis:
Just turn it off!
To mean only:
It just makes me bored.
To mean exactly:
He is just like his father.
Put *just* into the following sentences. What does *just* mean in each one?
1 Be quiet, please.
2 It was a mistake.
3 Thank you for the CD, it's what I wanted.

Speaking and Reading

1 Work in pairs. Write down the names of all the pop groups you can think of in one minute.

2 Work with another pair and compare your lists. Then answer these questions.
- Is pop music popular in your country?
- Who listens to pop music?
- Do you like pop music?

3 🔊 1.43 Read and listen to the extract from Nick Hornby's *High Fidelity*. How does pop music make the writer feel?

4 Work in pairs and discuss these questions.
- Do you think the author is being serious or funny?
- The writer thinks British people are very scared of violence in videos. Do people in your country worry about this? Do you think it is a problem?

Glossary:
melancholy (noun) – a feeling of being very sad and having no hope
miserable (adjective) – extremely unhappy

High Fidelity

What came first, the music or the misery? Did I listen to music because I was miserable? Or was I miserable because I listened to music? Do all those records turn you into a melancholy person?

People worry about kids playing with guns, and teenagers watching violent videos; we are scared that some sort of culture of violence will take them over. Nobody worries about kids listening to thousands – literally thousands – of songs about broken hearts and rejection and pain and misery and loss. The unhappiest people I know are the ones who like pop music the most …

Nick Hornby (1957–)
Nick Hornby is one of Britain's most popular contemporary authors. He frequently writes about sport and music. Many of the characters in his books have aimless or obsessive personalities.

High Fidelity (1995) is set in London and is about Rob, a man who works in a record shop. His girlfriend has left him. In the rest of the book, Rob examines his past relationships with women and with music. There was a film of the book in 2000 and a Broadway musical in 2007.

16 Unit 3 Music

Music Unit 3 17

Real world people

Reading and listening texts in *Global* are about real people and the real world.

Glossary

Many texts include a short glossary of difficult words.

Coursebook: extra material at the end of a unit

Function Globally

Every unit includes a *Function Globally* section. This contains frequent functional and situational language that is immediately useful outside the classroom.

Global English

Every other unit contains an extra reading lesson, called *Global English* featuring a text by David Crystal, which provides interesting information about the English language.

Global voices

Every other unit contains a listening section featuring authentic and unscripted recordings of a wide range of native and non-native speakers of English, which expose learners to real English as it is being used around the world today.

3 Function globally agreeing and disagreeing

Warm up

1 Work in pairs and look at the pictures from four different films. Match the pictures to the types of film in the box.

| action | comedy | drama | horror | musical |
| romantic comedy | science-fiction | thriller |

2 Describe the similarities and differences between the pictures.

3 What kinds of films do you like?

Useful language
• costumes   • in black and white
• martial arts

Useful phrases
• I think this one is a / an ...
• I've seen. / I've never seen ...
• This could be from India / Germany ...

Listening

1 1.44–1.46 Listen to three conversations about films and match each one to a situation. There is one situation you don't need.
a An interview situation, perhaps on television or on radio.
b A couple deciding what to rent at a DVD shop.
c Two friends coming out of the cinema.
d A teacher giving his opinions about films to a class.

2 Listen again and answer the questions.
Conversation 1: Did they both like the film?
Conversation 2: What kinds of films do they talk about?
Conversation 3: What kind of film does the woman want to see?

Language focus: agreeing and disagreeing

1 Read the sentences and mark *A* for agreeing, *D* for disagreeing or *I* for in between.
I agree. ___
Absolutely. / Definitely. ___
I don't agree (at all). ___
Well, maybe but ... ___
You're absolutely right. ___
That's what I think too. ___
Oh please! ___
That's right. ___
I sort of agree / disagree but ... ___
Exactly. ___

2 1.47 Listen and check your answers. Then listen and repeat the phrases. Try to copy the intonation.

Speaking

Work in pairs and choose **one** of the tasks below.
A Complete these sentences with your own ideas.
• Two great films are _____ and _____.
• Two great actors are _____ and _____.
• The best musician from my country is _____.
• The worst kind of music today is _____.

Compare your ideas with your partner. Do you agree or disagree?

B Decide how much you agree or disagree with these statements.
• Music used to be much better.
• Hollywood always produces the same kinds of films.
• There is a lot of exciting new art around today.
• Art galleries and museums are important for society.

Compare your opinions with your partner. Do you agree or disagree?

Unit 3 Function globally

Global English

The power of music
by David Crystal

Music has the power to engage all the emotions – from excitement to relaxation, from tears to laughter. But why does it have such power over us? The clue lies in babies.

The word *lullaby* has been in English since the Middle Ages. It's one of several, such as *rockaby* and *hushaby*, which show how generations of mothers have helped their children fall asleep through music.

5 Babies can hear in the womb about two months before they're born. Newborns prefer their mother's voice to that of a stranger. And they show preferences in music too. One research study played the same tune to a group of mothers every day throughout pregnancy; another group of mothers didn't hear the tune. When all the babies were born, their heart-rate was monitored while the tune was played to them. Only the 'musical' babies reacted to the tune.

10 There's something special about the music of the voice. From the moment a baby is born, the mother talks to it in an unusual way. Her voice ascends and descends from very high to very low – almost like singing in speech. And infants soon copy. You can hear them trying to sing from around nine months of age.

Melody, of both speech and music, is especially
15 significant. In another study, infants were shown two pictures of their mother. In one she was singing and in the other she was speaking. They looked for longer at the singing one.

Singing also simplifies our vocal behaviour: words are
20 often shorter, sounds are clearer and repeat more often, and they often rhyme. Nursery rhymes work so well because they combine these effects – clear rhythm, repeated sounds and rhyme. In the music of speech lies the foundation of poetry.

Glossary
clue (noun) – a piece of information that helps you to understand something
longer (adverb) – more time
monitor (verb) – to regularly check something
stranger (noun) – someone who you do not know

Warm up

1 Complete the nursery rhyme with the words in the box. Do you know this rhyme?

| all | blows | fall |

Rock-a-bye baby on the tree top,
when the wind _____
the cradle will rock,
when the bough breaks
the cradle will _____,
down will come baby,
cradle and _____.

2 Can you remember any nursery rhymes in your language? What are they?

Reading

1 Read the text. Which sentence is the best summary?
a Music and poetry are linked.
b We are affected by music from a very young age.
c Babies are more sensitive to music than adults.
d Lullabies are an English invention.

2 Read the text again. What do these words refer to?
1 it (line 2)   5 them (line 12)
2 It (line 3)   6 one (line 18)
3 that (line 6)   7 they (line 21)
4 it (line 11)   8 they (line 22)

3 Which of the facts in the text do you think are the most interesting? Compare your ideas with a partner.

Language focus

Look at the words in the box and put them into two groups: *music* or *babies*. Then translate them into your language.

| born | infant | melody | musical | nursery |
| pregnancy | rhyme | singing | tune | womb |

Speaking

Work in pairs and ask each other these questions.
When you were a child ...
• did your mother or father sing to you? What songs?
• did you have a favourite record or group? What was it?
• did you play an instrument? Which one?
• did you have music class at school? Did you enjoy it?
• did you use to sing? What songs?

Global English Unit 3

Listening

Students hear conversations in various situations which help contextualise the language and provide a model.

Putting it into practice

This is followed by a choice of speaking activity so that students can put the new language to use immediately.

Reading tasks

Each text is accompanied by different kinds of reading activity, which focus not only on comprehension, but also provide typical exam-type tasks that are useful for students preparing for an international exam.

Writing

Each unit focuses on a specific writing skill and a language point, presented within a particular genre. Learners' critical ability is developed by reading, analysing, and correcting one aspect of a model writing text.

Global review

Revision is crucial for language learning. Each unit contains review activities that cover the main grammar and vocabulary points.

Study skills

Developing effective study skills and strategies is an essential part of language learning. The study skills section in each unit focuses on a particular skill or strategy.

Preparation

Structured preparation tasks, useful language and paired activities guide students towards production of a final piece of writing.

Extra speaking and writing practice

Speaking and writing tasks based on the unit topic provide an extra opportunity to revise and consolidate the language from the unit in a freer and more open-ended format.

Writing models

Texts are based on authentic pieces of writing from international students at pre-intermediate level, reflecting the interests of a world-wide audience, and providing a realistic model within their capabilities.

---

3 Writing a review

Reading

1 Read Stefano's review of a concert he went to and answer the questions.
1 Who gave the concert?
2 What sort of singer is he?
3 Where was the concert held?
4 What happened during the concert?
5 Did Stefano enjoy the concert?

Last summer I went to a concert given by Vasco Rossi, he is one of Italy's most famous rock stars and one of the best live artists in the world. He is also a good songwriter, he writes great rock songs and also very nice love songs. He has many fans in Italy, and every summer he gives four or five concerts in big Italian stadiums, thousands of people go to listen to him there.

The concert took place in Rome's Olympic stadium, there were very many people there, all the tickets were sold out. I arrived at the stadium at three o'clock in the afternoon, I had to queue for six hours, I was very excited to see Vasco Rossi. The concert started at 9 o'clock in the evening, it went on for a very long time, maybe three or four hours. When Vasco Rossi started the concert everybody shouted, in the middle of the concert the crowd sang with him, it was very nice.

When the concert finished there were many security guards, everybody went home very quickly but without problems. I was very tired, I also went straight home, I was happy because of the excellent concert.

2 Would you enjoy the concert? Why?

Writing skills: sentences

1 You cannot join sentences with a comma. You need to start a new sentence using a full stop and capital letter. Stefano wrote:
Last summer I went to a concert given by Vasco Rossi, he is one of Italy's most famous rock stars.

He should write:
Last summer I went to a concert given by Vasco Rossi. He is one of Italy's most famous rock stars.

2 Find 12 more places where Stefano has joined sentences with a comma.

3 Join some of the sentences using *and*, *but* or *so*.

Language focus: adjectives

Make your writing more interesting by avoiding words like *nice*, *good* or *great*. Use your dictionary to find different words.

Improve Stefano's writing by using these words in the text.

| moving | powerful | talented | tender and expressive |

Preparing to write

1 Think of a concert you have been to or would like to go to. Make notes about it. Use the useful phrases below to help you.
Paragraph 1: Who was the concert given by? Give some information about the performer.
Paragraph 2: Where did the concert take place? Who was in the audience? What happened during the concert? How did you feel?
Paragraph 3: What happened at the end? How did you feel?

2 Work in pairs and share your ideas.

Describing a concert
* The concert was given by ...
* It was a live / open air / sell-out concert.
* It took place in a stadium / a concert hall / a field.
* The hall was full /packed / half empty.
* The audience cheered / clapped / shouted.
* The music was brilliant / powerful /moving.
* I felt excited / moved / happy.

Writing

Write a review of a concert. Use your notes to help you.

Global review

Grammar

1 Complete the sentences with the past simple or past continuous form of the verbs in brackets.
1 How much _____ (you / pay) for that painting?
2 I _____ (not / pay) anything. It was a present.
3 When we _____ (arrive) at the cinema, our friends _____ (wait) for us.
4 My grandfather _____ (find) a valuable manuscript while he _____ (work) in his attic.
5 He _____ (sell) it to the museum for more than half a million dollars.

2 Complete the sentences with the correct form of *used to* and the words in brackets.
1 What kind of music _____ (you / listen) to when you were a child?
2 I _____ (listen) to pop music. I _____ (not / like) classical music then, but I do now.

Vocabulary

1 Read the definitions and complete the words.
1 a large group of musicians who use instruments to play classical music   o _____
2 you can listen to live music here   c _____   h _____
3 an image of a person or animal, made of stone, metal or wood   s _____
4 you usually put books on these   s _____
5 a comfortable object to sit on   a _____

2 Complete the sentences with the correct word.
1 I used to be *angry / tense / frightened* of horses.
2 Sanna always has a happy face – she's a *sad / cheerful / scared* person.
3 I hate exams – they make me *anxious / relaxed / sleepy*.
4 As a child I used to feel very *miserable / bored / excited* about going on holiday – it was the best week of the year.

Speaking and Writing

1 Work in pairs. You are ill in bed and feeling miserable. Tell your partner how to find your favourite music and play it on your music player. Then swap roles and repeat.

2 Work in small groups. Write four sentences about your childhood using *used to* or *didn't use to*. One must be false. Take it in turns to read out your sentences and try to guess which one is false.

Study skills

Conversation partners

1 Work in pairs and discuss these questions.
* How often do you speak English outside class every week?
* In what situations do you speak English? For example, with friends or family, at work, in social situations etc.
* What do you talk about?
* How can speaking outside class help to improve your speaking ability?

> One way to practise speaking is to meet with a conversation partner between classes. Your partner can be someone from your English class. You can use some of your time together to practise what you have learnt in class.

2 Work in pairs. Make arrangements to meet as conversation partners this week.

★ Decide on a time and place to meet.
In school, before or after the class?
In one person's house at the weekend?
In a bar or café in the evening?
On the phone?
★ Decide how long you will meet for.
For fifteen minutes?
For half an hour?
Some other length of time?
★ Decide which of these topics you would like to talk about. Add your own ideas.
Finding out about each other.
Your taste in art, music or books.
Things you used to do in a previous school.
Feelings that you had this week.
Some things that you did this week.
Instructions for using something.

3 Make some notes after the meeting.
* What was the most helpful or interesting part of the meeting?
* What was difficult?
* What will you do differently next time?

eWorkbook

Comprehensive component for self-study

The *Global* eWorkbook represents an evolution in self-study materials for learners. Within a rich multimedia environment it provides a wealth of resources for the learner, enabling them to continue their studies at their own pace, and in their own time.

Language Work

The eWorkbook contains a wide range of activities which allow for extra practice and review of the language presented in the Coursebook. These activities cover all aspects of language learning. Grammar, Vocabulary, Listening and Pronunciation practice activities are available both as fully interactive activities and in a printable pen-and-paper format. There are also worksheets to practise reading and writing skills.

global

PRE-INTERMEDIATE

eWorkbook

 LANGUAGE PRACTICE

 PRINT AND WORK

 LISTEN

 WATCH

 ON THE MOVE

DICTIONARY

 WORD LISTS

 GRAMMAR HELP

 WRITING TIPS

 TESTS

 PORTFOLIO

CONTENT MAP

Tools for reference and support

The eWorkbook offers all the support the learner may need. For instance, links to the Macmillan Dictionary Online, Word lists per unit and grammar help organized by topic. The Writing tips section includes information on general aspects of writing, such as spelling, punctuation, paragraphing, etc.

Learning on the Move

The Global eWorkbook provides a wide variety of authentic extra listening and video materials supplied in commonly used file formats, so learners can load them onto their portable music and video players and study and review 'on-the-go'.

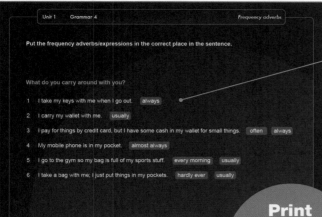

Unit 1   Grammar 4   *Frequency adverbs*

Put the frequency adverbs/expressions in the correct place in the sentence.

What do you carry around with you?

1 I take my keys with me when I go out. [always]
2 I carry my wallet with me. [usually]
3 I pay for things by credit card, but I have some cash in my wallet for small things. [often] [always]
4 My mobile phone is in my pocket. [almost always]
5 I go to the gym so my bag is full of my sports stuff. [every morning] [usually]
6 I take a bag with me; I just put things in my pockets. [hardly ever] [usually]

Interactive activities
Meaningful practice.

Video
Extracts from BBC programmes as well as original videos that can be downloaded and used on the move.

Print and Work
For those who prefer to work offline.

UNIT 10 **New & Old**

Vocabulary 3A
Transport

Write the form of transport under the pictures.

Vocabulary 3B
Transport

Choose the correct answers.

1 Which form of transport doesn't have wheels?
 a bicycle
 b ship
 c bus
2 Which form of transport has wings?
 a underground
 b plane
 c boat
3 Where do you catch a train?
 a stop
 b track
 c station

4 Which form of transport doesn't...
 a bicycle
 b motorbike
 c car
5 Which form of transport has a driver?
 a bicycle
 b plane
 c taxi
6 Which form of transport doesn't run on tracks?
 a underground
 b train
 c bus

Vocabulary 4
Transport verbs

Complete the texts with the correct words.

Commuting around the world.

Around the world, more and more people are (1) *getting to / getting on* their bicycles and cycling to work. In New York, for example, the number of people who (2) *drove / rode* to work increased by 35% from 2007 to 2008. Beijing, however, is really the city of bicycles, with more than 10 million bikes. An estimated 38% of Beijingers travel (3) *by bicycle / on bike* every day. However, cars are quickly replacing bikes, with around 3.3 million cars (4) *running / driving* around the city's streets in 2008.

The US city with the most taxis per capita is Bethel, Alaska. With no roads going in or out of this remote city, there are almost no private cars. To get to Bethel, you have to (5) *get in / get on* a plane or a boat. But if residents want to get across the city, they (6) *get in / get on* a taxi and (7) *get off / get out* on the other side of town.

Global Pre-intermediate eWorkbook © Macmillan Publishers Limited 2010

global
PRE-INTERMEDIATE   eWorkbook
WATCH   6
02.50 / 14.20

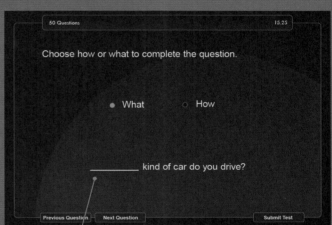

50 Questions   15.25

Choose how or what to complete the question.

● What   ○ How

_____ kind of car do you drive?

[Previous Question] [Next Question]   [Submit Test]

Listening
Comprehensive listening section, with tracks that can be downloaded and used on the move.

global
PRE-INTERMEDIATE   eWorkbook

| Word List | Grammar Help | Writing Tips |

acceptable
accepted
bring
basketball
dynamo
poodle
practical
twister
dynamo
poodle
practical
twister
words
speaker

Click the correct answer.

1. When do you not use commas?
 a. to join sentences
 b. to separate prepositional phrases
 c. to separate items in a list ✓

previous next

LANGUAGE PRACTICE
DICTIONARY
WORD LISTS
CONTENT MAP

Self assessment
Test generator and Common European Framework checklists for self assessment.

Tools
Comprehensive tools for self study.

global
PRE-INTERMEDIATE   eWorkbook

LISTEN ON THE MOVE

Literary Extracts | In Conversation | Vocabulary Builder | Useful Phrases

● Describing people
The human body
Feelings
Describing people and things
Work
● Technology
Time and money
House and home
Sports and activities
New words

Teacher's Book

Scott Thornbury: Making the most of learner-generated content

Learner-generated content is the language – either spoken or written – that learners produce, naturally and often spontaneously, during the course of a lesson, and which constitutes authentic communication. This distinguishes it from the language that is produced in order to answer comprehension questions and display questions (like "What is the past of *take*?"), or to do grammar exercises, or to perform role plays, or to write summaries, and so on.

Why use it?

Using learner output as lesson input is one way of involving learners more directly in the learning-teaching process. And research suggests that when learners have some control of the topic agenda and of the management of classroom talk, the lesson is more likely to match their particular learning needs, as well as being both more meaningful and more memorable.

When?

Learner-generated content can emerge at any stage of the lesson, and is often a by-product of some other activity, such as reading or listening. It can be deliberately prompted by personalisation tasks – that is, tasks that require students to use a pre-taught language item to talk about themselves – or by opinion-seeking tasks, such as when preparing learners to read a text, or by questions eliciting their response to the text they have just read. It can occur in the chat that opens a lesson. It can also be prompted when learners report on group-discussions, or on something they have read or heard prior to the lesson. Asking the learners to come prepared to every lesson with an item of interesting news is one way of formalising this procedure. But learners are more likely to generate original content if the classroom dynamic is conducive to informal, personalised talk, and if initiating such talk is welcomed by the teacher.

How do you make the most of it?

First of all, treat the personalisation stage – not as a test of pre-taught items – but as a potential launch pad for classroom talk. Let's say an individual learner has offered an opinion, or given some personal information, or referred to something going on in the world outside the classroom, and that you feel that this is a comment of general interest, and exploitable for the language 'affordances' (i.e. learning opportunities) that it offers. Use questions to encourage the learner to elaborate. Try to do this in as natural and conversational a way as possible. If the learner is stuck for words, feed them. Avoid correcting errors if this might inhibit the speaker. Instead, reformulate what the speaker is saying in a way that makes it more target-like. Draw others into the conversation. When the topic seems to have run its course, ask the students, working in pairs or groups, to write a summary of what was talked about, e.g. for an absent classmate. Collect the texts and use these as the basis for a more focused lesson, e.g. error correction. This could take the form of extracting a number of (unattributed) correct and incorrect sentences and asking the learners to identify them, and then to correct the incorrect ones.

Set up writing activities that replicate on-line social networking interaction. Students can 'chat' to one another in small groups using pen and paper. This conversation can then form the basis of a group 'blog'; these blogs are then passed around – or posted on the classroom wall – and commented on, before being returned to the original writers. This material is then available to the teacher for subsequent use and development.

Finally, exploit the texts and the topics in your course book as stimuli for learners' own comment and opinion. Learners may not always respond to the content of a text – but they *never* will if they are not invited to!

UNIT 3 Art & Music

Part 1

TEACH GLOBAL THINK LOCAL Lead-in

Write out pairs of art and artists, eg Michelangelo + David; da Vinci + Mona Lisa; Monet + Bridge over a pond of waterlilies, Van Gogh + Vase with Flowers, etc. (one or two can be the same as from Part 1). Put these onto small pieces of paper and give each student either a piece of art or an artist. Students mingle and find their matching partner. At the end, hear the pairs and elicit any information students know about the artist / the work of art. Students remain with their new partner for at least part of the lesson.

Vocabulary and Speaking (SB page 30)

1 Students match the words to pictures, either individually or in small groups, if they need to pool their knowledge.

Early finishers can predict how to say them, marking the word stress: all of them have the stress on the first syllable (except for /ˌself ˈpɔːtrət/). Drill the new words, chorally and individually.

a cave art
b statue
c sculpture
d sketch
e manuscript

Reading (SB page 30)

The text describes how four well-known pieces of art were discovered in strange and unexpected circumstances.

1 ▶ 1.33 Write the text heading on the board: *Discovered! True stories of how valuable works of art were found in unexpected places.* Tell them they are about to read some very interesting 'finds' or 'discoveries' of important pieces of art. Elicit the meaning of *valuable* (adj) /ˈvæljʊbl/ and *unexpected* (adj) /ˌʌnɪksˈpektɪd/.

Give them two minutes to complete the skim reading task: matching each text to a picture. Play the recording and check answers as they listen.

in a field b
Under a street c
On a wall f
At a market e

2 Refer students to the glossary (SB page 31) and check these words as appropriate, eg *What can you buy at a flea market? Have you been to one? Where?*

Students complete the sentences alone, then compare answers before whole class feedback. At the end, ask students which discovery they are most surprised by, and why. Also ask if students know of similar stories.

1 Aphrodite the goddess of love
2 the Louvre, France
3 electrical cables
4 the Museum of the Great Temple in Mexico
5 a reproduction of a Vincent Van Gogh
6 1.4 million dollars
7 a flea market
8 wooden picture frame

Note

...contain consonant clusters which ...students, eg manuscript, ...h, /skʌlptʃə/; sketch, /sketʃ/;

...are going to describe the ...h.

...phrases box before listening to ...tion, using one of the pictures, ...than if it's been drawn in pencil. It ...people. Most of them are girls, apart ...rom right-hand corner who looks like ...look thoughtful, and are not looking ...as if this picture was drawn from the ...tion, but the faces look real. This painting ...though one of the faces is Asian. It's probably ...century. I quite like this picture as the faces are ...and quite peaceful. There's something romantic ...it.

TEACH GLOBAL THINK LOCAL Extra activity

If your students are particularly interested in art, you could give them some extra fluency practice by asking them to rate the pictures in order of preference, giving reasons, working in threes.

Students ... or more pictures each.

Art & Music Unit 3 **11**

Teach Global Think Local

The Teacher's Book includes comprehensive teaching notes with answer keys and audioscripts, and detailed background and language notes.

It also provides 'Teach Global Think Local' ideas: extra activities that can be adapted to individual teaching situations.

Specialist essays

The Teacher's Book features a number of specialist essays, each focusing on a different aspect of language teaching. These have been written by a range of well-known and award-winning guest ELT authors and teacher trainers, and will be of interest to teachers of all levels of experience.

Teacher's Resource CD

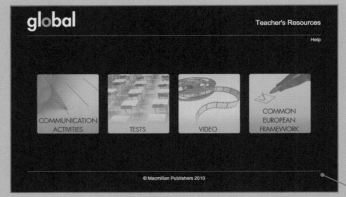

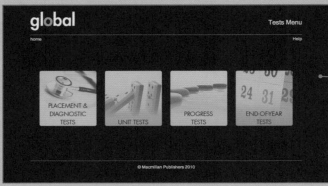

Communication activities, tests, videos

The Teacher's Resource CD includes printable communication activity worksheets that practise areas of language from the Coursebook units and printable communication activity worksheets to do at different stages of the course. In addition, it provides a wide range of tests (diagnostic, progress tests, end-of-year test etc) and additional video clips and video worksheets for the teacher.

Audio CDs

global PRE-INTERMEDIATE · INTERMEDIATE
Class CD 1 · s CD 2

Units 1–5 · Units 6–10
Tracks 1–75 · Tracks 1–90

© Macmillan Publishers Limited 2010

ISBN 978-0 230-03313-9 · 230-03313-9

The *Global* Pre-intermediate class audio is contained on two CDs. They include the listening material from the Coursebook and recordings of the literary extracts featured in the book

Website

The Global website consists of author blog, teaching tips, extra resources and much more.

www.macmillanenglish.com/global

Global Digital

Enhancing the teaching experience in the classroom

Global Digital is a digital component designed for classroom use. It can be used with an interactive whiteboard or with a computer and projector.

The Digital Book

The Digital Book allows the teacher to access and display an interactive version of any page from the Coursebook in front of the class. All of the relevant audio, video and reference materials are instantly accessible right on the page.

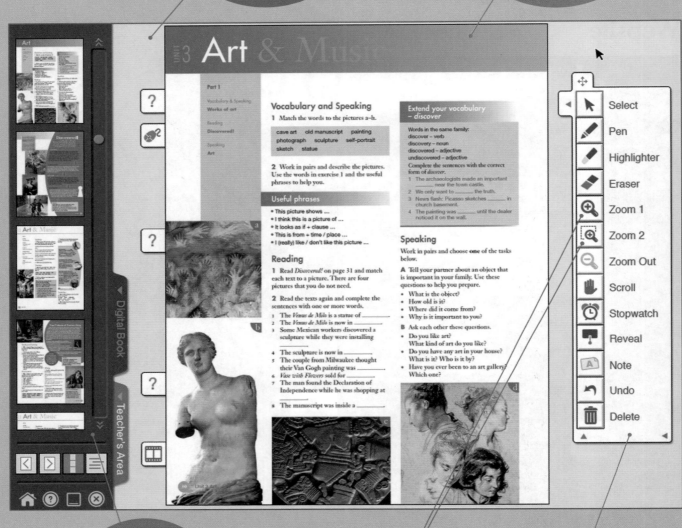

Navigation pane

The navigation pane allows you to select a page from anywhere in the book.

Zooming in and out

The Zoom tools allow you to zoom in either on pre-defined areas or any part of the page that you choose.

Toolbox

The toolbox provides a number of tools which enable you to interact with the Digital book page.

Navigation pane

The navigation pane displays thumbnails of the pages you have created in the Teacher's area.

The Teacher's Area

The Teacher's Area can be used to create your own material either before or during the class. You can insert and edit text and images, add links to pages from the digital book and insert audio and website links.

Select

Pen

Highlighter

Eraser

Text

Shape

Image

Audio

Hyperlink

Stopwatch

Reveal

Copy

Paste

Background

Undo

Delete

Open Game

Create Game

Teacher's Area

Games section

The games section provides interactive game templates to which you can add your own content.

Toolbox

A toolbox which includes some different tools from the ones for the digital book enables you to make annotations and create and edit materials.

Specialist essays

Introduction

Ideas about language teaching, like languages themselves, are subject to change. For much of the twentieth century different 'methods' were presented as the best way to learn or acquire a new language. Some argue that we are now 'beyond methods', or in a 'post-method' condition in the twenty-first century. However, suggestions and approaches, useful tips, techniques and advice for good teaching practice are still as important as they ever were.

We know that language teachers often like to be informed of the newest developments in our field. With current technology we know more about the English language than ever before. Additionally, we as teachers are harnessing technology and the internet in new and exciting ways that help us help our students in ways we could not have imagined twenty years ago. And yet, there are some things that remain the same in the classroom.

What follows are a series of short essays, each written by experts in the field. The aim of these essays is to provide you, the language teacher, with up-to-date information about your subject matter. Like the material in *Global* itself, they are thought-provoking pieces. We also believe that learning more about what we do is extremely useful for our ongoing professional development. We hope you find them useful.

Lindsay Clandfield

Contents

Lindsay Clandfield: Why *Global*?

Every book is a product of its times. Nowhere is this truer than in educational materials. Notions of how people learn, of what they learn and of what is important are shaped by the world around us and the period we live through. What then, are the times that have shaped *Global*?

We live in an era of fast communication. More and more people are gaining access to internet and quicker communications technology. This means that we are writing and reading more than before, be it emails, text messages, blogs or web pages. Language learners need to work on quick and unplanned writing (writing for fluency) just as they do for speaking.

We live in an era of information. New technologies enable us to communicate more and with more people, but they have also made more and more information available than ever before – and it is available faster. Much of this information is still in English. Students need to be able to access information and assimilate it quickly.

We live in an era of uncertainty. Precisely because so much information is out there, we are often unsure what is accurate and what is opinion or even misleading. To succeed in an information-rich world one has to learn how to discern, analyse and evaluate what one sees or hears. Fostering critical thinking skills has long been an important goal of educaton.

We live in an era of global English. One of the most important realisations in the field of English Language Teaching of the past decade or so is that English is an international language, spoken all over the world, by people with different accents and different 'Englishes'. A learner is just as likely, if not more likely, to use his or her English with another non-native speaker as with a native speaker.

Given all this, the goals of *Global* are threefold:

1   For your students to **learn English**. This, as for any language course, is the primary goal of *Global*, which reflects modern developments in language teaching and learning. There is a strong lexical focus as well as a complete grammar syllabus, language presentation and practice is highly contextualised with many opportunities for personalisation, and there is plenty of meaningful communicative practice which in *Global* extends to mean writing as well as speaking fluency. *Global* includes a wide variety of reading and listening genres and practises a range of reading and listening skills. With the addition of sections to develop functional language, writing and study skills and review language, we are confident this course provides your students with the tools to become competent users of the language.

2   For your students to **learn through English**. The texts and topics of *Global* are selected so that in every lesson you and your students will be learning something new. We have chosen material that is thought-provoking, interesting, intelligent and above all, real. We have also included tasks that encourage students to examine the information they receive critically, and to find out more about a topic if they are interested. Unlike many other courses, texts and topics steer away from the light human interest or celebrity-related story. We use real world information from a wide variety of domains and the power of literature to unlock students' self-expression.

3   For your students to **learn about English**. This course also includes a focus, through extra reading and listening activities, on the English language as a subject itself. What is it? How is it changing? What kinds of English are appearing around the world? What are the implications of this? We believe these are important questions, worthy of being touched on in the language class. It is why we asked the foremost world expert author on these matters, David Crystal, to contribute to this new and innovative thread of *Global*.

David Crystal: The future of Englishes: going local

When people talk about 'global English' they are usually referring to the common features which identify the variety we call standard English. Increasingly, however, attention has been drawn to the regional features which differentiate one part of the English-speaking world from another. So today we happily talk about British, American, Australian, South African, Indian, and other 'Englishes', and studies are accumulating of the way these varieties make distinctive use of pronunciation, orthography, grammar, vocabulary, and discourse. Much of the distinctiveness resides in the area of lexicology, the linguistic domain which most closely reflects cultural identity, and dictionaries have been compiled of the distinctive lexicons encountered in these regions.

It does not take long before these lexicons reach many thousands of words. When a country adopts a language as a local alternative means of communication, it immediately starts adapting it, to meet the communicative needs of the region. Words for local plants and animals, food and drink, customs and practices, politics and religion, sports and games, and many other facets of everyday life soon accumulate a local wordstock which is unknown outside the country and its environs. When someone in South Africa says 'The bakkie had to stop at a red robot', we need to know that a bakkie is a truck and a robot is a traffic-light. There are thousands of such words in a dictionary of South African English. And other parts of the English-speaking world display the same kind of creativity.

This seems to be the pattern, as English becomes a local alternative language. When a group of people in a country switch into English, for whatever reason, the subject-matter of their conversation inevitably incorporates aspects of their local environment. They talk about the shops, streets, suburbs, bus-routes, institutions, businesses, television programmes, newspapers, political parties, minority groups, and a great deal more. They make jokes, quote proverbs, bring up childhood linguistic memories (such as nursery rhymes), and recall lyrics of popular songs. All this local knowledge is taken for granted, and used in sentences without gloss. Visitors who hear such sentences, or read them in local newspapers, need to have them explained. Conventional dictionaries will not help, for they do not include such localisms, especially if the expressions are encyclopedic in character (referring to local people, places, institutions, and suchlike).

Every English-speaking location in the world has usages which make the English used there distinctive, expressive of local identity, and a means of creating solidarity. From this point of view, notions such as 'Swedish English' take on a fresh relevance, going well beyond traditional conceptions of English spoken with a Swedish accent, or English displaying interference from Swedish grammar. Swedish English, for example, I define as the kind of English I need to know about when I go to Sweden, otherwise I will be unable to converse efficiently with Swedish speakers in English. It would be amazingly useful to have a glossary of the English equivalents of Swedish cultural references, but I know of none. This seems to be a neglected area for any language.

We need regional cultural dictionaries or glossaries. It is something every region can do, and something to which everyone who learns English can contribute. It takes only an hour or so to accumulate a list of dozens of culturally specific items. And when these are written down, in the style of a glossary, it has an interesting effect upon the participants. They feel they have somehow made the English language their own. I suspect such projects also add greatly to their linguistic confidence and self-esteem, for no-one else in the world knows their home-grown variety of English as well as they do. And they can take pride in the fact that they have added their own small piece to the global jigsaw puzzle that comprises the English language.

David Crystal is honorary professor of linguistics at the University of Bangor, and works from his home in Holyhead, North Wales, as a writer, editor, lecturer, and broadcaster. He read English at University College London, specialized in English language studies, then joined academic life as a lecturer in linguistics, first at Bangor, then at Reading, where he became professor of linguistics. He received an OBE for services to the English language in 1995. His books include *The Cambridge Encyclopedia of the English Language* and *The Stories of English*. *Just a Phrase I'm Going Through: my Life in Language* was published in 2009.

Amanda Jeffries: Developing study skills and encouraging learner autonomy

Learner autonomy can be defined as the ability of a learner to take charge of their own learning, not only by learning specific strategies or study skills but also by developing an entirely new attitude to learning. A truly independent learner of English is aware of their learning needs and goals, can reflect on how they learn, has a positive and proactive attitude to language-learning, and can make the most of learning opportunities both in and out of class.

Study skills are strategies and approaches that can lead to more effective learning. The *Global* series follows a comprehensive study skills syllabus covering metacognitive strategies (thinking about, planning, and evaluating learning) and affective and social strategies (monitoring your attitude to learning and working with others) as well as dictionary and reference skills. It also develops specific strategies for learning and practising listening, speaking, reading, writing, vocabulary, and grammar more effectively. All learners are different and research suggests that effective learning depends on choosing the right strategy, or combination of strategies, for the task, the learning context, or the particular individual.

Why deal with learner autonomy in class?

Most teachers recognise the importance of learning effectively, but many have reservations about doing learner training or learning awareness activities in class: 'It wouldn't work with my group'; 'There's already too much to do in class'; or 'I wouldn't know where to start'. It is important to remember, however, that a focused and independent learner is not only more efficient but also more motivated. Moreover, learner autonomy activities provide a valuable extra practice opportunity.

How can I help my learners to develop these skills?

You may find some of the following suggestions useful in your teaching situation.

- Include short regular learner training slots in your timetable, so that your learners get used to the idea of study skills as a key part of their learning.

- Offer students a 'menu' of possible strategies for, say, planning an essay, or memorising vocabulary to help them choose the strategy that works best for them. Comparing ideas in pairs or groups can also suggest new and useful ideas. Suggest they try out a new strategy for a week and report back on how effective they found it.

- When doing class activities, share your aims with your students and suggest useful strategies; for example, explain that you are asking them to read primarily to understand the gist of a passage and offer good gist reading tips.

- Ask students regularly to note down or discuss how well they have learned and what they have enjoyed or found puzzling, and make resolutions for how to improve.

- Find out how your students learn. You could ask them to write you a short letter about their progress and write back with suggestions!

- Make students aware of the range of practice opportunities and materials available – in a library or study centre, online, or in the media. Students can also keep a record of work outside class that they can discuss with you.

- More advanced groups might find writing learner diaries a good way to reflect on their learning styles and preferences.

- Above all, show you are convinced that developing good learning habits is a valuable learning focus – that way, your own attitude is more likely to rub off on your students.

Amanda Jeffries teaches university students and works on teacher development programmes in Oxford. She has contributed to the Macmillan *Straightforward* and *New Inside Out* series. She has written the writing, study skills and review pages for the *Global* series, and is the co-author of *Global Advanced*.

Pete Sharma: Blended learning

The term 'blended learning' is a 'buzz' term, yet one that means different things to different people. The 'classic' definition of blended learning is a course consisting of traditional 'face-to-face' language lessons, combined with 'distance learning' i.e. the opportunity to study 'beyond the classroom'. Such a course can provide many benefits for language learners.

In our book *Blended Learning*, we suggest a broader definition, taking blended learning to mean a combination of classroom teaching and the *appropriate* use of technology. Technology such as an interactive whiteboard can be used inside the classroom to enrich the learning experience. In addition, the students could have 24/7 access to their interactive learning materials, allowing them to study at anytime, anywhere.

Principles

Whichever definition is used, new technology has had a major impact on language teaching and learning. We describe four key principles for successfully integrating technology into language teaching:

- Differentiate the role you play as a teacher, and the role the technology is playing. For example, the teacher can clarify 'fuzzy' areas of grammar. The interactive exercises on a CD-ROM could then offer extra practice in 'crisp' areas of language, with students receiving feedback from the computer.

- Teaching should be principled. In other words, there should be a sound pedagogical reason for using the technology.

- The technology should complement and enhance what the teacher does. It is not a replacement for the teacher.

- 'It's not what it is, but what you do with it'. The interactive whiteboard in itself is just a 'tool'. It is how teachers actually use it, to help provide engaging language lessons, which can lead to better learning outcomes.

Integrating technology into language courses

There are many ways to integrate technology into a language course. A teacher can:

- support their face-to-face teaching with a Virtual Learning Environment, a web based platform which learners can access at any time. The VLE can be used, for example, to post language feedback for students to study after a class discussion.

- run 'learner training' sessions to show students how to benefit from the digital material in the eWorkbook at the back of their course book. For instance, you can download the audio files to their mp3 players to allow learning 'on the go'; use the 'QuickFind' feature on their electronic dictionary, and download the free interactive version of the phonemic chart from the web.

- use technology before a class. Before a fluency lesson, email students a pre-discussion reading task to get them thinking about the topic.

- use technology during a class. If you use an interactive whiteboard, you can save the electronic flip-charts you create. This allows you to build up a bank of personalised digital materials including photographs and sound files to support each of the course book units.

- use technology after a class. Students focusing on writing can collaborate together to produce an essay using a wiki, a website which contains editable web pages.

If teachers continue to provide pedagogically sound and interesting lessons, and allow the technology to support learning both inside and outside the classroom, then a blended learning approach can certainly enrich the language learning experience of students.

References

Barrett, B and Sharma, P *Blended Learning* – using technology inside and beyond the language classroom (Macmillan, 2007); Jones, C (1986) 'It's not so much the program, more what you do with it: the importance of methodology in CALL' System 14 / 2, 171-178

Pete Sharma is an associate Lecturer at Oxford Brookes University, UK. He has written books on technology in language teaching, and is co-author of *Blended Learning: using technology in and beyond the language classroom* (Macmillan 2007). Pete is a Director of Pete Sharma Associates, which runs training in educational technology: www.psa.eu.com. He has edited the CALL Review, the newsletter of the Learning Technologies SIG of IATEFL, and blogs on technology at: www.te4be.com

Duncan Foord: How we can develop as teachers

Development means change and change is inevitable. You are not the same teacher (or person) you were a year ago. Working with a new coursebook, new students and colleagues, taking part in in-service training, preparing classes – all of these challenging elements of your day-to-day routine have changed you. You are always developing, you just have to decide how.

Our choices are framed by the culture we live in, the school we work in, government policy, students' expectations and so on. Some schools may encourage and support teacher development, others less so, but you will always have choices to make about how you teach and how you deal with challenges inside and outside the classroom. Focus on what you can do rather than what you can't.

Guiding principles

Just like a lesson, your working life needs some aims to guide your choice of development activities, your development plan, if you like. Here are six which I like.

- Take an interest in my students.
- Enjoy teaching.
- Take on challenges.
- Manage stress.
- Balance work and home life.
- Share my enthusiasm with others.

Give your teaching a 'developmental twist'

Here are some ideas for practical activities which are easy to integrate into your teaching routine and not time consuming.

- **Get feedback** from your students. Five minutes before the end of the lesson ask the students to write on a piece of paper three things they liked about the class and one thing they didn't like, or a 'suggestion' if they prefer. Thank your students and collect the papers in. In the next class (or via email) respond to the comments.

- **Make a short video** of your class. For this you need a small hand-held camera or mobile phone with video. Get a colleague or student to video your class for about 5–10 minutes. Watch the video afterwards more than once. The first few times you will be cringing at your appearance and mannerisms! After that you will notice more interesting things about your choice of language, gestures and facial expressions and get a good idea how your students see you.

- **Try activities out first**. Before you use a speaking activity, try it out with a colleague. Afterwards assess how much time you needed, whether the instructions were clear, if you needed preparation time, what language you used, whether your students would find it easy or difficult and what help they might need. Adjust your lesson plan accordingly.

- **Break your routine**. This can be a very good way to help you understand your teaching better and add an element of surprise and fun to your classes. For example, let one of your students become the teacher for ten minutes and you become a student, move the seating arrangement, supplement the coursebook text with one you find which will particularly interest your students…

- **Create a staff 'sharing board'**. This is a place where you can share materials and teaching ideas with your colleagues. Once it catches on, the board will help build staff rapport as well as provide a source of interesting lessons and save you preparation time.

Duncan Foord is the Director of the teacher training institution OxfordTEFL. He is responsible for teacher training and development in the company and teaches on Trinity Certificate and Diploma courses in the Barcelona centre. He is co-author (with Lindsay Clandfield) of *The Language Teacher's Survival Handbook* (It's Magazines, 2008) and *The Developing Teacher* (Delta Publishing, 2009) winner of the Duke of Edinburgh ESU English Language Award 2009 for Best Entry for Teachers.

Jim Scrivener: Pre-intermediate – a very teachable level

In many ways we can think of Beginner and Elementary levels as a necessary foundation. But they can also be quite hard work – to study and to teach. There are so many pieces of essential grammar and core vocabulary that just have to be in place before you can do anything terribly creative with English. The students have relatively little background knowledge or understanding of the language so explanations and tasks can sometimes feel slow or get bogged down – especially if the teacher is trying to only use English in class. Now, as students learn and get confident with these basic items, they can move on and start enjoying a different way of learning the language.

It's good to be a Pre-intermediate learner! And it's an enjoyable level to teach (usually!). Sweeping statements? Maybe – but let me offer a few personal impressions of this level that may or may not persuade you.

The learners now have a good stock of useful basic grammar and vocabulary and, because they do, their language use can suddenly start to blossom. Rather than each new item feeling like something separate and discrete, learners start to glimpse the bigger holistic picture of the language and new grammar or vocabulary can slot into its place alongside already-known language.

Students start to realise that they can actually do something with this strange language. Although they certainly still make lots of mistakes, in general, they can start to rise above the struggle to form a coherent sentence and begin using the language creatively to express what they want to say. They can get their meaning across. They can play with it, they can make jokes, they can start to enjoy it. These are huge steps.

Because of these things, it can be very enjoyable to teach Pre-intermediates. A teacher can talk with them in something much more closely approaching normal English and they will understand a great deal of what you say. Not only instructions and explanations and so on, but all that wonderful pre-lesson, in-lesson and post-lesson chit-chat, banter and gossip that tends to start growing a lot at this level.

Practice activities are liberated from being very form-focused. We can start to make assumptions that students already have other language that they can use and incorporate into the tasks they do. Students will work on form but can be much more creative about it.

And now, I'll stick my neck out and say that one of the best things about Pre-intermediates is that there is so much enjoyable grammar to teach! This may be a politically incorrect comment – as nowadays we do, for the most part, try to be very focused on *learner* needs. But there are teacher needs too! And I have a sneaking suspicion that many teachers really like working with a lot of the grammar items that typically come at this level.

I'm thinking of things like: past simple and past continuous, *used to*, futures, comparatives and superlatives, modals for prediction, conditionals. All nice meaty areas whose inarguable usefulness is immediately apparent to the students. All very 'teachable', lending themselves to interesting presentations, amusing narratives and anecdotes, visual demonstrations and active practice tasks. As students rise on to Intermediate and Upper Intermediate the syllabus of language items becomes more obscure, more fiddly, less obviously everyday. Pressure of exams starts to make students more aware of the need to be accurate and the explosion of joyous language use of Pre-intermediate can start to fade.

So, if you offer me my free choice of level to teach, I think I'll have Pre-int please. I wish you fun with this level too.

Jim Scrivener is Head of Teacher Development for Bell International based at Bedgebury School in Kent, UK, where he developed and runs the Online Delta course. He is the author of *Learning Teaching* (Macmillan), *Oxford Basics Teaching Grammar* (OUP) as well as the Teacher's Books and Portfolios for the *Straightforward* coursebook series (Macmillan).

Scott Thornbury: Making the most of learner-generated content

Learner-generated content is the language – either spoken or written – that learners produce, naturally and often spontaneously, during the course of a lesson, and which constitutes authentic communication. This distinguishes it from the language that is produced in order to answer comprehension questions and display questions (like "What is the past of *take*?"), or to do grammar exercises, or to perform role plays, or to write summaries, and so on.

Why use it?

Using learner output as lesson input is one way of involving learners more directly in the learning–teaching process. And research suggests that when learners have some control of the topic agenda and of the management of classroom talk, the lesson is more likely to match their particular learning needs, as well as being both more meaningful and more memorable.

When?

Learner-generated content can emerge at any stage of the lesson, and is often a by-product of some other activity, such as reading or listening. It can be deliberately prompted by personalisation tasks – that is, tasks that require students to use a pre-taught language item to talk about themselves – or by opinion-seeking tasks, such as when preparing learners to read a text, or by questions eliciting their response to the text they have just read. It can occur in the chat that opens a lesson. It can also be prompted when learners report on group discussions, or on something they have read or heard prior to the lesson. Asking the learners to come prepared to every lesson with an item of interesting news is one way of formalising this procedure. But learners are more likely to generate original content if the classroom dynamic is conducive to informal, personalised talk, and if initiating such talk is welcomed by the teacher.

How do you make the most of it?

First of all, treat the personalisation stage not as a test of pre-taught items but as a potential launch pad for classroom talk. Let's say an individual learner has offered an opinion, or given some personal information, or referred to something going on in the world outside the classroom, and that you feel that this is a comment of general interest, and exploitable for the language 'affordances' (i.e. learning opportunities) that it offers. Use questions to encourage the learner to elaborate. Try to do this in as natural and conversational a way as possible. If the learner is stuck for words, supply them. Avoid correcting errors if this might inhibit the speaker. Instead, reformulate what the speaker is saying in a way that makes it more target-like. Draw other learners into the conversation. When the topic seems to have run its course, ask the learners, working in pairs or groups, to write a summary of what was talked about, as if writing to an absent classmate. Collect the texts and use these as the basis for a subsequent lesson, e.g. error correction. This could take the form of extracting a mixture of (unattributed) correct and incorrect sentences and asking the learners first to sort them, and then to correct the incorrect ones.

Set up writing activities that replicate online social networking interactions. Learners can 'chat' to one another in small groups using pen and paper. This conversation can then form the basis of a group 'blog'; these blogs are then passed around the class – or posted on the classroom wall – and commented on, before being returned to their original writers. This material is then available to the teacher for subsequent analysis and development.

Finally, exploit the texts and the topics in your course book as stimuli for learner comment and opinion. Learners may not always respond to the content of a text – but they *never* will if they are not invited to!

Scott Thornbury teaches on an MA TESOL program for the New School, New York, and lives in Spain. He is the author of a number of books on language and methodology, including *Uncovering Grammar, Beyond the Sentence* and *An A-Z of ELT* (all published by Macmillan). His latest book, *Teaching Unplugged* (Delta Publishing) was co-written with Luke Meddings. He is currently the series editor for the Cambridge Handbooks for Teachers.

Rose Senior: Class-centred learning

Class-centred teaching is a framework for understanding the behaviour of effective classroom teachers that can help all language teachers to teach more successfully. As its name suggests, class-centred teaching foregrounds the class group and makes the learning and social wellbeing of the class the focal point of the teacher's attention. The holistic notion of class-centred teaching is based on the premise that cohesive classes (characterised by overall feelings of openness, trust, and mutual respect) provide optimum environments for language learning.

The class-centred framework is applicable to all classroom situations, to all teaching contexts, and to all teaching approaches. Although no teacher has a 100% success rate, class-centred teachers have a higher proportion of classes that 'gel' than those who do not. The good news is that all teachers can become class-centred. The starting point involves keeping in mind that each class must sense that it is going on a collective journey towards the achievement of worthwhile learning goals.

How do class-centred teachers behave?

Class-centred teachers:

- develop rapport with their classes, ensuring that their students regard them not only as teachers with a sound knowledge of English but also as integral members of their class groups (who can laugh at themselves or behave spontaneously when something unexpected happens, for example).

- treat all students fairly and with respect, appreciating that learning a new language is a risky business because of the possibility of making mistakes and appearing foolish.

- always maintain their authority while remaining friendly towards their students and establish codes of behaviour that support student learning and enforce them in ways that do not alienate or humiliate individuals.

- understand that once social processes that enhance learning have been set in motion, teachers should find it unnecessary to behave in authoritarian ways that enforce the 'me-versus-them' divide.

How can I teach in class-centred ways?

- Encourage whole-class involvement by engaging your students in a memorable or meaningful way at the start of each new lesson. (At intermediate levels this is particularly important, since the initial excitement of learning English may have worn off.) Think of alternative, engaging ways of having your classes complete mundane tasks such as grammar exercises, remembering that variety is the essence of good teaching and that there are many ways in which learning activities can be 'tweaked'.

- As you move around your class observing students you will find yourself naturally helping small numbers of students on the spot. As the need for additional words or phrases becomes apparent, write these on the board so that other students can benefit from your input. Make a note, too, of what needs to be expanded upon or revised. Then, at a later point, re-teach these items to the class as a whole.

- Remember that although lively behaviour is evidence of student engagement, noisy, fun-filled classrooms may not be reliable indicators either of student learning – or of student satisfaction. There will be times when it is more appropriate for students to be working purposefully and reflectively, either on their own or quietly with a partner. A collective feeling of whole-class learning will prevail when this happens.

The class-centred framework will help you keep in mind that your classes function as groups – and that effective teaching and learning involves keeping every class that you teach as unified as possible for the duration of the course.

Rose Senior is a language teacher, teacher educator and classroom researcher. Author of *The Experience of Language Teaching* (CUP, 2006), Rose presents at conferences, runs professional development workshops and writes on a range of aspects of classroom language teaching in both academic and teacher-oriented journals. She has a regular column in *English Teaching Professional*.

Jonathan Marks: Pronunciation: the right kind and the right time

Teachers sometimes feel unsure about what kind of pronunciation learners should be aiming for – British? American? or something else? – and about what is the right time in a lesson to focus on pronunciation. I hope this short essay will give you some pointers in these two directions.

What kind of pronunciation should my learners aim for?

If English is a global language, it obviously needs to be internationally intelligible. But it would probably be impossible to describe a type of pronunciation that would always guarantee intelligibility between any two speakers from any two parts of the world. It seems that consonant sounds – with the exception of the notorious 'th' sounds! – may be particularly important. A consistent set of distinctions between vowel sounds is important too, but the total number of different vowel sounds probably doesn't need to be as large as in standard native English. Word stress is probably important for intelligibility, and perhaps at least a basic intonation distinction between fall and rise.

There are other factors to consider, too. In some parts of the world there are well-established and widely-used regional pronunciations of English. In some countries, there may be prestige attached to British or American pronunciation, and learners may wish to aim for one of these or even be expected to do so in exams they plan to take.

At the same time, it's important for all learners to have experience of listening to, and 'tuning in' to, a wide variety of different pronunciations from around the world – which is why *Global* has introduced its Global Voices section.

When is the right time to focus on pronunciation?

1 Planned pronunciation activities

Sometimes you might want to plan and include an activity to practise a particular aspect of pronunciation. For example, if you notice that your learners systematically fail to make the distinction between the vowel sounds in pairs of words like 'cold' and 'called', you might devote a 10-minute spot to practising that distinction.

2 Introducing new language

Whenever you introduce new language, you should think about how it's pronounced, and whether learners are likely to need help with saying it. For example, if they're learning a compound noun such as 'reception desk' they need to know that the stress is on the first element, or if they're learning the idiom 'You must be joking!' they need to know that it has a standardised stress and intonation pattern.

3 Any other time!

A need for a focus on pronunciation can also arise at any other time. Let's say, for example, that a class discussion about different jobs turns to the topic of having to wear a suit at work. Some learners pronounce the word 'suit' correctly, and others say 'sweet' or 'suet'. Because 'suit' has become, for the moment, a key word in the discussion, it would probably be useful to intervene and establish the correct pronunciation. Or, let's say that learners have trouble understanding part of a recording which sounds to them like 'A bing go in there for ages'. You could help them by pointing out that: 'I've' is reduced to /ə/, the vowel sound in 'been' is shortened, the last sound of 'been' changes to 'ng' to make a smooth link with 'going', and the '-ing' of 'going' is changed to '-in'. You could also give them a chance to imitate the pronunciation on the recording – not necessarily in order to learn to speak this way, but because it will help them to develop an awareness of how words can become disguised in fluent speech, and to recognise such 'disguised' words.

Every lesson is a pronunciation lesson, because nobody can speak without pronouncing! Thinking about 'the right kind' and 'the right time' is a first step towards giving learners effective help with their pronunciation.

Jonathan Marks is a freelance teacher trainer, author and translator based in Poland. His publications include *English Pronunciation in Use - Elementary* (CUP 2007). He is a founder member of the IATEFL Pronunciation Special Interest Group, and currently the group's joint co-ordinator.

Ben Goldstein: Images and critical thinking

Using images in the language classroom is something we take for granted. However, images have been traditionally used as 'pictures' to stimulate or illustrate language, subservient to the written or spoken word, and therefore not always exploited to their full potential. Rather than asking learners simply to describe images, we can encourage them to reflect more deeply on them, to look beyond the frame and start to see images as cultural artefacts open to diverse readings. We can also allow learners to take a more active role by inviting them to bring their own images to class.

What kinds of images?

Digital technology has meant that we can now access and manipulate images as never before. Many of our learners have become experts in visualising experience, some communicate more easily through visual stimuli than verbal – this may be through photos on social networking sites, emoticons in text messages or avatars in virtual worlds. Alongside such images, it is easy for the ones we present in class to look outdated or irrelevant. Our challenge is to provide images that can truly resonate and motivate learners to take part in classroom tasks. To this aim the images in *Global* have been selected with the aim of moving away from typical language teaching representations of reality and to challenge our expectations. This is a fine starting point, but teachers should also be sensitive to local needs and interests when choosing images. Sensible criteria for selecting images might be summed up as: impact (will the images be able to stimulate or engage the learner on an imaginative level?), practicability (how easy is it for learners to access them?), familiarity (how well will the class recognize them or know how to respond?), opportunity for personalization (how can the learners make these images their own?) and openness to multiple interpretation (how many different readings can be drawn from a certain image?).

Where can you find them?

- Try image-sharing websites which allow you to search via key words or tags and exhibit or edit your own images.
- Create your own class page and ask learners to upload files, inviting them to comment on their own work and that of others.
- Use key words to search for miscellaneous images on the internet.

What can you do with them?

We can analyse images from three different perspectives: the affective, the compositional and the critical. The first is our emotional response to the image – how does it make you feel? The second is how the image can be analysed in terms of its relationship to text, for example the way it has been framed or captured and presented to the viewer. Finally, the critical perspective asks us to bear in mind the broader context in which an image appears, what messages does it convey and how is it intended to be read? Such an approach emphasizes the importance of bringing a social critique to our reading of images.

For example, imagine that you wanted to focus on a particular country in class. One idea would be to search for images that reflect something about this country's identity, customs, values, etc. Choose icons such as stamps, money, flags. Analyse these in class and collect different interpretations. Then set learners the task of finding their own visual representations of the place. Finally, source images of the learners' own country to find out how it is portrayed in different media. For example, what images are commonly found in tourist brochures of the learners' country and how representative are these in reality? As such, images can be an excellent way to encourage critical reading and intercultural awareness and consequently challenge stereotyping.

Ben Goldstein is a teacher, teacher trainer and materials writer. He teaches online at the Universitat Oberta de Catalunya in Barcelona and on the MA Tesol Program for the New School, New York. He is the main author of the *New Framework* adult coursebook series (Richmond Publishing) and author of a methodological handbook for teachers *Working with Images* (CUP). His main interests in ELT are the use of images, World Englishes and intercultural issues.

Teaching notes

Individual & Society

Coursebook

Unit 1	Language	Texts	Communicative skills
Part 1 SB page 6	Vocabulary Everyday objects Grammar Word order in questions Pronunciation The alphabet	Reading *The identity (ID) card*	Speaking Describing personal objects Exchanging personal information
Part 2 SB page 8	Vocabulary Describing appearance Extend your vocabulary – *look* and *look like* Grammar *What* and *How* questions	Reading Identity theft Listening Describing appearance and photo identification	Speaking Describing someone familiar Finding out real and false identities
Part 3 SB page 10	Vocabulary Relationships Extend your vocabulary – *in touch* Grammar The present simple and frequency adverbs	Reading *The six degrees of separation theory* Listening Explanation of the theory	Speaking Describing links in relationships and asking questions about family, friends and colleagues
Part 4 SB page 12	Extend your vocabulary – *place* Grammar The present continuous Pronunciation Linking words	Reading *CCTV is watching you*	Speaking Expressing opinions about CCTV Comparing what people do with what they are doing now
Function globally	Common social expressions / Social responses Listening to and matching situations and pictures Students roleplay short conversations with suitable responses		
Global English	David Crystal text: *Same language but different* Students talk about communication differences in language		
Writing	A personal description for a social networking site Joining sentences using conjunctions		
Global review	Grammar and vocabulary review Extra speaking practice		
Study skills	Students evaluate their methods for language learning		

Additional resources

eWorkbook	Interactive and printable grammar, vocabulary, listening and pronunciation practice Extra reading and writing practice Additional downloadable listening and audio material
Teacher's Resource CD	Communication activity worksheets to print and photocopy
Go global: ideas for further research	**Individual** – Ask students to find the origins of another everyday object **Society** – Ask students to choose a place to visit on Google Street View

Individual & Society

Part 1

Lead-in

Choose one object that you have in your bag or pockets, but do not show the students. Define this object without using the word, and students have to guess what it is, eg *It's something you use when you have a cold; it's usually white and it's made of paper* (*tissue*). Students then do the same in pairs with 3 'secret' objects in their bags or pockets.

Vocabulary (SB page 6)

1 Students work on their own, matching the object described to a word from the box, before comparing answers in pairs.

In feedback, ask students which piece of information they find surprising.

You may like to model and drill the word *chewing gum* (n) /ˈtʃuːwɪŋ ˌɡʌm/ and any other problem words.

a lipstick	d credit card
b mobile phone	e glasses
c chewing gum	

2 Before students start talking to their partner, put these questions on the board for extra discussion:
What sort/brand/type is it?
When and where did you get it?
When/how often do you use it?

Reading (SB page 6)

This is a text containing facts about ID (identity) cards.

1 💿 **1.01** Play the recording after the first task or during the second task, as appropriate for your students. Elicit some suggestions about what you can find on an ID card. For this first reading task allow 3–5 minutes.

Tell students that they do not need to worry about new vocabulary at this point. Ask for class feedback.

2 Give students time to read the task and to check any unknown words.

After re-reading the text, let them compare answers in pairs, before class feedback.

1	to travel to different countries
2	the UK, the US, Canada, Australia, Ireland and New Zealand
3	plastic
4	name, date of birth, address, phone number, nationality, profession, marital status
5	fingerprints, digital images of people's eyes

3 If your class make-up allows it, put students in mixed nationality groups and let them discuss the points in exercise 3.

To provide more opportunities to talk, ask groups to try to brainstorm two advantages and two disadvantages of having ID cards. Give or elicit an example, eg *you always have to carry it around with you.* Give students five minutes to do this.

(Other possible disadvantages are: *it takes away your privacy; it makes you feel like a statistic; it could lead to identity crime (fraud).* Possible advantages are: *it can be helpful to the police; it could be useful in an emergency situation; it is smaller to carry than a passport.*)

Ask students to give you their ideas and write them on the board, helping with any difficult vocabulary and taking the opportunity to input and upgrade any other language they need.

Grammar (SB page 7)

1 Your students will have met these forms already, so approach this as a test-teach (They attempt the task without help and then you help them if necessary).

Ask students to work alone on exercise 1, after doing an example together.

Students compare answers in pairs, then take class feedback. At this stage, elicit the grammar rules from the examples, using the board to highlight any relevant points, eg the auxiliary verb *do*, the main verb and the subject.

Then let students read the reminders under **Grammar**.

1	What do you do?
2	Do you speak any foreign languages?
3	What is your name?
4	What's your phone number?
5	Do you have any children?
6	Where were you born?
7	Where did you go to school?
8	Where do you live?
9	Are you married?
10	What is your date of birth?

Language note

In British English students may also come across *have got* to express possession (see 5: *Do you have …?* which could be expressed as *Have you got …?*). You may find that your students know or ask about this so be prepared to write the forms up if necessary. (See SB Unit 5 page 55).

2 Ask students to match the questions to the topics. These items are very useful as they typically appear on official forms which students may need to fill in.

Explain any items which cause difficulty, eg *education*, *marital status*.

1 Profession
2 Languages
3 Name
4 Phone number
5 Children
6 Place of birth
7 Education
8 Address
9 Marital status
10 Date of birth

3 Ask students to choose five questions they would like to ask someone and then do the task in pairs.

Monitor students, helping them with accuracy of form and pronunciation.

G Grammar focus

Show students the icon. Write page 132 on the board and ask them to find it. Show students the language summary on word order in questions.

You can use exercises 1 and 2 on page 133 for:

a) extra practice now
b) homework
c) review a couple of lessons from now.

The answers are on page 142 of the Teacher's Book.

TEACH GLOBAL THINK LOCAL Extra activity

Write four to six answers about yourself on the board, eg *33* (*What's your house number?*); *my husband and daughter* (*Who do you live with?*). Students find the right question (the one in your head) **and** should also use correct English. You need to indicate what the exact problem is when students ask you questions, eg (my husband and daughter) Student: ~~Who you live with?~~ You: *That's the right question here, but think about your English.* In the same way, students think of six answers about themselves, which they then show to their partner.

Pronunciation (SB page 7)

1 🔊 **1.02** This is an important diagnostic activity, to see how students cope with spelling and sounds in English.

Students listen to the recording and write the words as they are spelled.

Monitor as they are listening, and then let students compare answers.

In whole-class feedback, ask different students to spell out the words. You may need to drill individual letters.

1 T O R R A N C E
2 J A N S S E N
3 K E N T U C K Y
🔊 **1.02**
1 Man 1: Sorry, yes. My last name is Torrance. That's T O R R A N C E.
2 Woman 1: I live on Janssen Street. I'll spell that for you: J A N S S E N.
3 Man 2: Write this down. The name of the state is K E N T U C K Y. That's Kentucky.

2 Ask students to work in pairs and A spells these words to B. Monitor and assist, as appropriate.

You could also input relevant functional language here. eg:

My last name is Spatola, that's S P A T O L A.

My name is Scott, that's S C O double T. That's S for Spain and C for Canada. Have you got that?

3 Ask B students to spell the words to As.

TEACH GLOBAL THINK LOCAL Extra activity

If students find the pronunciation exercise difficult, ask them to put the letters of the alphabet into sound categories. Cut out a set of letters for each group of three, or simply write the alphabet on the board. Then ask students to group any letters with the same vowel sound. Give two or three examples to start with; if your students need it, also give the 'starter' phonemes for each sound group (see below).

/eɪ/ a, h, j, k
/iː/ b, c, d, e, g, p, t, v
/e/ f, l, m, n, s, x, z
/aɪ/ i, y
/əʊ/ o
/ɑː/ r
/uː/ q, u, w

Part 2

Speaking and Vocabulary (SB page 8)

TEACH GLOBAL THINK LOCAL Lead-in

Show students a photo of a close friend of yours. If you don't have one, draw a quick sketch on the board. Talk about his/her age, appearance, job, how you met. Spend most time on appearance, particularly how he/she has changed over the time you have been friends. At the end, let students ask questions about him/her.

1 Tell students that they are going to describe a friend or relative.

Students look at exercise 1 on page 8. Give them two minutes to think about what they are going to say.

Students then work in pairs to talk about their respective friends.

If necessary, you could clarify some of the words they are going to practise in exercise 2 beforehand, either visually, eg point to someone with *fair* hair, or with simple explanations, eg *a bald person has no hair*. It is likely that the following words will be new for at least some students: *bald, fair, medium-height, middle-aged, overweight, scar*.

2 Ask students to look at the spidergram with the circles and explain the task. Let students complete it alone, then compare answers in pairs.

Height – tall, medium height, short

Hair – short, bald, blond, curly, fair, straight, shoulder-length

Skin – dark, fair

Features – moustache, beard, scar, bald

Age – old, in her twenties, middle-aged, young.

Weight – fat, overweight, slim

Pronunciation note

Your students may find some of these words difficult to pronounce, often because the vowel sounds are diphthongs or long sounds: *bald* /ɔː/, *beard* /ɪə/, *curly* /ɜː/, *fair* /eə/, *height* /aɪ/, *middle-aged* /eɪ/, *weight* /eɪ/, *scar* /ɑː/, *shoulder(-length)* /əʊ/, *straight* /eɪ/. You could point out to students that *straight*, *weight* and *aged* all contain the sound /eɪ/ in spite of their different spellings. Drill these words as necessary.

3 Ask students to think of the friend they described in exercise 1 and to circle any words or phrases from exercise 2 which are relevant to him or her.

They should then describe their friend again, to a different partner, using the new words.

Listening (SB page 8)

These are four short conversations between two people discussing photos.

1 🔊 1.03–1.06 Let students look at photos **a–j** in silence for a few seconds. Students listen and choose four photos for the conversations.

1 A: Oh, when was this photo taken?
　B: That one? Five years ago, I think.
　A: Mmmm. It's quite a *good* photo of you.
　B: I don't know. I don't think I looked good with that beard.
　A: I think you look nice and intelligent.
(photo e)

2 A: How's the baby?
　B: Oh *great*. Great.
　A: It's a 'she', right?
　B: Yes, yes. I'll show you a photo. She looks like her father.
　A: Oh yes, bald just like her dad! How old is she?
　B: Six months now.
　A: She looks really happy. She's got a great smile.
(photo a)

3 A: Who's this a photo of?
　B: Don't you know? It's Bella!
　A: Bella? Oh yes! She looks so different here. How long ago was this?
　B: At the end of university.
　A: Wow. Her hair was much longer then, and so curly.
(photo j)

4 A: What does the suspect look like?
　　I can't hear you. What does the suspect look like?
　B: The suspect is a white, older man.
　A: Anything else?
　B: Just a second … yes. He's got grey hair and a moustache.
　A: What kind of car does he drive?
　B: An old white Volvo.
　A: Thanks.
(photo i)

2 Allow students to read the questions first, then to listen again.

Let students compare answers and, if necessary, replay the recording. Take class feedback.

1   Yes, she does.

2   Six months.

3   Her hair is shorter.

4   Grey.

3 First model an example to the class yourself. Then students work in pairs to describe the photos.

Extend your vocabulary – *look* and *look like*

Use the photographs from SB page 9 to focus on the target language. For example, say *He looks French* (photo i); *He looks like a film star* (photo h). Ask students to identify which photos they think you are referring to, then elicit the language you used onto the board.

Ask students what the difference is between the two forms, highlighting the difference (adjective or noun).

Let them read the rules under **Extend your vocabulary**.

Students then work in pairs to complete the exercise.

1   He looks like his father.

2   Are you OK? You look tired.

3   I look horrible in this photo.

4   That chair doesn't look comfortable.

Language note

Students typically muddle these two structures, saying for example: ~~he looks like angry, she like her mother~~ etc. Translation can be a useful way of getting students to focus on the differences. Ask students to translate the example sentences into their first language, if possible working with a partner sharing the same mother tongue.

Note that in the structure *to look like someone*, the verb *be* can replace *look*, eg *She is like her mother; She looks like her mother*. However, *be* can also refer to behaviour or character, eg *She's like her dad, always quick to get angry*.

TEACH GLOBAL THINK LOCAL Extra activity

Collect several photos of people from the internet or from magazines (about 6–10). Pass the numbered pictures around the class, with students working in pairs. Give students two minutes to write a mini-description in their notebooks next to each number, using either of the target structures, eg *She looks like a teacher* ; *She looks very friendly*. They should also include two facts about appearance, eg *She's got shoulder-length hair*. Stick up the collection of pictures on the board in order, with the numbers written underneath. Give a little extra time if necessary. Then re-group pairs into fours. Students read out their descriptions at random for their listeners to guess which one they are describing.

Grammar (SB page 9)

1 Before reading the text, put the following questions on the board: *What is identity theft? What are typical examples? How do thieves do it? How big is the problem and why? How can you protect yourself?*

Check that students understand the questions, then put them in threes to discuss.

Take whole class feedback. Do not focus on the Grammar section at this point.

Ask students to read the text and fill in the missing questions. In feedback on the task, first check the missing words, then ask students to close their books.

Ask the questions again, and students try to give you the answers to the questions. This allows students to focus on the message, as well as the language. If necessary, let them re-read the text, before re-asking the questions.

1   How

2   What sort

3   How many

4   How much

5   What kinds

TEACH GLOBAL THINK LOCAL Extra activity

If you feel your students would benefit from focusing on the form of the questions, then do so now: the rule regarding the use of an adjective after *how* is useful and also easy to teach. You could put the first two sentences from the grammar box on the board, with the bold words gapped, then elicit the words. Students should think of two more examples for each, in pairs. They can then read the grammar explanation in the box.

2 Let students work on their own initially to complete this task. You could put up the answers on the board, as an alternative to oral feedback.

1   What colour are your eyes?

2   What colour is your hair?

3   How long is your hair?

4   What month is your birthday?

5   How old are you?

6   What street do you live on?

7   How tall are you?

Individual & Society

TEACH GLOBAL THINK LOCAL Mixed ability

To make exercise 2 more pacy, and to suit **stronger students**, ask students to close their books and write down the numbers one to seven. Then read out each example exactly as in exercise 2, only saying each sentence twice. Students write down the correct sentence next to the number, or leave a blank if necessary. They should compare answers before feedback.

G Grammar focus

Show students the icon. Write page 132 on the board and ask them to find it. Show students the language summary on *What* and *How* questions.

You can use exercise 1 on page 133 for:

a) extra practice now
b) homework
c) review a couple of lessons from now.

The answers are on page 142 of the Teacher's Book.

Speaking (SB page 9)

1 The aim of this speaking activity is to practise the questions from exercise 2.

Give out a piece of paper to each student for exercise 1 and give time to students to write down the three pieces of information. Take in the pieces of paper.

2 Re-distribute the pieces of paper to different students, making sure that everyone has a new identity. Students need to realize that they are now the person on the paper.

3 Model the activity first, pretending to be one of the students. Their aim is to listen and find out who they are, judging from the answers. Put students in pairs.

Most students at this level will find the language relatively easy, but will nevertheless make slips when speaking. Monitor and collect some examples of language errors, to focus on after the activity.

TEACH GLOBAL THINK LOCAL Homework extra

If students need additional writing practice, ask them to write a description of one of their friends or family members, including some of the new lexis (SB exercise 2, page 8) and also the *look like* forms.

They should use at least 60 words, including details of their face, hair, height, weight, etc., as well as basic information (name, job, age, nationality, how they know him/her, interests, etc). They can include a photo if they wish!

Part 3

Vocabulary and Listening (SB page 10)

TEACH GLOBAL THINK LOCAL Lead-in

Ask students: *How well do you know your classmates?* Write these questions up for students to answer individually: *Who lives very close? Who speaks many languages? Who comes from a large family? Who enjoys learning English? Who's the youngest in the class? Who's a music lover?* Students compare answers in threes. Take open-class feedback and find out the answers!

1 Ask students to select three people from the class that they know something about. Put students in pairs.

Before they start sharing information, elicit some suggested areas to the board, eg *hobbies and interests, where from, travelling to school or work, weekends, pets, home,* etc.

2 **1.07** Ask students to look at the picture of Becky and make suggestions about her age, nationality, possible job, interests, personality, etc. This also consolidates the *look like/look + adj* forms.

Ask students to look at the words in the box in exercise 2. Check understanding by asking concept questions eg a concept question for *acquaintance* could be: *This is someone you know, but **how** well do you know the person?*

Drill the words and elicit where the main stress is: *acquaintance, classmate, colleague, neighbour.*

Point out the four names around the photo of Becky, then play the recording for students to decide on her relationship to them.

1.07

1 Pilar is my Spanish **neighbour**. She's on vacation in Mexico, and I've got her cat and her plants.

2 OK, Hans. Hans and I aren't really friends. He's more of an **acquaintance**. He's director of the German department.

3 Ken is a **colleague** of mine at the university. He teaches French, and I teach German.

4 I take a computer class in the evening. Sofia is my **classmate**.

---

3 Students read the questions before listening a second time.

---

1 She's on vacation.

2 No, she doesn't.

3 Yes, she does.

4 They are in the same computer class.

---

4 Provide a model of personal connections yourself, using the board and an oral description. Then tell students that they need to do the same, giving at least four names, as in the Becky diagram.

Give time for students to do this, then tell them to also think about three pieces of information for each of the names they have written.

Let students exchange information in pairs.

Listening and Reading (SB page 10)

This listening explains how the theory works, using the diagram in exercise 2.

1 💿 **1.08** Write *The six degrees of separation theory* on the board and ask students if anyone knows anything about it.

Pre-teach the following words: *bind – bound, planet, separate – separate*. Let students listen to and read the extract on page 11.

> 💿 **1.08** See SB page 11

Invite initial reactions to what they have read and point out the picture of the scientific model on page 11, which is a visual representation of the theory.

2 💿 **1.09** Tell students what they are going to listen to, instructing them to draw links between the names in the circle (SB page 10).

> The theory of Six Degrees of Separation works likes this. Imagine you and John are colleagues. John is married to Mary, but you don't know her personally. So you and Mary have one degree of separation. Mary has a sister, Jane. Jane and you have two degrees of separation. Jane's neighbour, let's call him Robert, works for a big hotel in the city centre. You and Robert, Jane's neighbour, have three degrees of separation. Robert doesn't own the hotel. He works for Mr. Smith, the president. You and Mr Smith … four degrees of separation. Mr Smith, because he's an owner of a big expensive hotel, he's often in touch with important people. He's friends with the Ambassador for example. So you and the Ambassador have five degrees of separation. And well, the Ambassador goes to New York three times a year, and he knows the Secretary General of the United Nations. So, if you make all the right connections it means that you and the Secretary General of the United Nations have six degrees of separation.

3 Tell students to listen again to explain the link between the people in numbers 1–3. Play the recording twice if necessary.

Let students compare answers before class feedback.

> 1   You and John are colleagues.
> 2   Jane and Robert are neighbours.
> 3   Mr Smith is friends with the Ambassador.

4 Let students read the examples first, and think about themselves or people that are close to them. Put students in pairs or threes to discuss whether they think the theory is true and if they can think of personal examples.

Monitor for any interesting points or examples, which you can then discuss later with the whole class. At the end students could also take a vote as to whether they believe the theory is true or not.

TEACH GLOBAL THINK LOCAL **Extra activity**

If your students need extra oral fluency practice, they could change pairs and think of someone well-known they have met, giving details of when and where they met. However, tell students that they can also choose to lie if they wish. Model this activity yourself, eg *I have met …* . Elicit up to ten questions from students about the encounter. Give convincing answers, even if the initial statement is actually false. At the end the students must decide if you are telling the truth or lying. Then students do the same.

Background note

'Six degrees of separation' refers to the idea that everyone on earth is connected to everyone else by a chain of only six steps, the first step being all the people a person knows, the second step being all the people known by those in the first step, etc. The theory has been developed and adapted by various thinkers and writers from different fields, interested in exploring the idea of human and social interconnectedness. For example, Frigyes Karinthy, a Hungarian author, writing in the 1920s and American psychologist, Stanley Milgram, working in the 1960s, looked into this theory. John Guare's play *Six Degrees of Separation*, helped to popularize the theory. Technology and globalization has produced a growing sense of social interconnectedness; a sense that the world is getting smaller. Thus, the theory seems particularly pertinent for our times.

Extend your vocabulary – *in touch* (SB page 10)

Write on the board: *I'm still _____ with a woman I met when I was at university. We phone each other every few months.*

Elicit the missing phrase and elicit any other phrases they know with 'touch'.

Ask individual students to read out the examples in the book (SB page 10) and after each one, ask students to try to paraphrase, eg *He is often in touch with important people*: *he often meets, emails or phones important people.*

Students then complete the exercise, first alone, then check in pairs.

1	in touch with
2	not in touch
3	keep in touch
4	lose touch

Language note

In these phrases with *touch*, *touch* can be replaced with *contact*. Note that in these phrases *touch* is a noun. Students probably already know *touch* as a verb.

Grammar (SB page 11)

Depending on your students, decide whether to remind them of the rules first, before doing exercise 1, or to let them tackle exercise 1 first, before looking at the rules. Students at this level are likely to be familiar with the rules presented, but still make slips, particularly in speech. Generally speaking, a test-teach approach is therefore appropriate.

1 Tell students they are going to read and talk about how people stay in touch.

Dictate the following question: *How often do you use: a) the phone b) texting c) face-book or other online social networks d) letters?*

Ask students to discuss *when/where/how often* or *how many/who to* with their partner.

They then turn to page 11 and complete the gap fill individually. As they are working, go around and monitor, making a note of any problems.

Students then compare answers in pairs. If the students have made a few slips, let them read the first two grammar rules under **Grammar** (SB page 11) and then re-check exercise 1, before whole class feedback.

TEACH GLOBAL THINK LOCAL Mixed ability

Allow students to work in pairs to talk through and possibly show their own online social network. Monitor to check that they are using the present simple for habits and routines.

1	keep	7	takes
2	use	8	puts
3	has	9	look
4	is	10	see
5	doesn't write	11	send
6	puts		

2 Students write the sentences out individually, then read the last two rules under **Grammar** (SB page 11). Take whole class feedback.

1	Becky talks to her parents on the phone three times a week.
2	She is always very friendly with the neighbours.
3	She often goes out with her colleagues.
4	She uses the internet every day to keep in touch with people.

G Grammar focus

Show students the icon. Write page 132 on the board and ask them to find it. Show students the language summary on the present simple and frequency.

You can use exercise 1 on page 133 for:
a) extra practice now
b) homework
c) review a couple of lessons from now.

The answers are on page 142 of the Teacher's Book.

Language note

You may want to point out to students that longer adverbs of frequency (expressions), such as *three times a week*, go at the end of the clause or can be placed at the start for emphasis (see also SB page 132).

TEACH GLOBAL THINK LOCAL Extra activity

If students need reminding of the present simple, then ask them to quickly re-read the texts and then to close their books. Put the following prompts on the board: *people (keep); people (use); every member (have); Jim (be); he (not write); he (put) and (put); his friends (look); they (send)*. Then students can reconstruct the text, either orally or in writing, depending on students' needs and timing. Students complete this in pairs, then check their sentences with the original text.

Speaking (SB page 11)

Refer students to the relevant pages and give them time to complete the questions on their own first, with you monitoring and assisting. Then put students in pairs to ask and answer the questions.

TEACH GLOBAL THINK LOCAL Homework extra

Ask students to find a recent message (e-mails or similar) that they have sent to friends or family in their first language. Ask them to translate it and then bring it in, for their partner to read. They can add any comments or additional relevant information to help their partners understand the message.

Part 4

Lead-in

Write *CCTV* and some prompts from the text on the board eg *When first used and why/Modern uses/Most common place for CCTV/City with most CCTV cameras* and ask students if they can come up with any information, working in groups of three. Then ask them to check on SB page 12.

Speaking and Reading (SB page 12)

1 Ask students to read and answer the questions individually, writing their opinion for question 3.

Then students work in pairs to discuss the answers to the three questions. Take feedback on exercise 1, but keep it fairly brief.

When discussing point 3 in particular, elicit some possible arguments for or against, but do so succinctly.

The text *Readers' response* (SB page 13) gives members of the public's responses to an earlier article entitled 'CCTV is watching you'.

2 Give students a time-limit of about two minutes – you could encourage students to read the first sentence only of each mini text as this is a gist reading.

In feedback, make sure that the genre, audience and context for these texts is clear, to aid understanding.

b   letters to a newspaper

3 Ask students to read the texts more closely, and allow more time for them to answer the questions. Pre-teach the word *crime(n)* and *criminal(n)*.

1   Tatyana Ivanov
2   Philip Richards
3   Kenneth Thomas
4   Rajit Gadh

Mixed ability

For stronger readers, you could add extra questions, pre-prepared on a slip of paper, eg *Do they all live in dangerous places?* (no – see Martha Klein's letter); *How are cameras like or not like security guards?* (they protect but are cheaper); *Which writers have quite similar opinions?* (Richards and Ivanov; Klein and Gadh).

4 Students work in pairs to find and note down the main arguments in the texts – two for and two against – then decide which they agree with.

In feedback, elicit the arguments to the board. Highlight useful language or collocations, eg *an invasion of our*

privacy, private life, dangerous society, make you feel safe, etc. Ask for any additional suggestions and encourage students to give full answers to the question: *Which arguments do you agree with?*

Refer back to what students wrote in exercise 1 (question 3). Ask students if any of them have changed their opinions.

Two arguments in favour: They make people feel safe; they reduce crime (Philip Richards); they give protection and are cheaper than security guards (Tatyana Ivanov).

Two arguments against: The government is watching us too much and this will extend into other areas of our lives (Rajit Gadh), The government is invading our privacy (Martha Klein).

Extra activity

Ask students to write their own letter, in response to the imagined text. You could also make the situation more concrete: *the school/college is thinking of putting up CCTV cameras on the premises.* Students write in to give their reaction.

Extend your vocabulary (SB page 12)

Ensure the students' books are closed. Write the word 'place' on the board to focus students, telling them they are going to look at different expressions with this word. Ask them if they can think of any expressions with this word, prompting them by using the examples given: *The festival _____(2 words) in October; I felt _____(3 words) there, I didn't know anybody.*

Students then open their books on page 12 and complete the exercise on their own, before comparing answers in pairs.

1   in the first place
2   in place of
3   all over the place
4   a very quiet place
5   it's not our place

Extra activity

Read out the five complete sentences from the texts containing the target 'place' phrases. Students listen and translate them into their first language, either alone or in pairs if your class is monolingual, writing them down. They then convert these back into English, paying particular attention to the target phrases. When students have checked their own versions with the original, get them to underline the translated 'place' phrases in their mother tongue versions, and to find out how many different words are used for 'place'.

Individual & Society

Grammar (SB page 13)

Before doing exercise 1, write the first two example sentences under **Grammar** on the board. Ask students to discuss in pairs why the present continuous is used.

Then refer students to the first two bullet points under the examples on page 13, and ask students to find and underline any other examples of the present continuous in the letters.

Then write on the board:
My co-workers and I _____ with CCTV cameras. Personally, I _____ that this is another example of government invasion of our privacy.

Elicit what the verbs are (*agree* and *believe*, respectively). Ask students why they are in the present simple and not continuous, then refer them to the third bullet point. Elicit examples from the students, eg *I like ice-cream.*

1 Tell students they are going to read another letter on CCTV. First give them one minute to read and find out if Lola is for or against CCTV. Do the first example together, eliciting why the present continuous is used and referring back to the grammar explanations.

Students then work alone to complete the task. They compare answers in pairs and should try and explain their choice, if necessary in L1.

1	am looking	4	need them
2	belong	5	don't like
3	don't understand		

Language note

The so-called 'stative' or 'state' verbs can often be used in a continuous form as an 'active' or 'event' verb with a change in meaning, eg *I'm having a bath* (*I am in the bath now*) versus *I have a dog* (*I own a dog*). The state verbs such as *own* or *believe* are used to describe something that is generally unchanging; it cannot be broken down into single actions or component parts.

Note that verbs such as *like* and *love* are sometimes used in the continuous form in spoken English, eg *He's really loving the course.*

Many languages show the 'temporariness' or the 'nowness' of the progressive form with adverbials, so they have only one present verb form where English has two. Where appropriate, try to find out in advance more about your students' first language, to help anticipate problem areas and to perhaps use the L1 to focus on concept.

2 Draw a stick figure of yourself on the board, and three other stick figures of people you know, with their names.

Demonstrate the activity, using both tenses, but keeping it natural-sounding, eg *This is my sister who's a nurse. She works in a local hospital in Wales, where she lives. She qualified about 3 years ago and she really likes her job. At the moment (look at watch), she's probably looking after the patients.*

Students do the same activity, but written down. Monitor and give assistance.

TEACH GLOBAL THINK LOCAL **Mixed ability**

For students who need to see the text, provide a written copy of your model. Let students read it and then re-highlight the use of the two different tenses. Ask students to complete the same task, with your help where appropriate.

3 Put students in pairs and allow them to compare what they have written. Remind students that they need to ask at least one extra question per person described. Be prepared to assist with question forms.

G Grammar focus

Show students the icon. Write page 132 on the board and ask them to find it. Show students the language summary on the present continuous.

You can use exercise 1 on page 133 for:

a) extra practice now
b) homework
c) review a couple of lessons from now.

The answers are on page 142 of the Teacher's Book.

Pronunciation (SB page 13)

1 🔊 **1.10** This exercise focuses on contractions. Let students listen to the recording as many times as they wish to count the number of words. Remind them that contractions are made up of two words.

Man: What are you doing? (**4 words**)
Woman: So, what do you do? (**5 words**)
Woman: Excuse me, we're trying to work. (**7 words**)
Man: You're *not* listening. (**4 words**)
Woman: How's it going? (**4 words**)

2 Ask students to listen again and write the sentences, while you monitor progress.

In feedback, write the sentences on the board and highlight any linking visually, eg *What are /ə/ you doing?* Drill the sentences, as a class and individually.

3 Put students in pairs and tell them to think of a context for each of the sentences, and a follow-on sentence. Do the first example as a whole class.

Monitor and check students are using the correct present forms. Ask some pairs to demonstrate their dialogues to the class.

Function globally: common social expressions

These lessons in *Global* are designed to provide students with **immediately** useful functional language. They all follow a similar format.

Warm up (SB page 14)

Aim: to introduce the topic via a quick speaking task or picture work.

Tips:

- Do not over-correct here, especially in speaking activities.
- Encourage students to use what language they can at this stage.

Listening (SB page 14)

Aim: to present the functional language in context via a conversation or series of conversations.

Tips:

- Ask students to read the questions first before listening.
- Play the recording all the way through for each task (there are always two tasks).
- For multiple conversations pause the recording after each one.
- If students find it very difficult, play the recording a final time and allow them to read the audioscript at the back of the book.

1.11–1.14

1
A: Hello.
B: Hello.
A: First time here?
B: Sorry?
A: I said, is this your first time here? At the conference.
B: Yes. Yes.
A: Well, hello. My name's George.
B: Hi George. Nice to meet you.
picture c, situation 1

2
A: Oh, look at the time. It's getting late.
B: What time is it?
A: Eleven o'clock. And I have a class tomorrow.
B: Oh. Well, okay then.
A: Yes. Thanks for everything.
B: No problem.
A: Goodnight.
B: Bye.
picture d, situation 2

3
A: And this is from me.
B: Aww. Oh my …
A: It's a dog! Isn't that great?
B: Er, yes. A dog. Thank you very much.
A: You're welcome. Happy Birthday.
picture b, situation 6

4
A: … hello? Oh hi, listen I'm on the train. It's not a good time right now …
B: Hey!
A: Wait a minute … Oh, I'm sorry. I didn't see you and …
B: That's all right.
A: Here, let me help you with your bag.
B: No, it's fine.
picture a, situation 7

Language focus: social expressions (SB page 14)

Aim: to draw students' attention to the items of functional language.

Tips:

- Make sure students have time to understand the form and meaning of the phrases, but you needn't translate them word for word.
- Students should be able to pronounce these phrases intelligibly, so drill them.

1	c
2	a
3	c
4	b
5	c
6	a
7	c

Speaking (SB page 14)

Aim: to allow students an opportunity to use this language in a meaningful, real-world context.

Tips:

- There is sometimes a choice of task. Any task involving reading a script will be easier than a task involving making students' own scripts. This gives you flexibility for mixed ability classes.
- Give students time to prepare this activity, and circulate and monitor carefully.
- Correct sensitively, paying particular attention to the target language.
- If time allows, ask students to repeat the task, but with a new partner.

Individual & Society

Global English

These lessons in *Global* have two main goals. The first is to give you and your students interesting information about English and language in general. The second goal is to provide students with practice in different kinds of reading comprehension tasks that they are likely to encounter in future study (for example, exams).

TEACH GLOBAL THINK LOCAL Pre-reading activity

To help students understand the author's overall point, ask them to first look at the heading 'Same language … .' Elicit what this means, using questions like: *Do you all speak your first language in the same way? What affects how you speak and what you say?* Try to elicit some ideas from the text, eg age, region, social class. In this way, you prepare students and also clarify words used in the text.

Warm up (SB page 15)

Aim: to engage students with the topic, and highlight potentially difficult vocabulary in the text.

Tips:
- Be generous in helping students here with any unknown words in the first task.
- Ask students to relate this task, wherever possible, to similar events or texts in their own lives. This will help them with the reading.
- You may want to give your students an overview of the text before they read, possibly even in their first language. Make it interesting and involving.

Reading (SB page 15)

Aim: to provide students with interesting information about English, and reading exam practice skills.

Tips:
- Be ready to help less confident readers, explaining words or ideas in simpler terms if necessary.
- Get students to read through the whole text once first before doing the tasks.
- Many of these texts have been graded slightly, or not at all. There is a glossary of difficult words. Get students to read that first and reassure them that you do not expect them to understand every word or idea.
- There are two tasks. The first is an easier task, often focusing on the gist of the passage. The second is a more difficult task, similar to reading exam questions.

---

1 The author mentions differences in geography, social class and technology

2

1 true

2 false (American English)

3 false (U speakers had lunch in the middle of the day)

4 false (emails vary from highly formal to highly informal)

5 true

6 true

Language focus (SB page 15)

Aim: to highlight an interesting or useful aspect of language in the text.

Tips:
- The language focused on here is to raise students' awareness; do not expect them to produce it immediately.
- This language is not tested or reviewed in future units, which means you have more flexibility with this material as to when and where you use it.

---

1 as different as chalk from cheese (line 2)

2 rare (line 14)

3 above all (line 16)

4 inconceivable (line 17)

Speaking (SB page 15)

Aim: for students to relate the material in the reading to their own language, culture and experiences.

Tips:
- This is a short speaking activity and can be done in whole class mode or in small groups.
- Wherever possible, ask students to think of and provide examples in their own language but explain them in English too.

TEACH GLOBAL THINK LOCAL Extra activity

Students work in threes to guess the meaning of these abbreviations used in emailing (write these on the board). Listen to their ideas, then tell them the answers: TTYL (talk to you later); BFF (best friends forever); BFN (bye for now); g2g (got to go); CUL8R (see you later); NP (no problem). You could get early finishers to make up a couple of their own for English phrases.

Writing a personal description

Reading (SB page 16)

1 Students read the text and choose the best description.

1	b

2 Ask students to compare themselves with Constanza. This task demands a closer re-reading of the text. If students comment on the incorrect language, tell them that this is a real example of a student's writing and that you will look at the language later.

Writing skills: looking for errors in your work (SB page 16)

1 Students work alone to find twelve differences.

I'm <u>twenty years old</u> and single. I <u>was born</u> in Valdivia ... .
I <u>am studying</u> journalism <u>at university</u> and I like <u>this course</u> <u>very much</u>.
<u>There</u> are four people in my family ... . We <u>also have</u> a dog called Kalu. <u>My father is a</u> photographer and my mother is <u>a</u> teacher.
In my free time I like swimming, listening <u>to</u> music, and seeing friends. In the future I hope to go to <u>the</u> USA <u>to</u> do a Master's ... .

2 Students should highlight their own mistakes using a coloured pen.

3 To help students answer this question, you could do a mini-survey. Write these adverbs up: *always, sometimes* and *hardly ever / never*. Students decide which one applies to checking their own writing. Discuss.

Language focus: joining sentences (SB page 16)

1 Write or project the sentences up on the board one at a time. Have the conjunctions ready, each one on a separate piece of paper at the side, stuck onto the board. Once the students have read the sentence and consulted in pairs, call one student up to the front to stick the correct conjunction into the sentence and to cross out the capital letter of the second sentence, for example:

My sister trained as a teacher/ ~~but s~~ ~~S~~*he's unemployed at the moment.*

Language note

In this sentence, *and* is also possible, eg if the previous utterance was: 'My brother trained as a lawyer, but he's unemployed'. *So* is also an option here, eg if job prospects for teachers are currently very poor.

1. I'm short and slim, <u>and</u> I have long curly black hair.
2. My sister trained as a teacher <u>but</u> she's unemployed at the moment.
3. I'm thirty years old <u>and</u> I'm married with two children.
4. Clodagh isn't a common name, <u>so</u> people often don't know how to spell it.
5. I have three sisters, <u>but</u> I don't have any brothers.
6. I was born in a small village, <u>so</u> I find living in a big city very strange.

2 This exercise focuses on avoiding unnecessary repetition, known as 'ellipsis'. Students work in pairs to find the unnecessary words in other examples.

1. I'm short and slim, and ~~I~~ have long curly black hair.
2. My sister trained as a teacher but ~~she's~~ is unemployed at the moment.
3. I'm thirty years old and ~~I'm~~ married with two children.
4. Clodagh isn't a common name, so people often don't know how to spell it.
5. I have three sisters, but ~~I~~ don't have any brothers.
6. I was born in a small village, so ~~I~~ find living in a big city very strange.

Language note

In this exercise, the smallest part of the sentence that is ellipted is the pronoun (or subject). The pronoun can only be omitted if it is the same subject as in the first clause (see example 4: 'people' cannot be ellipted as it is a different subject). If the auxiliary or the main verbs are the same as in the first clause, these too can be omitted.

Preparing to write (SB page 16)

Remind students to refer back to the corrected Constanza text from earlier, which serves as a model.

For the first category, *Name*, point out the *Writing about names* section. You could read this out to students; personalise it for yourself; then elicit examples from individuals. Give students at least ten minutes to complete this note-taking stage. Strong students could share their ideas in feedback.

Writing (SB page 16)

Timing of a writing exercise such as this can be tricky, as some students need longer than others. Establish a clear, generous time-limit at the start, asking the learners how long they think they will need. Give early finishers dictionaries to check their work.

Let students read and check each other's work, considering issues such as spelling, vocabulary and grammar.

Global review

These lessons in *Global* are intended to review some of the language and topics covered in the unit. They follow a similar format.

Grammar and Vocabulary (SB page 17)

Aim: to review the main grammar and vocabulary in the unit.

Tips:

- Students can do these exercises alone or in pairs, in class or at home, depending on their learning style and your teaching situation.
- Ask students to read the questions first to establish the grammar and vocabulary areas which are focused on.
- Encourage students to check their own answers by looking back through the unit.

Grammar 1	Grammar 2
1 Are you	1 'm trying
2 Do you	2 don't know
3 What is / 's	3 doesn't like / is looking
4 What do	4 doesn't speak
5 What colour	

Vocabulary 1

classmate, colleague, friend, height, neighbour, profession

Vocabulary 2

1 He's got short grey hair. He's slim. He's got a moustache.

2 She's young, with long fair hair.

Speaking (SB page 17)

Aim: to provide extra speaking practice that will review and consolidate language presented in the unit.

Tips:

- Before speaking encourage students to think first about what language they need to focus on from the unit, and a good way to start their conversation.
- Monitor as students are working and note any points for feedback at the end.

Model this activity first. Ask a student to throw a dice and then two stronger students should ask you questions about the person in the box which corresponds to the number thrown. Group students into threes, instructing them to do the same.

Study skills

Being a good language learner (SB page 17)

1 Check language initially, eg *willing* (adj), *take a risk, make a mistake, organised* (adj), *guess* (v), *notice* (v), *set goals, monitor progress, review* (v). Put these words up on the board and ask students to find them in the sentences. Then, in pairs, students try to explain the meaning of the words to each other.

Check students' understanding by using concept questions or synonyms / explanations, as appropriate, eg *when or how can a learner take risks in a classroom?*

Students then complete the questionnaire alone.

2 There are some words here which you may need to clarify first, eg *(language learning) strategy* (n), *improve* (v), *consistent* (adj). Let students add up their score, read what it means and compare with their partner.

Take class feedback to see what students think of their results and to encourage students to reflect further on their learning strategies, ie *Do you think you are a good learner? Why? Is this a useful questionnaire?*

3 Let students read and think about the first two points on their own. If possible, give examples from your own experience of learning another language. Pairs then discuss the three points.

In whole class feedback, ask students about their ideas in relation to the third point. If students' suggestions are rather vague, eg *you need to set goals when learning vocabulary*, then elicit from students how these can be made more specific, eg *you need to learn 15 new words / phrases every week*.

4 Monitor to check on learners' goals and to see if there are some general areas of weakness for the whole class – if so, think of a teaching strategy to deal with them. For example, if most students state they find it difficult to guess the meaning of a word/phrase, you could target this overtly, eg by providing exercises in deducing meaning from context when reading in future lessons.

Eating & Drinking

Coursebook

Unit 2	Language	Texts	Communicative skills
Part 1 SB page 18	Vocabulary Food Extend your vocabulary – *taste* Grammar Countable / uncountable nouns	Reading *Tastes comforting*	Speaking Finding out about eating and drinking habits Describing personal 'comfort food' Describing a dish they like
Part 2 SB page 20	Grammar Quantifiers Vocabulary In the kitchen Pronunciation /k/ and /tʃ/	Reading *Ten secrets … from the world's top kitchens* Listening Talk on Zao Shen	Speaking Talking about cooking Describing kitchens Discussing cultural beliefs about food / kitchens
Part 3 SB page 22	Vocabulary Containers and drinks Grammar The infinitive	Reading *The people behind the drinks*	Speaking Talking about kinds of drinks Writing Writing 'rules' for preparing a food or drink
Part 4 SB page 24	Vocabulary The human body Grammar The infinitive of purpose Pronunciation /tə/ and /tuː/	Listening Talk on water and the human body	Speaking Describing purposes of different objects Creating a questionnaire about drinks
Function globally	Eating out Roleplaying situations in restaurants		
Global voices	Listening to people describing dishes associated with home Listing foods and ingredients		
Writing	A description of food and drink Phrases to describe habits		
Global review	Grammar and vocabulary review Extra speaking and writing practice		
Study skills	Students evaluate their language learning over the unit		

Additional resources

eWorkbook	Interactive and printable grammar, vocabulary, listening and pronunciation practice Extra reading and writing practice Additional downloadable listening and audio material
Teacher's Resource CD	Communication activity worksheets to print and photocopy
Go global: ideas for further research	**Eating** – Ask students to find a photo of an interesting kitchen and bring it in to talk about **Drinking** – Ask students to find instructions in English on how to make a favourite drink and bring it to class

Part 1

Lead-in

Put the following words on the board. Ask students to put the food into three groups in terms of their personal preference – food they love; food they quite like; food they can live without. Model (part of) the activity, talking about your personal preferences:

*chicken   bread   local fruit   green vegetables   chocolate
potatoes   exotic fruit   pasta   cakes   rice dishes
pork   red meat   seafood   cheese   spicy food*

Students can then compare and discuss their preferences in groups of three.

Vocabulary and Speaking (SB page 18)

1 Ask students to look at the words in the box and the diagram below. Do the first example together, eliciting the answer. (*bitter: describing food*).

Students put the other words under the correct headings on the diagram in pairs. Check answers as a whole class and in feedback, draw students' attention to the schwa sound in *dinner*, *breakfast* and *bitter*: /ˈdɪnə/, /ˈbrekfəst/, /ˈbɪtə/. Ask students to listen and say what sound they hear; then repeat. Also drill *salty*: /ˈsɔːltɪ/.

> Food verbs – cook, eat, serve, taste. *snack* is sometimes used as a verb too.
>
> Kinds of meal – breakfast, dinner, lunch, snack.
>
> Describing food – bitter, fresh, salty, spicy, sweet.

2 Ask students to read the questions on their own first, then to circle the five questions they want to ask their partner.

Put students in pairs, then students ask and answer. As students are talking, monitor and highlight food vocabulary which is of interest or which is causing problems. Take note of these for feedback at the end (or on the spot if appropriate).

Also remind students that the present simple is the most natural form to use in these cases (see previous unit): this is because most of the questions relate to habits and routines, as well as likes.

Mixed ability

Early finishers can add extra food-related questions of their own.

Reading (SB page 18)

This is a short reading text introducing the concept of comfort food.

1 🔊 **1.15** Write *Comfort food* on the board. Elicit from students what they think it is, giving or eliciting an example.

Ask students to read the text in three minutes, responding to the question in exercise 1, as you want them to read quickly.

2 Students read again and make a list of information about each kind of food in the text. You may need to clarify some lexis from the text first, eg *childhood (n)*, *popular (adj)*. Give students time to compare answers in pairs.

When they have finished, allow students to look up any of the ingredients in the dictionary, eg *noodles*, *lentils* and *sauce*. For food items which your students are not likely to know, use the photos in the text or even bring some examples in.

3 Students close their books and tell each other about the four examples of comfort food.

Reading extra

If your students would benefit from a closer reading of the text, use these comprehension questions, either dictated or written on the board:

a   *How old is the word 'comfort food' ?*
b   *Are the four comfort dishes similar in any way?*
c   *Which of the four dishes would you like to try?*

4 Ask students to think of their two favourite comfort foods and to write them down. Put students into pairs or groups of three and mix nationalities, if possible. Students should find out if there are any similarities between their choices. Students may need to describe the ingredients of their dish, if their listeners are unfamiliar with it.

Take whole class feedback on any points of interest, and use this opportunity to pool useful new food lexis and to upgrade students' language: if students are finding it hard to express themselves, then provide the language they need immediately – this could be lexical (vocabulary), grammatical, or functional.

5 Divide the class into **A** and **B**. Ask group **A** to turn to page 126 and group **B** to page 128.

Tell them to work with the student next to them and make notes on their text (maximum 20 words), to help them remember it. Students can check their understanding of the text with you and with their partner.

Re-group the class into A and B pairs, and ask them to use their notes to re-tell the information to their new partner.

Extend your vocabulary – *taste*

Before students read the examples and comments, put the three unfinished sentences on the board and let them try to complete them in pairs (… *has a sweet taste*, etc).

Go around and monitor to see how students are doing. Let students refer to the explanatory comments in this section either in the middle or at the end of this activity, depending on how difficult they are finding it.

Grammar (SB page 19)

As your students are likely to be familiar with this grammar area, approach this as a test-teach, ie look at the grammar rules *after* they have tried the exercise.

1 Assuming that your students are familiar with the terms 'uncountable' and 'countable', write *U* and *C* on the board and model the task: say two of the items in exercise 1 and ask students if they are *C* or *U*. Remind students that before an uncountable noun you cannot say *a* or *an*, but should use *some*.

Students then work in pairs to categorise the items. At the feedback stage, pay attention to pronunciation. The following nouns may need drilling: *casserole, chocolate, cracker, noodle, sandwich, toast, vegetable*. Encourage students if appropriate to pronounce *chocolate* and *vegetable* with just two and three syllables, respectively: /ˈtʃɒklət/, /ˈvedʒtəbəl/.

> Countable: cracker, lentil, noodle, potato, sandwich, sweet, vegetable
>
> Uncountable: bread, cheese, meat, pasta, toast
>
> Both: casserole, chocolate, steak, pizza

2 Write the three foods *bread, chicken soup* and *baklava* on the board. Tell students that these are the comfort foods of the three people in the photos on page 19. Do the first example together, then students work alone, before checking answers in pairs.

Let students read the rules under **Grammar**, making necessary amendments. Monitor and assist, before whole class feedback.

> 1 some, a.
> 2 a, any, some.
> 3 a, –, –.

Ⓖ Grammar focus

Show students the icon. Write page 134 on the board and ask them to find it. Show students the language summary on countable/uncountable nouns.

You can use exercise 1 on page 135 for:

a) extra practice now
b) homework
c) review a couple of lessons from now.

The answers are on page 142 of the Teacher's Book.

Language note

The concept of countability and uncountability is one which exists in many other languages. However, what is countable in one language may be viewed as uncountable in another. The rule about using *some* in affirmative sentences and *any* in negatives and questions is a useful generalization for students. In actual use, it is not the form which dictates the choice of determiner: the word *any* is used where the amount is 'unrestricted', eg *If there are any problems, call this helpline.* In contrast, *some* has a restricted meaning, eg *Could you tell someone that there's been an accident?*

TEACH GLOBAL THINK LOCAL Extra activity

Draw three columns on the board and write *Countable, Uncountable* and *Both* as headings. Put students in teams and manage this as a board race, with students in their team-line at the board. Give a different coloured board pen to the first representative from each team and then dictate one food at a time, eg *lettuce*. The students rush up to the board and write the food in the correct column. Each student then passes the board pen to the next team member, so everyone has a go. Possible foods are: *pea, beer, noodle, rice, chicken, salad, lettuce, lamb, tomato, pork chop, sausage, pasta, yoghurt, cheese, potato,* etc. You could take spelling into account when scoring, eg they get an extra point for correct spelling.

Speaking (SB page 19)

1 Talk students through the ingredients of your favourite dish, who prepares it, when you eat it and why you like it. Then get students to look at the headings in exercise 1, and to think for a moment about which dish they will describe. Then give students time to make notes. Monitor and feed in necessary language. Remind students that they do not have to have exact amounts for the ingredients.

2 Put students into pairs and let them read the example. For fun, before starting, let them make a sketch of their dish. They can hold the paper up to their partner's nose at the start, saying: '*Smell this! Doesn't it smell delicious?*'

TEACH GLOBAL THINK LOCAL Homework extra

For homework, students write up their recipe, if possible including a relevant picture (of the finished item or ingredients). These can be displayed on the classroom wall. A recipe is a specific genre with specific layout and linguistic features, so give an example of your recipe, or another. Remind students to avoid just copying a recipe from the internet or a cookery book. If students are interested in cooking and cooking words, remind them that many video clips of people cooking in English are available on the internet, eg do a web search of: *chocolate mousse*, and clips are available.

Part 2

Reading and Speaking (SB page 20)

Lead-in

Ask students to look at the photo and to try to imagine life as a chef. In threes, students brainstorm positive and negative aspects of the job, eg + *you can be creative;* – *you often have to work very late.* Elicit an example first. In feedback, find out if any students know a chef, or would like to be one themselves, giving reasons.

1 Put students in pairs or small groups and tell students they have at least seven minutes to ask each other the four questions. If they finish early, add the following questions: *What makes a good cook? Are people born to be good cooks, or do they learn? Who are better cooks: women or men?* At the end, take feedback on any points of interest open class.

Pre-reading activity

An engaging way to approach this reading is to see if students can first guess any of the answers in threes. Put up about five of the problems or desired results on the board, eg:

1 To give soup a beautiful golden colour, ...

2 Too much salt in a sauce ? (Add) .....

3 Eggs will stay fresh if ....

After class feedback, students read to find out who was right.

2 🔊 1.16 Pre-teach *storage* (n). Students then read and listen to the text and put each tip into the correct category, working alone before checking in pairs.

a	1, 2, 5, 6, 7, 9
b	3, 6
c	8
d	4
e	10

3 and 4

Put students into different pairs to discuss these food tips. Students may know other interesting food tips, eg *if you want to get rid of the smell of garlic from your hands, rub your fingers on something made of steel.*

Afterwards, share any useful tips as a whole class. Before giving their tip, students should ask the class: *Do you know how to …?* Then, if no one knows the answer, they supply it.

Homework extra

If students enjoy this topic, get them to find more tips by either asking relatives or friends, or doing a web search using the key words: *tips for the kitchen* or *tips for cleaning* or *tips for storing food.* Ask students to find 5–10 interesting tips and report back next lesson in groups. Why not design a 'Secrets from the kitchen' poster for the classroom?

Grammar (SB page 20)

Ask students to read this section, starting with the examples. Then pairs think of two examples for each one, eg *I only use a little salt in my cooking; I use too much butter on my bread.* Encourage students to keep to the topic of food and food preparation.

1 Ask students to work individually to match the sentences and meanings. Check answers as a class.

1	c
2	e
3	b
4	d
5	a

2 Students work alone to complete the questions. In feedback, ask students why they selected either 'much' or 'many': some students may simply be completing the gap with what sounds better, but you want them to consciously focus on the rule here.

many, much, much, many, much, much

3 Ask students to find out how healthy their partner is by choosing four questions to ask. People answering the questions should use the expressions in the box, eg *I drink a little water with my meals but a lot when I am exercising.*

Early finishers can ask all of the questions to their partner. As pairs are working together, monitor for accuracy and note down any problems for feedback.

Ⓖ Grammar focus

Show students the icon. Write page 134 on the board and ask them to find it. Show students the language summary on *a lot of, a little,* etc.

You can use exercises 1 and 2 on page 135 for:

a) extra practice now

b) homework

c) review a couple of lessons from now.

The answers are on page 142 of the Teacher's Book.

Extra activity

Put the prompts below on the board: *stress, sleep, friends, vegetables, exercise, cigarettes, alcohol, leisure.* Tell students they are going to make a questionnaire for you, the teacher, to find out how healthy you are. They can use some of the questions in exercise 2, as well as these prompts and their own ideas. Students should write at least five questions, working in threes. Then they 'interview' you: each group asks one question in turn, and listen to make sure they're not asking the same questions. Then they can give you feedback as to how healthy you are!

Vocabulary and Speaking (SB page 21)

Get students to quickly read the list of kitchen things in the *Useful language* box, and to tick off the things that they have in their kitchens.

1 and 2

Give students the chance to look at the *Useful phrases* box. Elicit examples for each of the three sentences.

Students work in pairs to describe the pictures and the differences between them. Monitor, noting down any problems, particularly with countable and uncountable nouns, for later comment.

Mixed ability

For stronger students, you could remind them of the language of comparatives, in relation to countable and uncountable nouns, eg *there are fewer plates in this kitchen; there's less space in this kitchen.*

Pronunciation (SB page 21)

1 💿 **1.17** Introduce this activity by putting the two sounds on the board: /tʃ/ and /k/, and say that you are going to describe or define some words which contain these sounds (anywhere in the word).

Students listen and write down the words if they can, eg *you use it to eat your main meals in many cultures, and it has three sharp points (fork).* Use the words in exercise 1 under **Pronunciation**, avoiding the word *knife.* This activity provides intensive listening practice. Students compare answers, before checking with exercise 1.

Students work in pairs to group the sounds. You could try to elicit other examples too, eg *kitchen* contains both sounds.

/k/	/tʃ/	Both	Neither
cup	chill	chocolate	knife
quick	watch	picture	
fork			
cloth			
cook			

2 Students listen again and repeat. Afterwards they could try to think of similar examples. Common examples of words with /tʃ/: *cheese, church.* Other examples like 'knife': *knee, knit, knock, know.*

/k/: c, k, ck /tʃ/: ch, tch, t (+*ure*)
💿 **1.17**
chill   chocolate   cloth   cook   cup   fork   knife   picture
quick   watch

Pronunciation note

For some learners, the /tʃ/ sound is quite difficult to say. In particular, the consonant cluster in *picture* /ˈpɪktʃə/. **For stronger students**, you could introduce some exceptions: a few 'ch' words are not pronounced as a /tʃ/, eg *chemistry* and *chemical*; also *Christmas* and related words like *Christian*; words such as *chef* /ʃef/ or *Chianti* /kiːˈjænti/ are French and Italian respectively.

Listening (SB page 21)

1 Students work in pairs to discuss the picture. Ask for some ideas open class.

2 💿 **1.18** Students listen once to answer the questions and then tell you if they need to hear it again.

1 Zao Shen is the kitchen god.

2 He watches families and tells the other gods if a family is good or bad. He has the power to make families rich or poor. Zao Shen also protects the home from evil spirits.

3 In the kitchens of many homes in China, Taiwan and Southeast Asia.

💿 **1.18**
Zao Shen is the god of the kitchen. He is a figure in Chinese mythology. He watches families and tells the other gods if a family is good or bad. He has the power to make families rich or poor. Zao Shen also protects the home from evil spirits. Many homes in China, Taiwan and Southeast Asia have a picture of Zao Shen in the kitchen.

3 Students from some cultures will find this discussion point easier than others. You could as an alternative discuss the significance of certain foods associated with festivals or celebrations at different times during the year.

Background note

Zao Shen literally translates as *God or Master of the Stove,* (*stove* is another word for *oven*). Many Taoist Chinese gods are believed to protect the home and the family. Zao Shen plays an important role just before the Chinese New Year, when he reports back to the Emperor of the Heavens on how the family has behaved during the year. Just before New Year, Chinese families give offerings so as to get a positive report. After the report, they are either rewarded or punished.

Part 3

Speaking and Vocabulary (SB page 22)

Lead-in

Play the game: *I went to the (super)market and I bought some ... (eg sugar)*, etc. You start, saying the one item that you bought. Ask a strong student to go next: they need to first repeat your food item and then add their own item: *I went to the supermarket and I bought some sugar and some juice*. As each student takes their turn, the list gets longer and harder to remember. The last student gets a round of applause, if successful! You can play this at the end of the lesson or as a revision activity, using containers eg *a bag of sugar, a carton of juice*, etc.

1 Give students a time limit of two minutes to write down as many phrases as possible from the words in the box.

Hear one or two examples as a whole class and use this opportunity to focus on pronunciation: these phrases provide nice examples of both connected speech and also the schwa, eg a glass of /əv/ milk. Drill some examples, then students practise saying the others, first whispering quietly to themselves, then in pairs. Finally, hear some more examples whole class.

Mixed ability

For stronger students, you could introduce more challenge by giving additonal food container words, eg *jar* (of jam, honey); *tub* (of ice-cream, soft-cheese), *bag* (of oranges, frozen peas), *packet* (of crisps, cheese), *tube* (of tomato puree or mayonnaise, or toothpaste!), *tin* (of fruit or beans). Show, draw or describe these items to elicit the words; put these on the board and ask students to think of a food item that goes in it.

For your less strong students, cut up the container words and some food items, and ask groups of three to match them.

a glass of cola, juice, milk, beer, water, wine

a cup of coffee, tea

a mug of coffee, tea

a bottle of cola, milk, beer, water, wine

a carton of juice, milk

a can of cola, beer

Language note

These food and drink items occur so frequently with their associated container noun, that they are collocations. However, students and teachers should be aware that there are other possibilities dependent on context and culture, eg in some countries you drink a **glass** of tea, and you might give a **cup** of milk to a child. In US English, the word *can* is used in place of *tin* for food.

2 Students read the questions quietly and think of their responses for two minutes. Then put students into twos or threes to compare answers.

Listen to some answers and be prepared to input appropriate language, eg for the final question, if appropriate, teach the following: *it depends on* + noun phrase eg *the weather*; or *it depends how/what/who ...* eg *it depends how hot it is*.

Reading (SB page 22)

This reading text gives five mini factual descriptions of different drinks named after people.

1 Ask students if they know of any drink named after a person, showing / giving an example such as *Perrier*, or a well-known drink in your culture. Students work in pairs to look at the pictures and identify the drinks but do not read the texts yet.

2 🔊 1.19 Ask students to read the text and choose the best answer a, b, or c, checking students understand the phrase 'in common'. Give students a relatively short time limit of about three to four minutes. If necessary, clarify *19th century* in feedback, ie the 1800s.

a they are all more than 100 years old.

3 Ask students to read the texts in more detail and point out the glossary on page 23 before they complete the sentences. Allow pairs to compare answers before class feedback.

1	Guinness
2	Perrier and Dom Pérignon
3	Cappuccino and Earl Grey Tea
4	Earl Grey Tea
5	Cappuccino and Dom Pérignon

Background note

'Cappuccino' means 'little hood', which refers to the hoods that the monks wear.

4 Ask open class if students have tried any of these drinks. Invite students to comment on whether they like the drinks or not.

Extra activity

Write these words from the text on the board:

politician	company	brewery	monastery
mineral water	champagne	monk	bottle
Prime Minister	beer	product(s)	bubble(s)

All the words are job or product-related. Students check the meaning with a partner, then try to pair up the words. They can use dictionaries if necessary. Drill the words before taking feedback. **Stronger students** should try to justify their pairings, eg *you find bubbles in champagne.*

Suggested answers:

politician – Prime Minister

company – products

brewery – beer

mineral water – bottle

champagne – bubbles

monk – monastery

Grammar (SB page 23)

This is a fairly straightforward aspect of grammar, so let students complete exercise 1 before reading the comment.

1 As a warm up, ask students to work in pairs to discuss for a minute the best way to make tea. Put any new vocabulary on the board. Students read and complete the extract alone, then check in pairs.

Let students read the comment under **Grammar** before taking whole class feedback.

At the end, elicit the verbs or adjectives which come before *to* in the text. Write these on the board in two columns:

Adjectives using *to*:   Verbs using *to*:
(It's) easy   important   need   try   forget

1	(–)
2	to
3	to
4	(–)
5	(–)
6	to
7	to
8	(–)
9	to

Background note

George Orwell is a famous British writer. He was born in 1903 as Eric Blair in India, but he grew up in England (his mother was the daughter of a tea merchant in India). In his younger days he worked in the police force and also as a teacher; he also lived as a tramp for a while. As an adult he held strong political views as a socialist and democrat. His most famous novels are *Animal Farm* and *1984*, both written in the 1940's. He died from tuberculosis in 1950. As he was pro socialism but anti communism, his books were forbidden in the Soviet Union, but nowadays they have been translated into numerous languages.

2 Encourage students to use the target phrases (see exercise 3) and to write at least five rules. Do not draw attention to the use of the imperative at this point, eg *Don't forget to, Try to* etc., unless students are avoiding it in their writing.

3 Partners tell each other their rules. If students are familiar with their partner's topic, they listen to see if they agree with the guidelines.

Ⓖ Grammar focus

Show students the icon. Write page 134 on the board and ask them to find it. Show students the language summary on the infinitive with *to*.

You can use exercise 1 on page 135 for:

a) extra practice now
b) homework
c) review a couple of lessons from now.

The answers are on page 142 of the Teacher's Book.

Homework extra

Tea is a very popular drink all over the world, not least in the UK, where 165 million cups of tea are drunk every day! If your students are interested in the topic, they should go the UK Tea Council website: www.tea.co.uk. This site has lots of information on the history of tea, tea and your health, types of tea, etc. Ask students to choose an area that they find interesting, make notes and prepare to report back to a partner next lesson.

Part 4

Vocabulary (SB page 24)

TEACH GLOBAL THINK LOCAL Lead-in

Get a confident student to stand at the front of the class. This student will be your model. Write different parts of the body on sticky notes and attach them to the board, eg *leg, shoulder, wrist, forehead, mouth*, etc. Ensure that you leave some of the words out from Exercise 1. Nominate individuals to come up to the board and stick one note on the appropriate part of the body of the 'model'.

1 Challenge students to name as many parts of the body as they can, in two minutes, with books closed.

Ask the pair with the longest list to read theirs out. Students then complete exercise 1 on page 24.

> arm, back, ear, elbow, finger, foot, hair, hand, head, knee, leg, nose.

2 This exercise partially checks students' understanding of these words. Do the first example together, then let students check the task in pairs.

> I – blood, bone, brain, heart, muscle.
>
> O – nails, skin.

3 Students should be able to see most of the inside body parts in the picture.

As students are completing this task, listen to their pronunciation. Many of the target words are likely to need practice, eg from exercise 1: /ɪə/, /ˈelbəʊ/ and from exercise 2: /blʌd/, /bəʊn/, /breɪn/, /hɑːt/, /ˈmʌsl/, /neɪl/. Drill as appropriate.

Listening (SB page 24)

This listening is a formal talk about the biological facts of water, in relation to humans.

1 Focus students on the words at the bottom of the photo of the human body: *50 to 60% water*. Ask for students' response to this.

Introduce the listening: a talk about water. Pairs check their understanding of the words in the box together, then use dictionaries to look up the unknown words.

Double-check their understanding, eg ask a student to show you what 'breathe' is; ask students to name a food which has a lot of 'nutrients', with examples, etc.

Drill the students quickly on these words, so that they will recognize them when listening.

Ask students to predict how water is connected to some of these words, eg *How is water linked to temperature?*

2 ⏺ **1.20** Students listen and write down the parts of the body. You could tell them that there are six mentioned. Be prepared to re-play the recording or pause it as appropriate.

> The body parts mentioned are brain, eyes, blood, skin, bones, muscles
>
> ⏺ **1.20**
>
> Human beings need water to live. A human being can live for weeks without food, but only a few days without water.
>
> We often hear that our body is two thirds water, but what exactly does water do to help the human body?
>
> Water helps to protect important parts of the body, such as the eyes.
>
> The brain is 75% water.
>
> We also need water to breathe, and to keep our body temperature normal.
>
> Water carries nutrients and oxygen to all parts of the body. Blood is, in fact, 92% water.
>
> In addition, water helps to convert food into energy and removes waste from the body. It is also very good for a person's skin.
>
> Even the bones in our body are made up of 22% water.
>
> The human body gets water not only from water itself but also from other drinks and food. Water is a major part of many foods, particularly fruit and vegetables, which may contain from 85 to 95% water. Because the amount of water we need may change with climate, level of activity, diet and other factors, there is no one recommendation for how much daily water you need to drink. However, adults typically need at least two litres (eight cups) of water a day, from all sources.

3 Ask students to look at the numbers before they listen again. Elicit how these numbers are said, eg *two-thirds, twenty-two per cent*.

Tell students that the numbers are not necessarily in order in the recording. Students listen again. Monitor to see how much students have grasped, and re-play some or all of the recording as necessary.

> Human beings can only live **a few days** without water.
>
> Adults typically need at least **two litres** of water a day.
>
> Our body is **two thirds** water.
>
> The bones in our body are made up of **22%** water.
>
> The brain is **75%** water.
>
> Muscles are **75%** water.
>
> Fruits and vegetables may contain from **85 to 95%** water.
>
> Blood is **92%** water.

4 Students discuss how much water they drink in pairs. Take feedback on any points of interest.

Grammar (SB page 24)

Put this first sentence on the board:
Human beings need to drink water to _____. Elicit what the

verb might be and why the infinitive is used. Ask students what question it answers. (*Why*).

Students read the point under **Grammar**. If necessary, walk around the classroom, picking up objects to prompt similar responses with *to* + infinitive, asking: *Why do we use this / these?*, eg a pair of glasses (to see better), a board rubber (to rub out what's on the board), etc.

1 Do the first example together. Students work alone to write down the purpose of each object. Monitor here. Then students take it in turns to describe two different items to their partner.

TEACH GLOBAL THINK LOCAL **Mixed ability**

For **stronger students**, before they start exercise 1, cover the phrases in the box. They complete the activity on their own, then compare with the language used in the book.

a	to water plants	d	to purify water
b	to make ice cubes	e	to drink with
c	to breathe underwater	f	to serve drinking water

TEACH GLOBAL THINK LOCAL **Extra activity**

Put the following lists of words onto separate pieces of paper, A, B and C, making enough copies for your students.

A	B	C
clock	tea	scissors
eat	aspirin	pin
bicycle	computer	towel
glasses	dictionary	socks

Put students into groups of three A, B and C. Distribute the lists accordingly. They then define their 'secret' words to the other two, using the infinitive of purpose. Give an example or two for the class as a model first, eg *you use this to make yourself smell nice (perfume)*. As students play the game, pay attention to their use of the target language so that you can give feedback later.

2 Sketch picture prompts on the board first, based on the reading *More water facts* – don't worry if your pictures are not very artistic! Space the pictures out: *a shower, a toilet (if this does not offend), a bag of rice (marked 1kg)* and *a cow (marked 1 kg)*.

Elicit what the pictures mean in relation to water, if possible eliciting and clarifying the appropriate verb (see exercise 2) at the same time.

Finally elicit some ideas regarding the amount of water needed, eg *how much water do you use when you have a shower?*

Students read the text and complete it, first on their own. In feedback, ask students which piece of information is the most surprising.

1	to have
2	to flush
3	to grow
4	to produce
5	to provide

TEACH GLOBAL THINK LOCAL **Extra activity**

Ask students to look at the last line of the *More water facts* text. Ask them how they feel about this. Count up the number of students in the classroom and relate it to the figures '1 in 6 people' worldwide. Students discuss the following in groups of three.

1 *There is an international charity called 'Water Aid'. How exactly do you think this helps people?*

2 *How many countries do you think it works in? (17)*

3 *If you could have only half the amount of water that you use daily, how would you cut down? Think of some practical ideas.*

Students can also do a web search, with 'Water Aid' as key words.

3 Do the first example together as a model. Students work in pairs to think of as many alternatives as possible in six minutes.

To extend the activity, you could also add the following examples on the board:

Why do people go on holiday? / Why do people go in their gardens? / Why do people read (magazines)? / Why do people wear make-up?

G Grammar focus

Show students the icon. Write page 134 on the board and ask them to find it. Show students the language summary on the infinitive of purpose.

You can use exercise 1 on page 135 for:

a) extra practice now
b) homework
c) review a couple of lessons from now.

The answers are on page 142 of the Teacher's Book.

Language note

Sometimes students' answers will sound slightly more natural with *because* rather than *to*, eg *Why do people learn English? Because they have to* or *To get a better job*. The *because* clause gives a reason, but the *to* clause gives a purpose.

Pronunciation (SB page 25)

1 🔊 1.21 Ask students how to pronounce these before they listen, writing the examples on the board. They then listen to check.

Eating & Drinking

 1.21

It's <u>too</u> cold. /tuː/

You need <u>to</u> drink more water. /tə/

Language note

You may need to remind students of the difference between *too* and *very*. You can say *It's too hot in here* and *It's very hot in here*, but the meaning is not the same. In the first example, there is an idea of negativity, which is 'more than I need or like'.

2 **1.22** Ask students what they know about Tunisia. Elicit 'desert', then tell students they are going to listen to a short story. First let them just listen initially to find out what happened, books closed. Then students can listen again and read, paying attention to pronunciation. Finally, let students read aloud the story to each other, paying particular attention to the target sounds.

1.22 see Student's Book page 25.

Pronunciation note

To is usually pronounced in its weak form, but it is pronounced /tuː/ in short answers ending in *to*, eg *You can't go. But I want to!* It is also pronounced in the strong form when followed by a vowel, eg *I went to* /tuː/ *a shop.*

Speaking (SB page 25)

1 Give students two minutes to think of the complete questions in their heads, before checking the question formation as a whole class.

2 Task **A** is easier than **B** so if you allow students to make the choice, bear in mind that timing might be an issue (task A will be considerably shorter). If students are doing B, make sure you monitor as they are writing the questionnaire, to ensure that they are asking (reasonably) accurate questions. Consider pairings carefully, eg put a stronger student with a less strong one.

TEACH GLOBAL THINK LOCAL ## Mixed ability

For stronger students, you could get them to look more closely at the different uses of *to* and *too* in this example story. Give these headings, including the word class, if appropriate to your learners: *1 (an adverb) to show that someone or something is the same / also; 2 (an adverb) more than enough; 3 with a question word; 4 purpose; 5 (a preposition) before a noun.* Students can then work in pairs to solve the puzzle.

too hot = 2, hungry too = 1, to buy = 4, how to ask = 3, to pay = 4, spoke to the owner = 5, gave it to me = 5, oranges too = 1

Function globally: eating out

These lessons in *Global* are designed to provide students with **immediately** useful functional language. They all follow a similar format.

Warm up (SB page 26)

Aim: to introduce the topic via a quick speaking task or picture work.

Tips:

- Do not over-correct here, especially in speaking activities.
- Encourage students to use what language they can at this stage.

Listening (SB page 26)

Aim: to present the functional language in context via a conversation or series of conversations.

Tips:

- Ask students to read the questions first before listening.
- Play the recording all the way through for each task (there are always two tasks).
- For multiple conversations pause the recording after each one.
- If students find it very difficult, play the recording a final time and allow them to read the audioscript at the back of the book.

---

1 🔊 **1.23–1.25**

1 A: Good evening.

B: Hello. It's a table for two, please. We've got a reservation.

A: Name?

B: Moore, that's M, double O R E.

A: Ah, yes. Just this way.

A: Now, what would you like to order?

C: I'll have the fish.

B: Just a minute. I haven't seen everything on the menu yet.

C: Sorry, then can we have another minute to decide? **(picture c)**

2 A: Here you go. Anything to drink?

B: Sorry, I think there's a mistake here. I wanted a hamburger, not a hot dog.

A: OK, sorry. Just a minute. One hamburger please.

B: Thanks.

A: Anything to drink?

B: A diet Coke please.

A: Small, medium or large?

A: Small please. **(picture d)**

3 A: More coffee?

B: No thanks, I'm fine.

A: Did you enjoy your breakfast?

B: It was lovely, thanks.

A: Good.

B: Could I have the bill?

A: You have to pay over there for the buffet service.

B: Sorry, where?

A: Over there, next to the plants and the exit sign.

B: Oh, I see it. Thanks again.

A: You're welcome. **(picture a)**

2

1 The reservation is for two people under the name Moore.

   The man is ready to order.

2 The man ordered a hamburger, not a hot dog.

   He has a small drink.

3 No, she doesn't.

   Next to the plants and the exit sign.

Language focus: eating out (SB page 26)

Aim: to draw students' attention to the items of functional language.

Tips:

- Make sure students have time to understand the form and meaning of the phrases, but you needn't translate them word for word.
- Students should be able to pronounce these phrases intelligibly, so drill them.

---

1 and 2

🔊 **1.26**

1 What would you like to order?

2 I think there's a mistake here. C

3 Could I have the bill? C

4 Did you enjoy your meal?

5 Small, medium or large?

6 We've got a reservation. C

7 You have to pay over there.

8 It was lovely, thanks. C

9 A table for two, please. C

Speaking (SB page 26)

Aim: to allow students an opportunity to use this language in a meaningful, real-world context.

Tips:

- There is sometimes a choice of task. Any task involving reading a script will be easier than a task involving making students' own scripts. This gives you flexibility for mixed ability classes.
- Give students time to prepare this activity, and circulate and monitor carefully.
- Correct sensitively, paying particular attention to the target language.
- If time allows, ask students to repeat the task, but with a new partner.

Global voices

These lessons in *Global* are designed to provide students with exposure to authentic speakers of English from both native and non-native English backgrounds. They all follow a similar format.

Warm up (SB page 27)

Aim: to introduce the topic and highlight potentially difficult vocabulary the students will encounter.

Tips:

- Be generous in helping students with the vocabulary here, but let them try and work it out first.
- Circulate and monitor any speaking task, but be careful not to overcorrect.
- Follow up any short discussion pairwork with an open class discussion, asking students to report back what they said.

1			
1	lamb	4	candy and sweets
2	kebab	5	fry and boil
3	beetroot		

Listening (SB page 27)

Aim: to expose students to English spoken with a variety of accents.

Tips:

- The first time students listen, tell them you don't expect them to understand every word; some of it will be hard. This is because the text has not been scripted or graded in any way. It's what they would hear in "the real world".
- Pause after each speaker on the second listening, and don't be afraid to re-play the whole thing if students appear to need it.
- Students can read the audioscript at the back of the book if you / they wish.
- Try to avoid hunting for specific pronunciation or language errors. In real world communication not everyone speaks perfect English all the time, not even native speakers.

1 and 2			
1	Iran – kebab	4	Germany – schnitzel
2	Italy – pizza	5	US – candy
3	Russia – borsch	6	Spain – tortilla

3	Mo, Iran: e	Marlies, Germany: f
	Gianfranco, Italy: c	Matt, US: d
	Elena, Russia: a	Sonia, Spain: b

 1.27–1.32

Typical traditional Persian food. It consists of rice and minced lamb, kebabs and chickens and dried fruit.

Pizza. Of course not Pizza Hut but Napoli pizza. Yes, pizza, lasagne and pasta.

Borsch – is very interesting – it's like a salad. But it's boiled in boiling water, I don't know … with beetroot with onion, potato, with meat, or maybe with chicken, or maybe with turkey. Yeah, and it is very tasty really.

A schnitzel dish. It's kind of a meat, it's fried and you most often have it with French fries and salad or potato salad which is rather typical of German food again.

Candy makes me think of home. There are certain candy brands that whenever I see them they remind me of my childhood and they remind me of growing up in the United States.

Spanish tortilla makes me think of home and that's a very typical answer but I think it is a very simple dish which is made from eggs and potatoes and it's made like any other tortilla.

Language focus: listing ingredients

Aim: to raise students' awareness of a particular piece of language present in the listening.

Tips:

- This language is not included in tests or reviews, it is here to help students understand international English.
- Don't expect students to produce this language in an exercise or in conversation immediately.

1 a	2 a	3 b	4 b

Speaking (SB page 27)

Aim: for students to discuss the same or similar questions as the speakers in the listening.

Tips:

- The speaking tasks here are slightly more open to allow for students to explore the subject. Give them time to do this.
- If students are working in pairs, circulate and monitor. Make notes of incorrect language use to correct afterwards (or in a future class).

Writing: a description of food and drink

Reading (SB page 28)

Tell the students they are going to listen to a student's description of his country's food and eating habits.

Students listen with books closed and guess which country is being described. Read the text aloud (when you read, omit the words 'Brazil' and 'San Paulo'). Students give suggestions. Students should then work in pairs to re-tell anything they remember from the text.

1 Students read for gist. Give them two minutes to put a title with each paragraph.

1	b	3	a
2	d	4	c

2 Ask students to complete the sentences individually, then compare their answers in pairs before whole class feedback.

1	three	4	coffee and beer
2	lunch	5	varied / delicious
3	feijoada		

For early finishers, add some extra questions, eg *Is the food the same all over Brazil? What's the difference between lunch and dinner? Do Brazilians have a healthy diet?*

Language focus: describing habits (SB page 28)

1 Ask students to find and underline any examples in Gustavo's description of ways to talk about habits. Then read out the examples in exercise 1.

2 Students work alone to complete sentences 1–6. Monitor, referring back to the examples, to improve accuracy, as appropriate.

1	tend/like	4	normally/generally/usually
2	common/customary	5	common/customary
3	tend/like	6	normally/generally/usually

Language note

These three ways of talking about habits are different in form. We can use adverbs (*normally, generally, usually*), which typically come before the main verb, except for the verb 'be' when they follow it; we can use verbs (*like* or *tend*, followed by *to*); we can use adjectives (*customary* or *common*) in 'it is' clauses. You might find it useful to point out the different grammatical forms to students.

Writing skills: using commas (SB page 28)

Read out the examples, to demonstrate that the pause is the written equivalent of the comma. Students read the two examples aloud in pairs, focusing on intonation and pausing.

1 Students find more examples on their own, before comparing answers in pairs.

> For breakfast, we usually have coffee with milk.
>
> We also like to eat fruits such as bananas, papaya, melon or watermelon.
>
> We generally eat a portion of beans and rice with beef, chicken or fish and salad.
>
> for breakfast, at work, in restaurants, and so on.
>
> Here in Sao Paulo, we like to eat "feijoada".
>
> In the north of Brazil, people eat a lot of fish.
>
> In the south, it is common to have barbecues.
>
> In Minas Gerais, cheese bread is a speciality.
>
> In Bahia, the food is very spicy and hot.
>
> On special occasions or for celebrations, we drink caipirinha.

2 For variety, write sentences 1–3 on the board. Students practise saying them in pairs, then individuals come up to the board to add commas.

1	In China, typical dishes are rice, noodles and dumplings.
2	Noodles are made with flour, eggs and water.
3	For breakfast, people tend to have coffee, bread and jam.

Preparing to write (SB page 28)

1 Inform students of the genre / audience that they are going to be writing for: a class magazine. Let them take notes on their own, using the paragraph titles to help.

2 Put students in same nationality pairs or threes if possible to discuss and make further notes together. Refer them to the bullet points for describing meals and dishes.

Writing (SB page 28)

This could be done at home or in class, alone or in pairs. Refer them to Gustavo's model. Encourage students to do at least two drafts. At the first draft stage, comment on: accuracy of grammar / vocabulary; organisation; overall clarity. Encourage students to use a computer for the final draft, where possible, and relevant visuals. The descriptions could form a class display, or a magazine-type booklet.

Global review

These lessons in *Global* are intended to review some of the language and topics covered in the unit. They follow a similar format.

Grammar and Vocabulary (SB page 29)

Aim: to review the main grammar and vocabulary in the unit.

Tips:

- Students can do these exercises alone or in pairs, in class or at home, depending on their learning style and your teaching situation.
- Ask students to read the questions first to establish the grammar and vocabulary areas which are focused on.
- Encourage students to check their own answers by looking back through the unit.

Grammar

1 I need to get more sleep.
2 English people drink a lot of tea.
3 You drink too much coffee.
4 I use a coffee machine to make my coffee.
5 How many biscuits do you want?
6 Could I have a little sugar in my tea, please?
7 *Correct*
8 I have too few eggs to make a cake.
9 Don't forget to buy some noodles.
10 *Correct*

Vocabulary

1	carton	6	finger
2	mug	7	knee
3	frying pan	8	bone
4	knife	9	vegetable
5	sink	10	serve

Speaking and Writing (SB page 29)

Aim: to provide extra speaking and writing practice that will review and consolidate language presented in the unit.

Tips:

- Before speaking encourage students to think first about what language they need to focus on from the unit, and a good way to start their conversation.
- Before they do the writing practice, ask students to either make notes or discuss ideas with a partner to activate useful language.
- Monitor as students are working and note any points for feedback at the end.

Study skills

Evaluating your language learning (SB page 29)

1 Give students a few minutes to re-familiarise themselves with the unit. Then students can discuss in pairs what they found easy or difficult and perhaps what they liked or didn't.

2 Clarify the words 'accurately' and 'confidently'. Do the first example together: *I can describe my eating and drinking habits*, eliciting responses from two different students. This exercise encourages students to start evaluating their own language, and developing self-awareness. It marks a shift in thinking, from letting the teacher do all the assessing, to the students themselves.

3 Let students compare their answers. It would be useful to take in, note down or take whole class feedback on any areas of difficulty which are widely felt in the group, for further work. At this stage, also get students to reflect on the purpose of this exercise in terms of their learning.

4 Students read Stefan's own evaluation and underline phrases about ability, having elicited the first example together. In feedback, board the different ways, drawing attention to issues of form: *I'm quite / not good at …(noun); I find it difficult to …(verb); I need to …(verb); I need more practice in …(noun)*. Elicit real examples from individuals, using the target language.

5 Give students time to think about their own language ability under the areas given. If necessary, your students may make notes. Students should think of at least one suggestion for each area, before listening to their partner. Remind students how to give suggestions, eg *you should …; it's a good idea to …; it's important to / that you … *. Pair up students to discuss.

Finally, listen to some of the suggestions together: this is a good way to increase students' knowledge of available strategies, as well as to focus on accuracy of language.

6 As this is a reflective and personal task, let students work alone in class or at home. Depending on students' previous learning experience, be prepared to give rationale for this activity. Ask students to give concrete examples or details, where possible: most students tend to write quite general comments at this level and usually need training in this aspect.

Art & Music

Coursebook

Unit 3	Language	Texts	Communicative skills
Part 1 SB page 30	Vocabulary Works of art Extend your vocabulary – *discover*	Reading *Discovered!*	Speaking Describing different art forms Talking about art / important objects
Part 2 SB page 32	Grammar Past simple and past continuous Vocabulary Furniture Pronunciation Past simple regular verbs	Reading *The picture of Dorian Gray*	Speaking Describing furniture Writing Reading and writing opening sentences for a short story
Part 3 SB page 34	Vocabulary Audio and video equipment and instructions Extend your vocabulary – describing decades Grammar *Used to* Pronunciation *Used to* and sentence stress	Listening Lecture on the history of sound recording	Speaking Talking about kinds of music and listening habits Discussing situations in the past Writing Writing instructions for using music equipment
Part 4 SB page 36	Vocabulary Feelings Extend your vocabulary – *just*	Listening Talk on music in film and TV Reading *High Fidelity*	Speaking Students connect music with feelings and images
Function globally	Agreeing and disagreeing Listening to opinions about films Students identify and talk about kinds of film		
Global English	David Crystal text: *The power of music* Students talk about nursery rhymes and early musical experiences		
Writing	A review of a concert Using adjectives and conjunctions		
Global review	Grammar and vocabulary review Extra speaking and writing practice		
Study skills	Students arrange conversation partners for practising English		

Additional resources

eWorkbook	Interactive and printable grammar, vocabulary, listening and pronunciation practice Extra reading and writing practice Additional downloadable listening and audio material
Teacher's Resource CD	Communication activity worksheets to print and photocopy
Go global: ideas for further research	**Art** – Ask students to find examples of Oscar Wilde's wittiest quotes and bring them to class **Music** – Ask students to visit Andy Price's Sound and Images website to hear more examples of his work

Part 1

Lead-in

Write out pairs of art and artists, eg *Michelangelo + David; da Vinci + Mona Lisa; Monet + Bridge over a pond of waterlilies, Van Gogh + Vase with Flowers,* etc. (one or two can be the same as from Part 1). Put these onto small pieces of paper and give each student either a piece of art or an artist. Students mingle and find their matching partner. At the end, hear the pairs and elicit any information students know about the artist / the work of art. Students remain with their new partner for at least part of the lesson.

Vocabulary and Speaking (SB page 30)

1 Students match the words to pictures, either individually or in small groups, if they need to pool their knowledge.

Early finishers can predict how to say them, marking the word stress: all of them have the stress on the first syllable (except for /ˌself ˈpɔːtrət/). Drill the new words, chorally and individually.

a	cave art
b	statue
c	sculpture
d	sketch
e	old manuscript
f	painting
g	self-portrait
h	photograph

Pronunciation note

Several of these words contain consonant clusters which may cause difficulties for students, eg *manuscript,* /ˈmænjʊskrɪpt/; *sculpture,* /ˈskʌlptʃə/; *sketch,* /sketʃ/; *statue* /ˈstætʃuː/.

2 Tell students that they are going to describe the pictures in pairs in English.

Students read the *Useful phrases* box before listening to you give a model description, using one of the pictures, eg (d) *This picture looks as if it's been drawn in pencil. It shows five faces, of young people. Most of them are girls, apart from the one in the bottom right-hand corner who looks like a young boy. The faces look thoughtful, and are not looking at the artist. It looks as if this picture was drawn from the artist's imagination, but the faces look real. This painting looks European, though one of the faces is Asian. It's probably from the 20ᵗʰ century. I quite like this picture as the faces are beautiful and quite peaceful. There's something romantic about it.*

The model is longer and more detailed than what students will produce, but provides ideas.

Students look at the pictures for two minutes and write down some notes in their **first** language to stimulate ideas, working if possible with a partner with the same mother tongue.

Students then change pairs and talk about two or more pictures each.

Extra activity

If your students are particularly interested in art, you could give them some extra fluency practice by asking them to rate the pictures in order of preference, giving reasons, working in threes.

Reading (SB page 30)

The text describes how four well-known pieces of art were discovered in strange and unexpected circumstances.

1 🔊 **1.33** Write the text heading on the board: *Discovered! True stories of how valuable works of art were found in unexpected places.* Tell them they are about to read about some very interesting 'finds' or 'discoveries' of important pieces of art. Elicit the meaning of *valuable* (adj) /ˈvæljʊbl/ and *unexpected* (adj) /ʌnɪksˈpektɪd/.

Give them two minutes to complete the skim reading task: matching each text to a picture. Play the recording and check answers as they listen.

In a field b
Under a street c
On a wall f
At a market e

2 Refer students to the glossary (SB page 31) and check these words as appropriate, eg *What can you buy at a flea market? Have you been to one? Where?*

Students complete the sentences alone, then compare answers before whole class feedback. At the end, ask students which discovery they are most surprised by, and why. Also ask if students know of similar stories.

1	Aphrodite the goddess of love
2	the Louvre, France
3	electrical cables
4	the Museum of the Great Temple in Mexico
5	a reproduction of a Vincent Van Gogh
6	1.4 million dollars
7	a flea market
8	wooden picture frame

Extend your vocabulary – *discover* (SB page 30)

Write the word *discover* on the board, and elicit the word class (*verb*). Elicit other words belonging to this word family, giving prompts, eg *noun? adjective?* Students then complete the exercise in pairs.

TEACH GLOBAL THINK LOCAL Mixed ability

Stronger students can write two more gapped sentences using the same word family, as in the examples. They can read these out or put them on the board at the end, for other students to complete.

```
1  discovery
2  discover
3  discovered
4  undiscovered
```

TEACH GLOBAL THINK LOCAL Extra activity

The texts contain several natural examples of referencing. Write these sentences on the board or OHP. Students should try to complete these sentences without looking at the texts.

*In 1820 **a Greek peasant** was working in his field when _____ found several blocks of stone.*

*In 1978, **workers** were putting down electrical cables when _____ discovered a huge sculpture.*

*A couple from the USA asked **an art dealer** to look at a painting in their home. While he was walking through the house, _____ dealer saw **a different painting** … On March 10, 1991, _____ painting sold for $1.4 million.*

Elicit suggestions to the board, writing in the missing words in a different colour. Students check in their books if necessary. Students are likely to find the last point the most interesting, the change from 'a' (general) to 'the' (specific). Draw coloured arrows in each example, showing how the referencing works, eg in the first example:

In 1820 a Greek peasant was working in his field when he found … .

There is a focus on articles in Unit 10.

Speaking (SB page 30)

Give students time to decide which task they want to do, and then to think about what to say. Consider whether your students would benefit from a model from you.

If they choose **A**, they can draw a little sketch of the item first. This will help to focus them – it does not matter how artistic students are! Students should give as much detail as possible, so set a minimum time-limit, which you can choose together with the students, eg 1–2 minutes.

Monitor as students are talking in their pairs, and take notes. Give feedback later on any points of interest, as well as relevant language points.

Part 2

Speaking (SB page 32)

TEACH GLOBAL THINK LOCAL Lead-in

Tell students their task is to interrupt you as many times as possible with questions, to stop you from finishing the description of your day, within three minutes. Start like this: *At the weekend / On my last day off, I got up early and decided to go to an art gallery. I sometimes really feel the need to see some art. As a child I used to paint. Anyway, I had a big breakfast, and then took the bus to the gallery …. and so on.* The students interrupt you with questions, eg: *What time did you get up exactly? Which art gallery did you go to? What kind of art did you like as a child?* etc. Students then do the same in threes, with one person talking and two interrupting.

1 Let students look quickly again at the pictures on pages 30 and 31, for one minute. Students read the unfinished sentences in exercise 1 in pairs, and try to continue them orally; they work in pairs to recall any information at all about the separate discoveries. All of these sentences contain the past continuous.

2 Ask students to check their memories with the texts themselves.

Grammar (SB page 32)

1 Ask students to work alone to put the verbs into the past simple. They can refer back to the texts to check.

```
arrived, asked, bought, discovered, found, got, paid, saw,
sold, took
```

2 Let students put the verbs into two categories, and check answers on the board.

Draw two columns, headed 'Regular' and 'Irregular'. Then call out the verbs (and extra ones, such as: *be, go, drink, eat, wear*) to individual students, for them to write in the appropriate column.

```
Regular – arrived, asked, discovered,
Irregular – bought, found, got, paid, saw, sold, took
```

Ask individuals to read out the three example sentences. Ask students which of the examples are **not** the past simple, eliciting them to the board: *Yorgos **was working** in his field when he found …; While he **was walking** …, the dealer saw … .* Elicit the name of the tense, and if possible why it is used.

Draw a time-line on the board and ask concept questions, eg *Why did Yorgos stop digging?* (because he found some stone blocks). *What's the main information in the sentence?* (He found some stone blocks). *Which is the 'background' information?* (He was working).

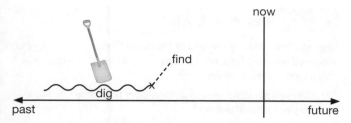

Yorgos was digging in the field when he found some blocks of stone.

Finally, ask students to read and find at least two more examples of the past continuous in the text *Discovered!* Ask them where they found most of the examples: *in the beginning, middle or end of each text?* (Most are at the start as they give background information).

Language note

Be aware that some students will find the past continuous form difficult to use actively. However, it's important to expose students to spoken and written examples of it in use at this level.

The continuous aspect is used to show what is happening at a particular time:

I can't talk now, I'm washing my hair (right now, at <u>this</u> point in time)

I couldn't talk this morning, because I was washing my hair. (just then, at <u>that</u> point in time).

These actions are / were in progress at this / that point in time. For this reason, when telling a story the past continuous (or past progressive) is often used to set the scene for an activity that interrupted it. The progressive aspect is often shown by words such as 'while' or 'when', eg *<u>When/while</u> he was working in the garden, he found some gold coins* OR *He was working in the garden <u>when</u> he found some gold coins.*

In many languages, the progressive aspect does not exist as a verb form and the 'progressiveness' is conveyed via the context, or via adverbials which mean 'at the point when' or 'while'.

3 Ask students to look at the three mini pictures in the text. Tell them they will find out about three more discoveries, and use the visuals to elicit what these were.

Students work individually on the grammar task. Monitor carefully as students are doing this activity, to see how difficult students find the differentiation task between past simple or past continuous. Students compare answers in pairs.

In whole-class feedback, ask students why they have selected which tense, and if necessary, help by using time-lines and concept questions such as: *Which is the background information in the example? What was the main event in the story? Which verb forms are used?*

1	were digging
2	discovered
3	were
4	found
5	was looking
6	was
7	put
8	visited
9	were examining
10	saw
11	identified

G Grammar focus

Show students the icon. Write page 136 on the board and ask them to find it. Show students the language summary on past simple and past continuous.

You can use exercise 1 on page 137 for:

a) extra practice now
b) homework
c) review a couple of lessons from now.

The answers are on page 142 of the Teacher's Book.

TEACH GLOBAL THINK LOCAL Extra activity

Ask students to complete these sentences in threes. Encourage them to be as imaginative as possible, doing the first one together. Students can keep to the topic of discoveries, or let their imaginations run!

1 *60 year old Freddie Smith was walking his dog one day when …*
2 *The two young girls were working in their school garden when …*
3 *While he was clearing out his cellar …*
4 *… when she discovered a huge dinosaur bone.*

Monitor and assist with language as necessary. Take feedback at the end. Give praise, particularly for the most interesting sentence completions.

Vocabulary (SB page 32)

1 Before students talk about the picture in pairs, check their pronunciation, in particular: *curtain* /ˈkɜːt(ə)n/; *carpet* /ˈkɑːpɪt/; *mirror* /ˈmɪrə/.

Students look closely at the picture and tell their partners what sort of person lives in this house, giving the following prompts orally to students: *age, nationality, job, sex, likes / dislikes.*

armchair; carpet; coffee table; curtains; lamp; shelf; sofa; wall; window.

Extra activity

For stronger students, before starting exercise 2, you could put the following adjectives on the board or on a handout:

modern; fashionable; antique; valuable; fancy patterned; plain; unusual; comfortable

Clarify any words as necessary and drill. Then students complete exercise 2, trying to use at least three of these adjectives.

2 Pair students. You could add the following prompts randomly over the board, to help students to provide more details of each item they talk about in the pair chat: *What does it look like? Where did you get it? How long have you had it? What are your feelings about it? What would you like to change about it?*

Reading (SB page 33)

1 🔊 **1.34** The text is an extract from the novel *The Picture of Dorian Gray*. Tell students they are going to both listen and read to a part of a novel by Oscar Wilde. Students first look at the picture of Wilde, and at the cover of the book, then read the information on Wilde. Ask students open class: *Is Wilde still alive? What did he write?* Introduce the book: it is a novel about a young man called Dorian Gray who is not a very nice person. He has a portrait of himself in his house, which he likes to look at. Clarify 'portrait'. Students read and listen.

> 🔊 **1.34** See Student's Book page 33

Mixed ability

Most students will benefit from re-hearing / reading the text. If you feel students still need further guidance to help them understand the text, set these questions:

Cross out the *incorrect* option.

1 The painting was:
a) on the wall   b) in the library   c) in the bedroom

2 The painting was:
a) of Dorian   b) of Basil   c) different

3 The face in the painting was:
a) beautiful   b) cruel   c) unkind

4 Dorian wanted:
a) to stay young   b) the painting to grow old   c) to grow old

1c 2b 3a 4c

> The picture was growing old instead of Dorian.

2 Students read the questions in exercise 2. Before discussing, ask students to write down some short answers on their own. Monitor and assist where appropriate.

Extra activity

Tell students that by the end of the novel Dorian's portrait – his real self – is very ugly, not just old. Then students discuss the following points in threes.

1) *Can you usually 'know' a person from their face?, ie tell if they are kind or unkind?*

2) *Is it better to be good 'inside', or to have a beautiful appearance? Is physical appearance important at all?*

3) *How do men and women try to stay young and beautiful these days? Do you think this desire is more common these days than before? Why?*

Background note

Oscar Wilde is better known for his plays, and this was his only published novel, completed in 1891. Dorian begins the novel as a beautiful, likeable young man, but he quickly changes, becoming very cruel and increasingly single-minded. He effectively exchanges his soul for beauty, and therefore loses all sense of morality and pursues a life driven purely by his ego. By the end of the novel, although he keeps his handsome, youthful appearance, Dorian loves no one but himself, and has even murdered to get what he wants. He finally destroys his portrait in a rage, and in doing so, kills himself and assumes his real age.

Pronunciation (SB page 33)

1 🔊 **1.35** If you think your students are able, they should try to complete exercise 1 before listening.

> 1 decided – yes
>
> 2 walked – no
>
> 3 stopped – no
>
> 4 looked – no
>
> 5 opened – no
>
> 6 remembered – no
>
> 🔊 **1.35**
>
> 1 Dorian decided to go to bed.
>
> 2 He walked along the hall.
>
> 3 Suddenly Dorian stopped.
>
> 4 The painting looked different.
>
> 5 Quickly, Dorian opened the curtains.
>
> 6 He remembered his exact words.

Language note

When the infinitive ends in these unvoiced consonant sounds, eg /k/, /ʃ/, /p/, /t/, /s/ then the past simple ending is pronounced /t/, eg *push, pick.* If it ends in a /t/ or /d/ sound, then the past simple ending is pronounced /ɪd/, eg *pat, nod.* If it ends in /m/, /n/, /l/, /v/ or a (semi)vowel sound, then the past simple ending is pronounced /d/, eg *sigh, climb, marry.*

2 Model and drill the students, as appropriate.

3 Let students i) first whisper the verbs quietly to themselves, ii) check the pronunciation as a whole class, iii) say them to each other (one infinitive each in turn, with their partner saying the past simple form in response), iv) repeat the activity with a different partner, but this time faster.

At the end, ask students to think of other verbs which fall into each of the three categories, asking students to write up their examples on the board in three circles: /t/; /ɪd/; /d/.

Writing (SB page 33)

1 Ask different individuals to read out the opening lines of the four stories and pause after each one for students to think.

2 Put students in pairs. If your students need support in terms of ideas, take one of the examples from exercise 1 and elicit suggestions of how to continue. Write up the first line, then the next three sentences of this story as a class.

Students choose their opening line and start to write in pairs (or alone, if students prefer). Give a time limit of about four minutes and monitor to see if they need extra time.

3 Ask students to swap stories with another person or pair, if they are comfortable doing this. Tell them to continue the new story with an additional three sentences, but not finish it.

Students then return the story to the original writers who can conclude their story. Students pass the completed stories around, for all to read. Take these stories in, and use them for diagnostic work.

TEACH GLOBAL THINK LOCAL Extra activity

For less strong or less imaginative students, give them the option of writing about something more tangible. Ask them to look back at the texts on p 31 and 32. Students work alone or in pairs to choose one of the stories, and to write it as a diary entry, in the first person. They should imagine that they are the 'discoverer', filling in their diary. Start them off as follows: *Today was an amazing day, which I will never forget. It started quite normally. I … .*

Part 3

Speaking (SB page 34)

TEACH GLOBAL THINK LOCAL Lead-in

You could bring in different examples of music that you particularly like. Play a sample of each one, eliciting responses from students: *What kind of music is it? Do you like it? Why/ why not?* Tell students why you like each one. Inform students that they will get a chance to talk about their own taste in music later (Speaking exercise 3).

1 Write the following prompts on the board: *instruments, people and jobs, place, sound, your feelings.*

Ask students to work individually to find differences between the pictures, and to look at the *Useful language* and *Useful phrases*, clarifying any vocabulary if necessary. Give an example yourself, then let students make notes.

2 Put students in pairs to compare differences, then ask for a few examples from different pairs for class feedback.

3 Put students into different pairs. If students know each other reasonably well, ask them to predict their partner's answers to the questions.

Students then check in pairs to see if their predictions were right.

Vocabulary (SB page 34)

1 Elicit from students where one can see these signs, to establish the context. Then students work alone to unscramble them.

2 1.36 Ask students to listen and check their answers, and repeat after the recording.

1.36
1 play
2 rewind
3 fast forward
4 stop
5 pause
6 eject

3 Students work alone initially to match the words to the pictures. They compare answers and answer the question. You could also add: *How often do you use X? Where do you keep it?*

audio cassette g	MP3 player b
CD c	record f
DVD player d	record player e
headphones h	video cassette a

4 **1.37** Students complete the gap fill individually, before listening to check.

> **1.37**
>
> Right, to use this DVD player, first you **plug** it in here. To turn it **on**, just press this **button**. Now press eject and put the disc in the tray. Close the tray and press play to **watch** the film. To turn **up** the volume, use this button. If it's too loud, turn **down** the volume with this button. And, to turn it **off**, press here.

5 Students write instructions in pairs.

> **TEACH GLOBAL**
> **THINK LOCAL** **Mixed ability**
>
> If students find this difficult, encourage them to talk about a CD player as this description will be very similar to the model text.

Monitor as they are writing, referring them to the model for relevant points of grammar, eg zero *if* clauses; use of the imperative; infinitive of purpose.

> **TEACH GLOBAL**
> **THINK LOCAL** **Extra activity**
>
> Students change partners so that they are working with someone with a different item. Students first tell their partner what the object is, then they give oral instructions. For each separate instruction that they hear, the listening partner mimes the action, to demonstrate understanding. Then partners swap roles.

Listening and Writing (SB page 35)

This listening is a lecture about the history of sound recording.

1 At the start, ask students to discuss the order of the music gadgets, then to arrange them from oldest to newest on the board on a cline: put pictures of the items on card; get visuals from the internet, or simply write out the words for students to come up with the order. Make sure that students agree on the final order.

oldest   newest

	audio cassette		DVD player	
record player records		Video cassette CD		MP3 player

2 **1.38** Students listen to check their predictions. Note that not all the words in Vocabulary Exercise 3 are mentioned.

> record; record player or gramophone; audio cassette; video cassette; CD; DVD player; MP3 player
>
> **1.38**
>
> In 1877, Thomas Edison made one of the first ever sound recordings. Edison predicted that sound recordings would be used for office dictation, speaking books, education, talking clocks and music.

In 1903, the first records were released with recordings on both sides. People used to listen to these on record players called gramophones.

In the nineteen-twenties sound recording met film. The first films with sound were called 'talking pictures'.

In 1962 the company Philips introduced the audio cassette tape player. One year later the first discotheque in America opened in Los Angeles.

The seventies and eighties saw the introduction of VHS video, cassette walkman and CD. The CD revolutionised the music industry.

It was in the early nineties that digital music and video appeared. In 1996 the first digital music player was sold in Japan. One year later the first MP3 player came out but it wasn't until the beginning of the 21st century that digital music and MP3 players really began to become popular. In 2001 Apple released the first iPod, a portable MP3 player.

The history of sound recording has always been to make devices that are smaller, but contain more sound. The first record played for only six minutes and needed a large machine to play it on. The current generation of music players go in your pocket and can hold more than 15,000 songs, video and photographs.

3 Give students time to read the notes before they listen again.

> **TEACH GLOBAL**
> **THINK LOCAL** **Mixed ability**
>
> If you think your students are able, they could work with their books closed: they imagine they are college students, taking notes on important points in a lecture. Then students open their books and try to complete the text, working in pairs to share information after a few minutes. This is a considerably more challenging task.

> Thomas Edison in **1877**.
>
> office dictation, speaking **books**, education, talking **clocks** and music.
>
> people play **records** on **record** players.
>
> first films with sound – called **talking pictures**.
>
> Philips introduces audio cassette: **1962**.
>
> 1963: first **discotheque** opens in Los Angeles.
>
> 1970s-80s: VHS video, cassette walkman and **CD** – ends era of the record.
>
> 1996: first digital music player sold in **Japan**.
>
> 2001: Apple iPod, a popular **MP3 player**, appears.
>
> Current music devices can store **15,000** songs, video and **photographs**.

Extend your vocabulary (SB page 35)

Write the word *decade* on the board, eliciting the meaning. Let students complete the sentences, referring to the explanatory notes.

Students then change the sentences so that they are true for themselves, writing them down to aid memorisation. Then students compare their sentences in pairs.

1	the eighties
2	the sixties
3	the seventies and eighties

Extra activity

To practise this lexical area, ask the following general knowledge questions:

1 *When did the first person step on the moon? (in the 1960s / in the 60s).*

2 *When did the second world war end? (in the 1940s / in the 40s).*

3 *When was the Queen of England born? (or adapt to local context) (in the 1920s / in the 20s).*

Students then work in threes to think of three more questions each, which they then pose to the rest of the class. You could do this as a team game.

Grammar (SB page 35)

1 Students read the points under **Grammar**, then ask them to look at the photo and say how their lives were different.

Students then rewrite the four sentences with the target language. Students make at least two additional sentences of their own, based on the photo. Monitor carefully in this controlled practice activity, to check for accurate use of the target language.

In feedback, write at least two of the examples up on the board, and focus if necessary on meaning and form:
Most women used to be housewives.

Ask concept check questions, eg *Are most women still housewives?* (Answer: probably not); *Were they housewives on one occasion?* (No, all the time).

1	Most women used to be housewives.
2	People didn't use to have lots of things.
3	Most families didn't use to have a television.
4	Some families used to have a radio in the living room.

2 Elicit the question form, using question 1 from exercise 1: *What did women use to do?* Write this up on the board. Students then complete the task alone.

1	What music did you use to listen to?
2	Where did you use to go to school?
3	Did you use to have long hair?

3 Put students in pairs. As they are using the questions in exercise 3, encourage the use of the weak form of *to* /tə/.

G Grammar focus

Show students the icon. Write page 136 on the board and ask them to find it. Show students the explanation of *used to*.

You can use exercise 1 on page 137 for:

a) extra practice now

b) homework

c) review a couple of lessons from now.

The answers are on page 142 of the Teacher's Book.

Language note

Conceptually this structure is not difficult. However, there is a potential confusion with the form *to be used to (doing)*, eg *I'm used to living in this city now, but at first I found it strange.* Do not mention this at this level unless it arises.

In actual usage, *used to* phrases are interspersed with past simple and other relevant tenses, avoiding repetition. Once the concept of a repeated habit or state is established, it typically changes to the past simple, eg *Some families used to have a radio. Very few had a TV at the time.*

Pronunciation (SB page 35)

1 🔊 1.39 Students first try to say the two sentences to each other, as naturally as possible. Hear one or two examples, then listen and compare with the recording. Elicit the position of the stresses and the schwa (the weak form). Drill chorally and individually.

My **brother used** to **play** the **guitar**.

I **didn't use** to **listen** to **classical music**.

2 Students work in pairs to mark the stresses in the example sentences (grammar exercise 1, SB page 35).

🔊 1.40

1	Most women used to be housewives.
2	People didn't use to have lots of things.
3	Most families didn't use to have a television.
4	Some families used to have a radio in the living room.

3 🔊 1.40 After listening and checking, students change pairs and repeat the sentences, this time paying close attention to their pronunciation.

Homework extra

Students choose a topic below and prepare a mini-presentation of 90 seconds for next lesson. They should discuss the past and the present; what has changed. Elicit one or two examples in class, eg *Families used to have only one phone in the house. Phones were bigger ...* They do research at home, and find relevant visuals.
TRANSPORT   TELEPHONES   MUSIC   EDUCATION   SOCIAL LIVES

Part 4

Lead-in

Write up the adjectives from exercise 1 randomly over the board. Check students are familiar with most of the words. You provide mini-situations to describe one of the words at a time, using the starter sentence: I felt this when …, eg *I felt this when I was watching TV last night. I was eating toast and wearing comfortable clothes. I'd just finished all my marking.* (Answer: *relaxed*). Students listen, and write down the answer, to compare later with their partner. Start with the easier adjectives.

Vocabulary (SB page 36)

1 Students match the words from the sentences to the words in the box in pairs. New lexis is likely to be: *cheerful* /ˈtʃɪəfl/, *miserable* /ˈmɪzrəb(ə)l/, *anxious* /ˈæŋkʃəs/ and possibly *calm* /kɑːm/.

Students discuss the meaning of the words in pairs, then check their understanding in a monolingual dictionary, if possible. When checking the task, drill the words.

Put the new adjectives on the board and elicit the preposition, where appropriate, eg *frightened of; scared of, anxious about*, etc.

> cheerful = happy, calm = relaxed, miserable = sad, frightened = scared, sleepy = tired, anxious = tense

Language note

You may want to remind students of the structure:

X	+	make(s)	+	object pronoun	+	adjective/ verb:
↓		↓		↓		↓
Doing homework		makes		me		(feel) happy

The gerund is looked at more closely in Unit 5.

2 Students should write these sentences down. Monitor to check for accuracy, in particular with regard to the target lexis.

Students read out their sentences in groups, to find any similarities. Take whole class feedback on any points of interest, at the same time focusing sensitively on accuracy of the target lexis.

3 🔘 **1.41** Ask students if any of them mentioned music in exercise 1: some people use music to calm or relax them. Elicit other ways people use music, eg some people listen to heavy metal to help release anger!

Students listen and note their feelings on hearing the music, then compare their reactions in pairs.

4 Instruct students to imagine a film scene which goes with the music extracts. They read the four questions.

Play the recording (quite loudly!) and elicit some initial suggestions, then replay it. Encourage students to be imaginative.

5 Students compare ideas in pairs. Take whole class feedback on interesting areas as this stage links to the next one.

Listening (SB page 36)

This listening text is a monologue: an expert (Price) describes the importance of music in film, giving examples.

1 🔘 **1.42** Before listening, focus students on the picture and details of Andy Price, getting one of the students to read the description. Elicit the kind of music such composers might choose to show *sadness* and *anger*, considering the type of music and the instruments.

If possible, play some film music your students are likely to recognise, while students try to name the film.

Students listen and tick the feelings he mentions.

> scared, tense, calm, safe, sad
>
> 🔘 **1.42**
>
> Music has always been a very important part of film and television. A film can be completely transformed depending on the kind of music you use.
>
> For example, if you want the audience to feel scared you want to use some kind of tension music. Here is an example of music that makes people feel tense or scared. It uses violins played on a very high note and very quickly.
>
> Gentle music is good for making an audience feel calm and safe. I use guitar, violin or even piano. This kind of music is good with love scenes.
>
> I sometimes use choral music for certain special scenes, or to make people feel sad. I use this for when a character dies in a film.
>
> Finally, sometimes individual characters or ideas in a film have their own kind of music. I did the music for the British television programme *Robin Hood*, and every time the character of Robin appears you hear this kind of music. It uses trumpets, which are always good instruments for heroes.
>
> In the past, to record the music for a film, the orchestra used to play in front of a large screen showing the movie, so the composer could get the timing just right. Now with computers, it isn't so necessary. Everything is much easier, and we do a lot of the work in the studio.

2 Give students time to read the text first and to ask any questions, before listening. Clarify the word 'audience'.

To facilitate the listening task, allow students to predict in pairs what the answers are first. Play the recording again. Be prepared to pause the recording and / or to replay parts.

UNIT 3 Art & Music

1	has always been	4	sad
2	scared	5	trumpets
3	love scenes	6	used to play

Background note

Robin Hood is an English folk tale dating from Medieval times. Robin Hood and his gang of men lived in the woods in central England, and stole from the rich to give to the poor. This romantic and moral legend has been the topic of films, TV series, comics and plays.

3 After checking answers in pairs, if necessary get students to check with the audioscript. Ask students if any information was surprising or interesting for them.

Extend your vocabulary – using *just* (SB page 37)

To focus students, write the word 'just' and the numbers 1–5 down the board. See if students can give you 5 example sentences / phrases with the word 'just' in. If possible, try to elicit examples with different meanings of 'just'.

Then ask students to identify examples with similar or different meanings. They may mention examples which are not in the book, eg *He's just left!* (only a moment ago); *I'm just making a cake* (at this time).

Students read the examples and complete the task in pairs.

1	Just be quiet please. (for emphasis)
2	It was just a mistake. (means 'only')
3	Thank you for the CD, it's just what I wanted. (means 'exactly')

Speaking and Reading (SB page 37)

1 and 2

Put students in pairs to write names of pop groups, but if this is not suitable for your students, go straight to the discussion in exercise 2.

3 1.43 Introduce the extract from *High Fidelity*. Pre-teach the words: *misery (n)* (remind them of 'miserable', exercise 1, SB page 36), *violent (adj)*, *violence (n)*, *gun (n)* and *melancholy (n)* (see glossary). Students work in pairs to answer the question. You could conclude by playing students a sad, heart-rending pop song of your choice.

Pop music makes the writer feel miserable.

4 Ask students to work in pairs and discuss these two questions. You could write up the following: *Do you think that films and computer games are violent? Can you think of examples?*

Function globally: agreeing and disagreeing

These lessons in *Global* are designed to provide students with **immediately** useful functional language. They all follow a similar format.

Warm up (SB page 38)

Aim: to introduce the topic via a quick speaking task or picture work.

Tips:

- Do not over-correct here, especially in speaking activities.
- Encourage students to use what language they can at this stage.

1

| picture a | musical | picture c | romantic comedy |
| picture b | horror | picture d | action |

Listening (SB page 38)

Aim: to present the functional language in context via a conversation or series of conversations.

Tips:

- Ask students to read the questions first before listening
- Play the recording all the way through for each task (there are always two tasks).
- For multiple conversations pause the recording after each one.
- If students find it very difficult, play the recording a final time and allow them to read the audioscript at the back of the book.

1

Conversation 1 c

Conversation 2 a

Conversation 3 b

 1.44–1.46

1 A: So, what did you think?

　　B: I don't know. Horror films, well, they should be thrilling, you know, be a bit scary.

　　A: I think so too.

　　B: And that film wasn't.

　　A: Oh come on, it was.

　　B: No, I don't agree. It – was – not – scary.

2 A: Now, you believe that there are too many big budget action films in the cinema.

　　B: That's right.

　　A: And that there should be more space for films from around the world. More world cinema.

　　B: Exactly. There are lots of great films from other countries, but we only see our own American films here. And I don't think that's right.

A: I agree with you there, John. So what films do you think we should see?

B: Well …

3 A: What about this one?

　　B: What, a musical?

　　A: I know you think that musicals are terrible.

　　B: Absolutely, you're absolutely right. They are awful!

　　A: Well, maybe but … I read this one was different. We always see the same films anyway.

　　B: Oh please. We see lots of different films. Last week we saw a French film.

　　A: Fine, you choose the DVD then.

2

Conversation 1: No, they didn't.

Conversation 2: Action films and World cinema.

Conversation 3: A musical.

Language focus: agreeing and disagreeing (SB page 38)

Aim: to draw students' attention to the items of functional language.

Tips:

- Make sure students have time to understand the form and meaning of the phrases, but you needn't translate them word for word.
- Students should be able to pronounce these phrases intelligibly, so drill them.

---

1 and 2

 1.47

Agreeing	Disagreeing
I agree.	I don't agree at all.
Absolutely.	Oh please!
Definitely.	**In between**
You're absolutely right.	Well, maybe but …
That's what I think too.	I sort of agree but …
That's right.	I sort of disagree but …
Exactly.	

Speaking (SB page 38)

Aim: to allow students an opportunity to use this language in a meaningful, real-world context.

Tips:

- There is sometimes a choice of task. Any task involving reading a script will be easier than a task involving making students' own scripts. This gives you flexibility for mixed ability classes.
- Give students time to prepare this activity, and circulate and monitor carefully.
- Correct sensitively, paying particular attention to the target language.
- If time allows, ask students to repeat the task, but with a new partner.

Global English

These lessons in *Global* have two main goals. The first is to give you and your students interesting information about English and language in general. The second goal is to provide students with practice in different kinds of reading comprehension tasks that they are likely to encounter in future study (for example, exams).

TEACH GLOBAL THINK LOCAL Lead-in

Tell students a nursery rhyme in English, if possible with pictures or mime. There are also plenty available on video-sharing sites such as *YouTube*, which you can show. Afterwards, elicit the term *nursery rhyme*, clarifying the words 'nursery' and 'rhyme'. Before students do the warm-up, elicit the word for a nursery rhyme which helps a baby sleep: *lullaby*.

Warm up (SB page 39)

Aim: to engage students with the topic, and highlight potentially difficult vocabulary in the text.

Tips:

- Be generous in helping students here with any unknown words in the first task.
- Ask students to relate this task, wherever possible, to similar events or texts in their own lives. This will help them with the reading.
- You may want to give your students an overview of the text before they read, possibly even in their first language. Make it interesting and involving.

> blows, fall, all

Reading (SB page 39)

Aim: to provide students with interesting information about English, and reading exam practice skills.

Tips:

- Be ready to help less confident readers, explaining words or ideas in simpler terms if necessary.
- Get students to read through the whole text once first before doing the tasks.
- Many of these texts have been graded slightly, or not at all. There is a glossary of difficult words. Get students to read that first and reassure them that you do not expect them to understand every word or idea.
- There are two tasks. The first is an easier task, often focusing on the gist of the passage. The second is a more difficult task, similar to reading exam questions.

> **1**
> We are affected by music from a very young age.
>
> **2**
> 1 music
> 2 word
> 3 the voice
> 4 the baby, infants
> 5 the picture
> 6 sounds
> 7 nursery rhymes

Language focus (SB page 39)

Aim: to highlight an interesting or useful aspect of language in the text.

Tips:

- The language focused on here is to raise students' awareness; do not expect them to produce it immediately.
- This language is not tested or reviewed in future units, which means you have more flexibility with this material as to when and where you use it.

> Music: tune, musical, singing, melody, rhyme
> Babies: womb, pregnancy, born, infant, nursery

Speaking (SB page 39)

Aim: for students to relate the material in the reading to their own language, culture and experiences.

Tips:

- This is a short speaking activity and can be done in whole class mode or in small groups.
- Wherever possible, ask students to think of and provide examples in their own language but explain them in English too.

TEACH GLOBAL THINK LOCAL Extra activity

Students work in pairs (with different first languages, if your class-make-up allows it). They tell each other a nursery rhyme in their first language. Their partner listens and enjoys the rhythm. The speaker can then explain briefly what it is about, where relevant.

Writing a review

Reading (SB page 40)

1 Tell students about a concert that you have been to, giving details: what kind, when, where, what happened.

Students share information in pairs about a concert (any sort) that they have been to. They read Stefano's review and answer the questions. Students compare answers before class feedback.

1 Vasco Rossi	4 everyone shouted and sang
2 rock	5 yes, very much
3 Rome's Olympic stadium	

2 Students compare their feelings about the Rossi concert in pairs. Then, if possible, play some Vasco Rossi music and get their response.

Background note

Vasco Rossi (born 1952) is a well-known Italian singer and song-writer. His career has spanned over 30 years and he is nowadays extremely popular, both at home and abroad.

Writing skills: sentences (SB page 40)

1 Write up the first example and ask students what is wrong. Prompt with the word 'Punctuation'. Ask a student to read out the correct sentence in their books.

2 Find another example together as a whole class, then students work alone to find twelve similar examples, before comparing answers.

> **Paragraph 1:** … Rossi, he …; … songwriter, he …; … stadiums, thousands …
>
> **Paragraph 2:** … stadium, there …; … there, all …; … afternoon, I …; … hours, I …; … evening, it …; shouted, in …; … him, it …;
>
> **Paragraph 3:** … guards, everybody …; … tired, I also …; … home, I …

3 Write up this example from the text: *He is also a good songwriter; he writes great rock songs and also very nice love songs.*

First separate the sentence into two, as in exercise 1, then ask for an alternative: elicit how to keep one sentence, with the help of another word (see exercise 3): *He is also a good songwriter _____ he writes great rock songs and very nice love songs.* Write up the conjunctions: *and, but* and *so.*

Tell students to find at least three places in the text where they can join sentences or clauses together in this way, writing out the new sentences. Monitor and assist. In feedback, if you have the facilities, use an OHP or projector as it helps to see the changes.

> … He is also a good <u>songwriter, and he</u> writes great rock songs
>
> … Italian <u>stadiums. Thousands</u> of people go to listen to him there.
>
> The concert was held in Rome's Olympic <u>stadium, and there</u> were very many people <u>there, so / but all</u> the tickets were sold out.
>
> … the <u>afternoon, and I</u> had to queue for six <u>hours. I</u> was very excited to see Vasco Rossi.
>
> … 9 o'clock in the <u>evening, and it</u>
>
> … everybody <u>shouted, and in</u> the middle of the concert the crowd sang with <u>him. It</u> was very nice.
>
> When the concert finished there were many security <u>guards. Everybody</u> went home very quickly but without problems. I was very <u>tired, so I also</u> went straight <u>home, but I</u> was happy because of the excellent concert.

Language focus: adjectives (SB page 40)

If you have dictionaries with a thesaurus, where alternative words are provided for the target item, show how these work, using the words *nice, good* or *great* (see the *Macmillan Online Dictionary*). Then pairs do the exercise in the Student's book, using their dictionary to check the meaning of the new synonyms too.

> the most talented live artists
>
> a talented songwriter
>
> very tender and expressive/moving love songs
>
> powerful rock songs
>
> it was very moving

Preparing to write (SB page 40)

1 Ask which concerts students have been to. For students who have not been to a pop concert, suggest a folk or classical concert (they could also review a gallery, exhibition or fair). Refer students to the guidelines in exercise 1. Give students time to make notes.

2 Ensure that students are now working in different pairs. Check the words in the *Describing a concert* box.

Students talk through their notes to their partner, this time trying to use full sentences. Give listeners a brief check-list to listen for: *Where exactly-town + venue; when; who with; performer(s); sort of concert; how full; what happened; response from audience; the music; your partner's feelings both during and at the end.*

Writing (SB page 40)

Students write their review in class or for homework. Remind them that this is an informal review, different from those in magazines or newspapers. Highlight two areas to focus on: longer sentences and accurate use of commas and using alternative adjectives.

Global review

Grammar and Vocabulary (SB page 41)

Aim: to review the main grammar and vocabulary in the unit.

Tips:

- Students can do these exercises alone or in pairs, in class or at home, depending on their learning style and your teaching situation.
- Ask students to read the questions first to establish the grammar and vocabulary areas which are focused on.
- Encourage students to check their own answers by looking back through the unit.

Grammar ex 1	Grammar ex 2
1 did you pay	1 did you use to listen
2 didn't pay	2 used to listen / didn't use
3 arrived / were waiting	to like
4 found / was working	
5 sold	
Vocabulary ex 1	**Vocabulary ex 2**
1 orchestra	1 frightened
2 concert hall	2 cheerful
3 statue	3 anxious
4 shelves	4 excited
5 armchair	

Speaking and Writing (SB page 41)

Aim: to provide extra speaking and writing practice that will review and consolidate language presented in the unit.

Tips:

- Before speaking encourage students to think first about what language they need to focus on from the unit, and a good way to start their conversation.
- Before they do the writing practice, ask students to either make notes or discuss ideas with a partner to activate useful language.
- Monitor as students are working and note any points for feedback at the end.

Study skills

Conversation partners (SB page 41)

1 Students first read through the bullet-point questions quietly, before sharing ideas. Take whole class feedback, then try to elicit ways to exploit or make opportunities to speak English, eg *joining a club*. Write these up on the board. Suggestions here will depend on your context: if your group is monolingual, learning English in their home country, then opportunities for speaking English will be more limited.

Focus students on the note about conversation partners at the end of exercise 1. Invite responses.

Depending on your students, you could also approach this task by giving students individual feedback slips:

Name:

Would you like to have a conversation partner? Why / Why not?

Who would you like to pair up with? (write 3–5 names):

This is more private and avoids potential embarrassment. You may choose to leave exercise 2 until you have seen students' responses.

2 Even if pairs are not sure about meeting up as conversation partners, doing this task could help them decide. Students pair up with someone they might work with as a conversation partner (let them choose, if appropriate).

Pairs should add additional topics to the third section and/or to break down the initial suggestion: *Finding out about each other eg family, home, favourite food, feelings about English, feelings about the course*, etc. Remind students that they are talking here <u>about</u> meeting for a conversation, not <u>having</u> the conversation.

At the end, again elicit students' feelings about having a conversation partner. If keen, ask students to arrange to meet by a given time, eg within ten days. Tell them you will be asking for feedback on the 'experiment'. Alternatively, set up a conversation group, if you have at least four interested students: students meet once a week, perhaps before or after class, with a different student-selected topic each week, eg your weekend; hobbies; music; favourite place, etc.

3 You can only do this task if (enough) students have actually met! This task is quite challenging as it demands a certain level of awareness. Provide prompts: *conversation topics; level of understanding of your partner; place you met; level of interest; level of success* (in %).

Students discuss their meeting in groups. At the end, they write down their individual responses, so that you know whether to exploit this idea further.

Hopes & Fears

Coursebook

Unit 4	Language	Texts	Communicative skills
Part 1 SB page 42	Vocabulary Adjectives and synonyms Grammar Future hopes and plans	Reading *When I grow up …*	Speaking Ranking importance of personal qualities Talking about childrens' hopes Discussing hopes and plans for the future
Part 2 SB page 44	Vocabulary Aid organisations Pronunciation Word stress Grammar Future plans and intentions – *be going to* / present continuous	Listening Interview with two aid workers Reading *Pandora's box*	Speaking Talking about aid organisations Talking about personal plans and intentions
Part 3 SB page 46	Grammar Future prediction and ability – *will* / *be able to* Vocabulary Phrases and phrasal verbs with *get*	Reading *Famous dystopias in literature* *Farenheit 451*	Speaking Speculating on the future Imagining a utopian world Writing Writing predictions
Part 4 SB page 48	Vocabulary Geographical features Extend your vocabulary – *-ed* / *-ing* adjectives Grammar Future time clauses with *if*, *when*, *after*, *before*	Listening Conversation about *An inconvenient truth*	Speaking Asking and talking about reducing individual carbon footprints
Function globally	Making offers and decisions Roleplaying travel situations		
Global voices	Listening to reasons for learning English Synonyms / words easily confused		
Writing	Emails: formal / informal styles Writing an email invitation		
Global review	Grammar and vocabulary review Extra speaking and writing practice		
Study skills	Students learn how to find the right dictionary entry		

Additional resources

eWorkbook	Interactive and printable grammar, vocabulary, listening and pronunciation practice Extra reading and writing practice Additional downloadable listening and audio material
Teacher's Resource CD	Communication activity worksheets to print and photocopy
Go global: ideas for further research	**Hopes** – Ask students to interview ten people and ask them about their hopes for the future. Make them into a form of word art (see http://www.wordle.net) **Fears** – Ask students to find the trailer for An Inconvenient Truth. Visit the film's official website to find out more: www.climatecrisis.net

Hopes & Fears

Part 1

Lead-in

Tell students about someone who you really admire and why. Students do the same for themselves – give thinking time and allow them to make notes. Students talk in threes. Take brief class feedback and ask students to give reasons for their choice – did they choose X because of their personality, talent, money, good-looks? This requires students to consider their personal values and links to the next stage.

Vocabulary (SB page 42)

1 Refer back to the reading on Dorian Gray page 33. Students tell each other in pairs what they can remember about the extract and the novel. Remind students that he made the choice to stay young and good-looking over everything else.

Students read the phrases in exercise 1 and work alone to order the qualities in order of importance.

Mixed ability

Add extra phrases on the board, giving students time to think where they would position these in order of importance: *being happy with yourself; living in a nice, comfortable home; having good friends; having a loving family; having a secure job*

After comparing answers, invite class feedback. Ask students to try and justify their responses if they feel able to.

2 First ask students to quickly look through the adjectives in the box and to tell you how many words are new to them. If there are four new ones or more, then elicit / clarify the meaning, so that the task is manageable. Drill the students on the new items.

Pronunciation note

Note the schwa, eg /ˈeksələnt/, /ˈklevə/, /ˈhænsəm/, /ˈwʌndəfəl/, /ˈɔːfəl/. You could also highlight the silent 'd' in 'handsome' and the pronunciation of the first vowel in 'awful'.

being **good-looking**: beautiful, handsome.
being **intelligent**: clever, smart.
being **rich**: wealthy, well-off.
having **good** health: wonderful, excellent.

Language note

Handsome is usually used for (adult) men, or for women with a strong face. *Beautiful* is usually used for women and young children. *Good-looking* is typically used for adult men and women. In spoken English, *good-looking* is more usual than *handsome* for describing men.

3 Elicit the answer as a whole class.

Extra words: awful, terrible
synonym: bad

4 Ask students: *Do the things you want from life change as you get older? How?* Give students a personal example to show how your own priorities have changed / will change, putting the examples on the board, using the target phrases suggested.

Students do exercise 4. Monitor and assist as students are writing. Students then compare ideas with a partner. Pick up on any areas of interest as a whole class.

Reading (SB page 42)

This text is a random collection of thoughts about the future, expressed by young children.

1 Ask students to look at the pictures and tell them they are going to read about different children's hopes, given in a survey.

Elicit some suggestions about the kind of hopes these children might have. Ask students to read the statements and make a choice of a, b or c. Take whole class feedback.

c

Mixed ability

For less strong students, ask them to provide examples from the text of a) and b). In pairs they write down at least three examples for each category.

2 Students re-read the text and choose the two most interesting quotes. At this stage, help individual students with any vocabulary queries. Students compare choices in pairs.

3 Students work in pairs or threes to discuss the questions. Provide an additional question for early finishers: *What age do you think the children in the survey were and how do you know?*

Reading extra

Ask students to look back at the text and decide what the hope tells us about the child; his/her fears; his/her situation, eg *I'd like to have less pollution in my city* – she might live in a very crowded city; *I'd like my dad to understand me one day* – he probably has a poor relationship with his father. Students choose four examples that they think are interesting. They will be using modals such as *might, may* or *must*; adverbials such as *maybe* or *perhaps*, or simply verb phrases such as *we think* … . Highlight these either before or after the activity, as appropriate.

Grammar (SB page 43)

1 Students work in pairs to try to remember as many of the children's hopes for the future as possible. First elicit an example and make sure students use full sentences and talk in the first person, eg *I want to have a nice house.*

As they talk, write up any of the target language they use on the whiteboard in full sentences, eg *I hope to …; I want to … .* At the end, highlight the target phrases.

Refer students to the Grammar examples and information. Clarify the word 'definite' if necessary.

Then students complete exercise 1 alone, writing the examples down. Monitor and assist, referring students back to the Grammar rules. Students compare sentences.

> 1 I hope to get a good job.
> 2 I'm going to get a good job.
> 3 I'm looking forward to getting a good job.
> 4 I'm planning to get a good job.
> 5 I want to get a good job.
> 6 I would like to get a good job.

TEACH GLOBAL THINK LOCAL **Extra activity**

As a preparation for the text in exercise 2, dictate these:

a *More English boys than girls hope to pass their driving test when young.*
b *More boys than girls are looking forward to having children.*
c *All children say they want to live in a peaceful world.*
d *Only a small number of children think of the developing world.*

Students decide in pairs if these are true or false before reading.

(*a* T *b* F *c* F *d* F)

2 This text summarises findings from research in which schoolchildren were questioned about their future.

Ask students to work alone initially.

> 1 to go
> 2 to get
> 3 to pass
> 4 having
> 5 to have
> 6 living
> 7 to get

G Grammar focus

Show students the icon. Write page 138 on the board and ask them to find it. Show students the language summary on future hopes and plans.

You can use exercise 1 on page 139 for:

a) extra practice now
b) homework
c) review a couple of lessons from now.

The answers are on page 142 of the Teacher's Book.

TEACH GLOBAL THINK LOCAL **Extra activity**

This exercise focuses on ways to talk about numbers and statistics. Write the following on the board. Elicit the full phrases. Note that only some of them are in the text in exercise 2:

a T_____ m_____ o_____ the children hope to go to university or college.(*the majority of*)
b M_____ o_____ the children were optimistic. (*most of*)
c A s_____ n_____ (of …) were pessimistic. (*a small number*)
d A f_____ (*a few*) were pessimistic.

Students work in pairs to use the phrases to describe their classmates, eg *a large number of students come to English classes on foot.*

Speaking (SB page 43)

1 First ask students to look at the list in the box and to select two areas for you their teacher to talk about. By discussing the ideas that they choose, this serves as a model. Give students two minutes to choose three ideas for themselves and think about what to say.

2 and 3
Pair students. Tell them that the listener should ask at least one question after each idea. Students need to keep talking until you make a signal, eg ring a bell or clap. Wait at least thirty seconds in each case. As students talk, monitor and focus on accuracy of the target language, noting details for later.

TEACH GLOBAL THINK LOCAL **Extra activity**

Write the names of different people familiar to your students on separate pieces of paper, eg *Usain Bolt (the fastest male 100m and 200m runner)*. Give each pair two different names. They write at least three hopes that each person might have for a) the immediate future b) the longer-term future, eg for Bolt a) *I'm looking forward to the Olympic Games.* b) *I'd like to be a good example to young black Americans.* Write up the different names on the board. Students then read out their secret person's hopes and see if others can guess their person.

Hopes & Fears

Part 2

Speaking and Listening (SB page 44)

Lead-in

To stimulate interest and to introduce the word 'aid', show students pictures by doing an image search on the web using the key words: *aid organisations,* or charity names such as *Oxfam* or *Save the Children.* Discuss as a class: *What do these organisations do? Where do they work? How do they raise money?*

This listening is an interview with two aid workers discussing their next post.

1 Students look at the graph and discuss the questions in pairs.

2 🔊 **1.48** To help students get a more global understanding first, write these two questions on the board: *Do you think Josh and Helle's new job with an aid organisation sounds a) difficult b) a positive or negative experience?* (it sounds quite difficult, but a positive experience).

Then ask students to listen again to order the interviewer's questions / comments in exercise 2.

1	So, tell us about yourselves.
2	What are you going to do there?
3	How did you become aid workers?
4	What is the most important thing in your job?
5	Thanks for your time.

🔊 **1.48**

Interviewer:	_____
Josh:	OK, well. My name's Josh Gross and this is Helle Hansen.
Helle:	Hi.
Josh:	And … well, we're aid workers with the Danish organisation Milene Nielsen Foundation. Helle, do you want to … say something about it?
Helle:	It's starting a new project in Guatemala next month. We're going to be in a small village …
Josh:	In the mountains.
Helle:	In the mountains. It's a very poor place.
Interviewer:	_____
Helle:	We're going to work with the children there.
Josh:	Basically, we're going to be responsible for the children during the day. Playing, cooking …
Helle:	Cleaning …
Interviewer:	_____
Josh:	I'm a teacher originally, and Helle has a background in child psychology. We both wanted to help people.

Helle:	I fell in love with Guatemala when I was there on a holiday two years ago. The people are friendly and the country is beautiful. I remember thinking: "I'm coming back here one day."
Josh:	It's going to be my first time in Guatemala. I'm looking forward to going on this trip very much.
Helle:	Yeah, me too.
Interviewer:	_____
Josh:	Good question. I guess I would say that hope is the most important thing. If you don't have hope, you don't have anything.
Helle:	Yes, this is especially true when you're working with people who have, really, lost hope. If you have hope, well that helps you keep going.
Interviewer:	_____
Josh:	Thanks. We'll let you know how it goes.
Helle:	Thank you.

3 Students work in pairs to share suggestions about these words before they listen again.

The aid organisation is Danish.
Guatemala is where they are going to do volunteer work.
Helle came to Guatemala on holiday two years ago.
They are starting a project in a village.

4 Put students in groups of three to answer the question and think of any positive or negative aspects of the job.

After the discussion, ask for feedback open class. (*Possible suggestions are:* **Positive** *– job satisfaction; an interesting experience; the chance to improve things; usually short term contracts; good team work; probably nice, like-minded colleagues.* **Negative** *– difficult living conditions; poor pay; frustrating because of insufficient money/politics; being an outsider; living away from family / friends.*)

Finally, ask students again whether they would like to do such a job and why / why not.

Listening extra

Students look at the audioscript and find examples of the target language for plans and hopes, eg *I'm going to …*

Vocabulary and Pronunciation (SB page 44)

1 Ask students to work in pairs to complete exercise 1 and then check any words in a monolingual dictionary.

Mixed ability

Early finishers work on word families in pairs: predicting the adjective (except for *war* and *natural disaster*). Students work together and then check their predictions with you / the dictionary. Encourage students to make logical guesses, eg to add 'ed' or 'ful' suffixes.

disease 4	pollution 7
homelessness 2	poverty 1
hunger 3	war 5
natural disasters 6	

2 Ask students how many syllables are in 'war' and 'natural' and show on the board how to represent word stress with small and large circles. Then ask them to complete the chart by writing a word on each line. Let students compare answers in pairs.

3 **1.49** Students listen to the words and check the stress, then repeat each word after the recording.

1.49

war O
natural Oo
hunger Oo
disease oO
poverty Ooo
homelessness Ooo
disasters oOo
pollution oOo

Homework extra

Ask students to re-read the audioscript of the interview with Helle and Josh. Imagine that the interviewer then asked: *Can I ask why you both became aid workers? What are the negative and positive sides to the job? What's the hardest thing about your job?* Students continue the interview. Give a minimum word count, eg 80 words.

Grammar (SB page 45)

1 Ask students to remember at least five facts from the listening about the aid workers, eg they worked for a Danish organisation.

Write up these two gapped sentences and elicit the missing words:

We _____ work with the children. (are going to)
The organisation _____ a new project in Guatemala. (is starting)

Elicit the meaning of the target structures by asking concept questions, eg *going to*: *When did they decide? Just now or some time ago?* and *present continuous*: *Is this a possibility, or is this sure? Has the organisation already made arrangements?*

Let students read the information under **Grammar**.

Language note

The two structures are sometimes interchangeable in use. They are both used for future plans, but where the situation is more fixed, the present continuous tends to be used, eg where you know details such as when, who with, where. When talking about plans which you have limited control over and do not know the details of, it is unnatural to use the present continuous: *I'm buying a big house when I'm older.* See example 3, exercise 2, SB page 45.

Typically students at this level prefer to use 'will' or possibly 'going to'. Students sometimes find it hard to use present continuous for future reference, having initially learnt it for the present (see Unit 1).

Students complete this exercise alone first, then compare answers in pairs. In feedback, zoom in on the present continuous example: *the organisation is starting a project next month*. Ask students why this is in the present continuous, asking concept questions, eg *Is it certain? Where? Do they know exactly where in this country? When?*

1	Incorrect – is starting
2	Incorrect – is going to work
3	Correct
4	Correct
5	Incorrect – It's going to be

2 Ask students to choose the correct form to complete each question. Elicit the first one as an example, reminding students that sometimes both options are possible. Then students work individually.

If students need help with the question form, elicit the forms onto the board.

1	are you doing	4	Are you working
2	Are you going	5	Are you going to study
3	Are you going to read		

3 Ask students to ask you the questions first, and focus in on the features of natural speech, eg contractions, linking and the schwa (see **Language note** below). Then pairs work together.

G Grammar focus

Show students the icon. Write page 138 on the board and ask them to find it. Show students the language summary on future plans and intentions.

You can use exercises 1 and 2 on page 139 for:

a) extra practice now
b) homework
c) review a couple of lessons from now.

The answers are on page 142 of the Teacher's Book.

Language note

In terms of pronunciation, the auxiliaries are reduced or contracted in fluid speech, eg They're going to work with the children there.

What are /ə/ you going to do after class?

'Going to' becomes: /gəʊɪŋtə/, or even /gənə/ with the 'to' pronounced as a weak form.

In exercise 2, SB page 45, in the short answer 'meeting a friend' the subject and auxiliary are omitted via ellipsis, a common feature of spoken English. Learners tend to give a full answer where fluent speakers might not. You could highlight this to students.

Reading and Speaking (SB page 45)

This is a text summarising the story of Pandora's box from ancient Greek mythology. Your approach to this text will depend on how much your students already know.

Put the words *Pandora's box* on the board and see if students know anything about this story, pointing to the picture. Pre-teach *trouble* (in the text *trouble* is similar to *problem*) and *despair*.

Write these questions on the board for students to answer on a first reading: *What was Pandora's box? What was the one trouble she did not let out? Was this a good thing? Why / why not? How do you think people felt when she changed her mind?* Check these open class.

Students then discuss the three more general questions in pairs.

Background note

Greek myths are the stories of the Ancient Greeks and they are about heroes, gods, mythological creatures, the world and culture. This myth of Pandora is mentioned in many different stories and is interpreted in different ways. It tries to give one explanation as to why evil exists.

Hope was considered to be negative by the Greeks: it gives you the false idea that you can control the future and does not let you live properly as it distracts you from the present.

Part 3

TEACH GLOBAL THINK LOCAL   Mixed ability

This unit focuses on *will* for future predictions. Decide if your particular students would benefit from having a break between this and the work on the present continuous / *going to* in this unit, or if they are ready to cope with this focus now.

TEACH GLOBAL THINK LOCAL   Lead-in

This activity will work best if students have the same or similar backgrounds. Put authors' first and last names on two separate pieces of paper, eg *William + Shakespeare*; *Leo + Tolstoy*, choosing writers your students will be familiar with. Give out the halves of the names to different students. They mingle to find their other half, then together try to name any works written by the author. They may need help from you to translate their titles into English. Take whole class feedback.

Reading (SB page 46)

The three texts are summaries of the three novels, *1984*, *Brave New World*, and *A Handmaid's Tale*.

1 Students work alone and write down three titles of novels or plays that they studied at school. Discuss in threes a) what sort of books they were b) briefly what they were about and c) if they liked studying them.

Then students continue the discussion by talking about the two points in exercise 1. Take some whole class feedback on points of interest.

2 Elicit any details that students know about the three books on page 46 or their film adaptations. If possible show the film posters, by doing a web search and typing in the name of the book, and then *film*.

Tell students that the books all have similar themes, as they are all 'dystopias', referring them to the glossary on SB page 46.

3 🔘 1.50 The three texts are summaries of the three novels, and all describe oppressive regimes.

Pre-teach the words 'government' and 'control' from statement b, exercise 3.

Students complete the reading task and compare answers in pairs.

a	tick
b	tick
c	–
d	–

4 First of all, write these words on the board and let students discuss the meaning in groups of three: *enemy* (n), *nuclear accident / disaster* (n), *pregnant* (adj); *slave* (n) and *factory* (n). If necessary, let students refer to dictionaries.

Check understanding by asking concept questions, eg *How long are women usually 'pregnant' for? What happens in a 'nuclear disaster'? What sort of things are made in a 'factory'?*

Remind students that they do not need to understand every word to complete the comprehension task.

Monitor closely to see how challenging they find the task. Students compare answers in pairs.

When taking class feedback, ask students to refer to specific lines from the summaries to support their answers.

1	HT (many women are infertile – line 4)
2	1984 (line 3)
3	HT (nuclear accident – line 3)
4	BNW (people don't know war – line 2)
5	BNW (create babies in factories – line 5)
6	1984 (even people's thoughts – line 6)
7	1984 (fall in love – a crime – line 9)
8	BNW (line 3)

5 Divide students into pairs and elicit their reaction to statement 1 in exercise 4, referring them to the *Useful phrases* box.

Monitor and note down any linguistic points that you would like to highlight afterwards.

Take whole class feedback and pick up on any interesting views or comments.

Background note

1984 was written in 1948. It has political, social and sexual themes. The book has an anti-totalitarianism message and is in many ways a description of post-war Britain. The novel has been translated into 62 different languages.

Brave New World was written in 1932. Huxley gave a frightening view of the future, when other novels were describing 'utopias'. Huxley was describing the fear of losing one's individual identity in an increasingly scientific world.

A Handmaid's Tale was written in 1985. Atwood was heavily influenced by Orwell. It explores the themes of women, politics and power and though frequently a school text, is considered by many to be anti-religious and over-explicit sexually.

All of these novels have been adapted for the cinema, TV, radio and stage.

TEACH GLOBAL THINK LOCAL Reading extra

To focus students on prepositions, write the following on the board:

a The novel is set _____ the future, in London. (in)
b Winston works _____ the government. (for)
c He is getting tired _____ life. (of)
d They fall _____ love. (in)
e Adults are divided _____ five social groups. (into)
f He has to choose _____ joining them or dying. (between)
g Offred learns _____ an underground resistance group. (about)

Students fill in the gaps alone, without looking at the texts. Check answers.

Students close their books and test each other in pairs, making sure that the student being tested does not see the board. The other reads the first half of each sentence up to the preposition, eg *The novel is set ...* . Their partner completes the sentence from memory, using the correct preposition. Swap roles and repeat. Encourage students to record the new language.

Grammar (SB page 47)

Using your fingers to represent each word, elicit the missing words in these two sentences, taken from the Grammar section:
There _____ _____ only 3 countries in the world. Women _____ _____ _____ _____ _____ have babies. Ask students concept questions: *Is this talking about the present or future?* (Future); *Are they talking about plans?* (No); *What are these?* (Predictions).

Students read the two bullet points about usage under **Grammar**.

Language note

Students often find the different choices of future forms confusing. Indeed, in many languages there is only one form used to convey the notion of futurity.

Will has many different uses as it is a modal auxiliary verb, but is often seen by learners as 'the future tense', leading to unnatural sentences such as: *I'm sorry I can't come, I will go to the dentist this afternoon.* Usually the choice is determined by the context and the speaker's perception of the event, eg

She's going to bake a cake.
This is a plan.
She'll make a cake.
This could be a prediction (based on knowledge of her behaviour), a warning, a promise, etc. These functional headings often help learners to understand 'will'.

Pronunciation note

Will is usually contracted to *'ll*, the so-called 'dark l' which learners find difficult to hear or produce, so drilling this may help.

UNIT 4 Hopes & Fears

1 Do the first example together (*The government will control society through the media*), then students work alone. This is a transformation exercise: the aim is to focus on manipulation of form rather than focusing on meaning.

> People won't be able to read or own books.
>
> The population will get all their information from the television.
>
> They won't know their history.
>
> Firemen won't stop fires, they will start them.

Background note

Fahrenheit 451 was first published in 1953 and was Bradbury's most popular novel. The novel is a critique of American society. It describes a world where people live for pleasure, one where reading is forbidden. Bradbury felt that television destroys literature. 451 degrees fahrenheit is the temperature at which a book starts to burn independently. The book has been made into a film.

2 Ask students if they know the word which means the opposite of *dystopia*. Write *utopia* on the board and try to elicit what this might be. Let them read the definition in their books.

Elicit a couple of examples from students and then let them work on their five predictions in pairs. If necessary, put some prompts on the board: *family life; health; work; lifestyle; money; happiness, food, travel* etc.

Then re-group students into fours, and let them decide on the six best ideas.

Let students read other groups' ideas at the end, by sticking the lists up around the room. Finally, they should vote for the best utopia.

Ⓖ Grammar focus

Show students the icon. Write page 138 on the board and ask them to find it. Show students the language summary on prediction and ability.

You can use exercises 1 and 2 on page 139 for:

a) extra practice now
b) homework
c) review a couple of lessons from now.

The answers are on page 142 of the Teacher's Book.

Vocabulary (SB page 47)

1 Tell students that they are going to look at one of the most common words in the English language: one of the top five most commonly used verbs. Students guess what it is (top five: *be, have, do, say, **get***).

Students read exercise 1 and complete the table. Then encourage students to think of other examples to add to

the list if possible, as a class, eg **become:** get angry, get hungry, get sick; **receive:** get the post, get his present; **arrive:** get to your destination, get home.

> become: getting tired; get pregnant; get interested
>
> receive: get their information
>
> arrive: get to

TEACH GLOBAL / THINK LOCAL — Alternative procedure

This approach contextualises the target lexis. Draw a stick figure of a man called Charlie, with a sad face. Tell the story about him. Every time you pause, elicit suggestions silently (raise eyebrows / use a hand gesture, etc, to signal). It does not matter if students do not give the correct suggestions.

*Charlie was very, very bored with his life. He wanted to **get away** from his humdrum life, his job as a (pause) … bank clerk, dealing with difficult customers and non-stop counting. He had no (pause) …. fun any more. That night, he decided to change his life. He (pause) … packed his (pause) … bag and had an early night. In the morning he (pause) … **got up** with the birds and set out on a round the world trip. After two weeks of **getting around** mainly on foot, he had only travelled about 150 km and he felt very (pause) …. tired. He realised that he was actually missing even his (pause) … job! That night, when sleeping in a cheap hotel, all his things – his bags and his money – (pause) … were stolen. He decided to (pause) … return home. When he **got back**, he **got together with** (pause) … some old friends in the local pub. He also started to talk to the pretty (pause) … barmaid. He decided that (pause) … his life back home wasn't so bad after all!*

Re-read the text without pausing. Students re-tell the story in pairs. Then elicit the target phrases with 'get', eg *He wanted to … .*

2 If you did not use the alternative procedure above, put the words on the right in exercise 2 on the board, eg *return* (v). Students in pairs try to think of a synonym with *get* for each of the five verbs, then complete the exercise.

1	b	4	e
2	d	5	c
3	a		

3 Clarify the situation: this is a perfect world. Ask the first two questions to confident students. Give a minute's thinking time. Ask students to work in pairs to ask and answer the questions.

TEACH GLOBAL / THINK LOCAL — Homework extra

Students write a single diary entry, from a utopian world. Start like this (put on the board and elicit ideas): *I woke up at 9.30 am, with the sun shining through the window onto my _____ (describe) bed. I got up and had _____ for breakfast (what?), then went to _____ (place) to _____ (why?).* Students continue it.

Part 4

Lead-in

Before class do an image search online with the key words: *polar bear* and *coral reefs* and show students selected images. Elicit why we should be worried: the polar bear's habitat / survival is threatened by melting ice; 60% of the world's coral is predicted to have died by 2030, due largely to warming waters. Elicit the global problem: *climate change* or *global warming*. Write these up on the board. Ask students if they can give other examples of climate change.

Vocabulary (SB page 48)

1 Students complete the missing words, alone initially, without a dictionary. Then they work together in pairs.

2 **1.51** Ask students to listen and check their answers, then repeat the words after the recording. Drill any tricky words, eg *flood* /flʌd/, *ocean* /ˈəʊʃən/ and *desert* /ˈdezət/.

🔊 **1.51**

1 Europe – stronger **storms** and increased chance of **floods**
2 Africa – **lakes** and **rivers** disappearing
3 New Zealand – **oceans** getting warmer
4 Mexico, US – Numerous **forest** fires
5 Africa – Area of **desert** increasing
6 Greenland – Glacial **ice** melting

Extra activity

Students have a group discussion on climate change. Tell them you will ask groups for their opinions and comments in seven minutes (give less or more, as appropriate). Students choose a representative to take notes and report back. Dictate these:

Have you felt or seen any signs of climate change yourself?

Can you remember any other examples of climate change which you have heard of?

Are we causing climate change or is it a natural thing?

What do you think is going to happen?

Listening (SB page 48)

This listening comprises different people giving their opinions about the film and its message.

1 Students write down the name of the most terrifying film they have seen, then discuss in threes.

Ask students to look at the poster on page 49 and respond to the two questions. Explain this is not a typical 'horror movie'.

2 🔊 **1.52** Students listen and compare ideas in pairs before feedback. If you have the technology, you could also watch a clip of this film on video sharing websites.

Do a web search using the key words: *An Inconvenient Truth film* or go to *www.climatecrisis.net*

The film is about future problems related to global warming.

🔊 **1.52**

1: An Inconvenient Truth? Isn't that a documentary from a few years ago about global warming? No. I haven't seen it, no. I heard it was interesting.

2: Well, of course I knew about global warming a bit before I saw the film … but, well …. wow. I mean, it really makes me think about what I'm going to do. If we don't do something now, we'll have serious problems in the future.

3: All I want to say is that I saw this film. It was a great documentary, and it's very very important.

4: Oh, yes I remember this film. I saw it after Al Gore won the Nobel peace prize. I learned a lot. It was different from a usual Hollywood film.

5: I didn't like it. These kinds of documentary films are always frightening. And anyway, when this climate change happens, I'll be dead. So I don't want to worry about it now.

6: I haven't, but my son saw this film at school, in his geography class. He was talking about it all evening. He said: "You'll think differently after you see it." I think it's good that he learns about this kind of thing at school.

---

3 Give students time to read the statements for each speaker first. Write the name *Al Gore* up, explaining who he is. Play the recording and monitor – play the recording twice at this stage, if necessary.

Students compare notes before whole-class feedback.

1	F	4	F
2	F	5	F
3	T	6	T

Background note

Albert Gore (born 1948) is an American politician. He was the Vice-President under President Bill Clinton from 1993–2003. He is also a businessman and environmentalist. He wrote *An Inconvenient Truth* and starred in the Academy-award winning documentary based on the book, although some of the claims made are not universally accepted. He won the Nobel Peace prize (2007) for his work on climate change.

---

4 Students respond to the question as a whole class. Encourage students to give reasons. If one of the students uses an *-ing* or *-ed* adjective, write the sentence on the board in preparation for the next stage.

Extend your vocabulary – -ed /-ing adjectives (SB page 48)

Students read the explanation and choose the correct words individually. Monitor to check that students have grasped the difference between the two types of adjective. Take feedback.

1 boring	3 worrying	
2 relaxed, surprised		

TEACH GLOBAL THINK LOCAL **Extra activity**

Students think of a film / book which made them feel: *surprised, tired, interested, bored, amused, excited, scared / frightened, depressed, relaxed* (clarify as necessary). Write up:

After / while watching / reading / doing X, I felt _____ (adj). It was (a) really _____ (adj) (film, book)

Provide an example yourself. Students write three full sentences about themselves, then compare notes.

Grammar (SB page 49)

1 Elicit an example of the target language first, eg *when I next _____ (go) on-line, I _____ (try)to buy the DVD of An Inconvenient Truth.* Check students know 'main clause' versus 'if/when' clause – students need this to do exercise 1.

As students are completing the gap-fill alone, monitor and note or point out errors relating to form. Take class feedback and point out the different order of the clauses in 4 (the main clause is first).

1 don't do, will have	3 happens, will be	
2 look, will see	4 will think, see	

Language note

The 'if' clause (subordinate clause) takes a present structure and for students this can seem odd when referring to the future. They might say, *when I will return home tonight, I'll cook dinner*.

2 Students work in pairs, both writing full sentences. Monitor.

In feedback encourage students to contract the auxiliary, eg *If the weather is good tomorrow, I'll probably go for a walk.*

If you feel your students could manage, input some examples of 'tentative language' eg *I think + I'll ... ; I'll probably ...*

G Grammar focus

Show students the icon. Write page 138 on the board and ask them to find it. Show students the language summary on future time clauses.

You can use exercise 1 on page 139 for:

a) extra practice now
b) homework
c) review a couple of lessons from now.

The answers are on page 142 of the Teacher's Book.

TEACH GLOBAL THINK LOCAL **Extra activity**

Write the following on the board:
1 *When / if I meet the love of my life, ...*
2 *When / if I become rich, ...*
3 *When I retire, ...*
4 *When I speak perfect English, ...*
5 *When / if I become a successful X, ...*
6 *When I pass all my exams, ...*

Students work in twos or threes with a dice. They take it in turns to throw the dice and after each throw, one student completes a correct sentence of that number.

Speaking (SB page 49)

TEACH GLOBAL THINK LOCAL **Extra activity**

Students close books. Write the words *To stop climate change, we have to ...* on the board, eliciting examples before students work in threes to brainstorm more ideas in two minutes. If your students need prompts, write words on the board eg *plastic food packaging; a packet of seeds; a light-bulb; car-keys, a bin,* etc. Listen to suggestions as a whole class, inviting students to give reasons.

1 As a lead-in to the questionnaire, introduce the task, then write up the first question on the board: Elicit two more possible questions. Students then read the six questions and think about their own answers.

2 Focus attention on the follow-up question in each case, which should be asked if their partner gives a 'yes' answer. Students work in pairs to ask and answer the questions. They should note down their partner's answers.

3 Students may find they still need to ask more detailed questions to their partner to complete this task.

Take whole class feedback to find out who is the most environmentally aware.

Background note

Your 'carbon footprint' is a measure of the amount you as an individual / group affect global warming and therefore the environment. It is a way of conceptualizing the damage we do by measuring the carbon dioxide produced in units.

Function globally: making offers and decisions

These lessons in *Global* are designed to provide students with **immediately** useful functional language. They all follow a similar format.

Warm up (SB page 50)

Aim: to introduce the topic via a quick speaking task or picture work.

Tips:

- Do not over-correct here, especially in speaking activities.
- Encourage students to use what language they can at this stage.

Listening (SB page 50)

Aim: to present the functional language in context via a conversation or series of conversations.

Tips:

- Ask students to read the questions first before listening.
- Play the recording all the way through for each task (there are always two tasks).
- For multiple conversations pause the audio after each one.
- If students find it very difficult, play the audio a final time and allow them to read the audioscript at the back of the book.

---

1 and 2

Conversation 1: situation 3. The bill is £2.75

Conversation 2: situation 1. His friend is going to drive him.

Conversation 3: situation 4. She is going to take the 6.50 train.

💿 **1.53–1.55**

1 A: Oh. Look at the time. My train's leaving soon.
   B: Shall I pay for these?
   A: That would be great.
   B: OK. Wait. I don't have enough for both of them.
   A: Hold on. How much is it?
   B: 2.75.
   A: I'll pay for it. Here's five. I really have to go now though.
   B: Thanks again. Have a good trip, and see you next Monday!
   A: Bye! See you Monday.
2 A: Hey! What time do you need to get to the airport?
   B: I'm planning to be there two hours before the flight. Why?
   A: Well, look at the time. The airport train leaves in five minutes.
   B: Oh no.
   A: I'm sorry, we were talking and I didn't see the time …

   B: No, don't worry. I … I won't take the train. I'll take a taxi.
   A: A taxi? They're quite expensive. Let me drive you to the airport.
   B: Really? That would be great. Thanks.
   A: No problem. We can continue our conversation in the car.
3 A: Can I help you?
   B: Yes, thanks. Erm, I … I've missed my train. Can I use this ticket for the next train?
   A: Yes, you can. The next train is the six o'clock fast train. You'll need to pay an extra ten euros for that. Or you can take the six fifty train and you don't have to pay anything extra.
   B: Okay, I'll take the six fifty train then. Thank you.
   A: You're welcome.

Language Focus: offers and decisions (SB page 50)

Aim: to draw students' attention to the items of functional language.

Tips:

- Make sure students have time to understand the form and meaning of the phrases, but you needn't translate them word for word.
- Students should be able to pronounce these phrases intelligibly, so drill them.

---

1 will

2 and 3

 1.56

1 A: Are you ready to order?
   B: Yes. I**'ll have** a salad.
2 A: I don't understand this.
   B: That's all right. I**'ll help** you.
3 A: The next train is in twenty minutes.
   B: **Shall** we **take** it or wait?
4 A: Here, let me take those bags.
   B: Thanks, but it's OK. I**'ll carry** them.

Speaking (SB page 50)

Aim: to allow students an opportunity to use this language in a meaningful, real-world context.

Tips:

- There are sometimes a choice of tasks. Any task involving reading a script will be easier than a task involving making students' own scripts. This gives you flexibility for mixed ability classes.
- Give students time to prepare this activity, and circulate and monitor carefully.
- Correct sensitively, paying attention to the target language especially.
- If time allows, ask students to repeat the task, but with a new partner.

Global voices

These lessons in *Global* are designed to provide students with exposure to authentic speakers of English from both native and non-native English backgrounds. They all follow a similar format.

Warm up (SB page 51)

Aim: to introduce the topic and highlight potentially difficult vocabulary the students will encounter.

Tips:

- Be generous in helping students with the vocabulary here, but let them try and work it out first.
- Circulate and monitor any speaking task, but be careful not to overcorrect.
- Follow up any short discussion pairwork with an open class discussion, asking students to report back what they said.

> **2** Other reasons might include: I'd like to travel; I need to speak English with my relatives / my colleagues; I want to read English books in the original; my boss has told me to; I need it to get into university; I love the sound of the language, etc.

Listening (SB page 51)

Aim: to expose students to English spoken with a variety of accents.

Tips:

- The first time students listen, tell them you don't expect them to understand every word; some of it will be hard. This is because the text has not been scripted or graded in any way. It's what they would hear in "the real world".
- Pause after each speaker on the second listening, and don't be afraid to replay the whole thing if students appear to need it.
- Students can read the audioscript at the back of the book if you / they wish.
- Try to avoid hunting for specific pronunciation or language errors. In real world communication not everyone speaks perfect English all the time, not even native speakers.

> 🎧 **1.57–1.62**
>
> 1 I'm learning English because it will be helpful for my career. **(5)**
> 2 I am learning English because first of all I want to be a teacher of English in my country. **(4)**
> 3 I would like to work for some companies who work in Canada and USA and they need really good English skills and I have to speak English very well and to work for them. **(3)**
> 4 Well I believe that English is very important nowadays as you cannot continue studying without using English because it's the international language nowadays. **(8)**
> 5 I am learning English because I love it. I love the English culture, the American culture, its movie, its music. **(10)**
> 6 English is a world language so we need to study English. It is essential. And personally I want to be a politician or I want to be a diplomat, which my father wants. So I think English is the most important thing for a politician or a diplomat so that is why I am studying English in Britain now. **(9)**

Language focus: synonyms

Aim: to raise students' awareness of a particular piece of language present in the listening.

Tips:

- This language is not included in tests or reviews, it is here to help students understand international English.
- Don't expect students to produce this language in an exercise or in conversation immediately.

> 1 actually
> 2 university studies
> 3 obvious

Speaking (SB page 51)

Aim: for students to discuss the same or similar questions as the speakers in the listening.

Tips:

- The speaking tasks here are slightly more open to allow for students to explore the subject. Give them time to do this.
- If students are working in pairs, circulate and monitor. Make notes of incorrect language use to correct afterwards (or in a future class).

Writing an email to a friend

Reading (SB page 52)

1 and 2
Find out if students know anything about Edith Piaf, show them a picture or play her music. Then students read the two emails. Ask open class if they have seen or would like to see the film and encourage them to give their opinions.

> They arrange to go and see *La Vie En Rose*.

Background note

Edith Piaf is a well-known French singer and songwriter (1915–63), a French icon. Two of her most famous songs are: 'La vie en rose' and 'Non, je ne regrette rien'. She had a rather tragic life and this was dramatized in the film 'La vie en rose', released in 2007.

Writing skills: informal style (SB page 52)

1 Point out that these emails are very like informal letters. Check the meaning of *salutation* and *contraction*. Students check what they know about informal writing to friends.

a	F	c	T
b	T	d	F

2 Students work independently initially, then check their answers in pairs. You could write the changes on the board.

1	I'm writing …	8	… acting's brilliant
2	I'd like to see …	9	I'd love to …
3	It's a drama …	10	I'd really like to …
4	It's had very good …	11	My sister's …
5	It's the true story …	12	… it's great
6	I've heard …	13	I'll see you …
7	… music's beautiful …		

Language note

This raises students' awareness of how audience affects choice of language. Students tend to either overuse or underuse contractions in both formal and informal writing. Informal written style is closer to spoken English, using different, higher frequency vocabulary, contractions and ellipsis (when the 'grammar' words are omitted, eg *(I'll) See you (on) Friday)*.

3 Ask students to work in pairs. Note that some of these answers may differ depending on context, age and personality of the reader / writer.

Hello Laura (I)	Yours sincerely (F)
Dear Laura (F)	Bye for now (I)
Hi Laura (I)	Regards (F)
Best wishes (Q)	Yours (Q)
Cheers (I)	

Language focus: making invitations and arrangements (SB page 52)

1 Ask students to choose whether the expressions are formal or informal. Students work with a different partner from the previous exercise.

1	F	5	F	9	F
2	I	6	I	10	I
3	I	7	I	11	F
4	F	8	F	12	I

2 Students can work in pairs if they wish. Encourage them to use informal expressions from exercise 1 to help them.

Preparing to write (SB page 52)

Introduce this by describing a film that you have recently seen, using some of the phrases under *Describing a film*.

Give students time to read the useful phrases. Focus students briefly on the use of *star* as a verb.

Write up any new words on the board and drill them, eg *thriller* (n) /ˈθrɪlə/; *documentary* (n) /dɒkjəˈmentəri/ and *review* (n/v) /rɪˈvjuː/. Students then describe their films in pairs.

Writing (SB page 52)

Remind students that the tone should be informal and to refer to Laura's text and to the Language focus (exercise 1 and 2) for support. If appropriate, use a local cinema guide, or the internet. Encourage students to develop the central paragraph, and give brief details of the film. Remind students this paragraph should encourage their friend to join them.

Monitor as students are writing, focusing on issues of style and clarity. Ideally, write and send the emails on computer. Take in the finished emails for diagnostic purposes.

Global review

These lessons in *Global* are intended to review some of the language and topics covered in the unit. They follow a similar format.

Grammar and Vocabulary (SB page 53)

Aim: to review the main grammar and vocabulary in the unit.

Tips:

- Students can do these exercises alone or in pairs, in class or at home, depending on their learning style and your teaching situation.
- Ask students to read the questions first to establish the grammar and vocabulary areas which are focused on.
- Encourage students to check their own answers by looking back through the unit.

Grammar

1 are you doing	5 buy / will be able
2 to get	6 going
3 to learn	7 am starting
4 'm going to buy	8 gets / will melt

Vocabulary

Natural disasters: storm, flood, forest fire

People with a lot of money: wealthy, well-off

People helped by aid organisations: poor, homeless

Geographical features: ocean, lake, desert

Speaking and Writing (SB page 53)

Aim:

to provide extra speaking and writing practice that will review and consolidate language presented in the unit.

Tips:

- Before speaking encourage students to think first about what language they need to focus on from the unit, and a good way to start their conversation.
- Before they do the writing practice, ask students to either make notes or discuss ideas with a partner to activate useful language.
- Monitor as students are working and note any points for feedback at the end.

Study skills

Using your dictionary: finding the right entry (SB page 53)

1 Familiarise yourself with the entries in the learners' dictionaries beforehand. If possible, to aid feedback, project the relevant entries for exercises 1–5 onto the board.

2 Students check in a monolingual dictionary. In feedback, clarify the purpose of the exercise. Read the comments under Exercise 2 aloud. Ask students if they can think of other examples like 'orange'.

3 Elicit from students the typical word classes for these three words, before searching in the dictionary. Ask students to check the meaning too (sometimes the meaning is related, eg *heat* (n) and (v), but *pretty* (adj) and (adv) and *fair* are not connected). In these three cases the pronunciation remains the same, despite changes in meaning.

1	heat: noun, verb
2	pretty: adjective, adverb
3	fair: noun, adjective

---

4 Remind students that there may be several meanings for one class of the word in the dictionary. Be prepared to help students unused to reading phonemic script.

---

1 tear (verb) /teə/ to pull something so that it separates into pieces; tear (noun) /tɪə/ a drop of liquid that comes from your eye when you cry.

2 close (verb) /kləʊz/ to move something to cover an open area; close (adj) /kləʊs/ only a short distance away.

---

5 First students cover the menu of meanings 1–6. They then read the example sentences in pairs and decide what 'green' means in each case. Students then find the relevant meanings from the list.

1	3
2	2
3	5

Work & Leisure

Coursebook

Unit 5	Language	Texts	Communicative skills
Part 1 SB page 54	Vocabulary Jobs and Work Extend your vocabulary – *job vs work* Grammar *Have*	Reading *Profile of an Indian call centre worker*	Speaking Discussing jobs and preferences
Part 2 SB page 56	Grammar Modal verbs Vocabulary Work issues Pronunciation Strong and weak forms	Listening Conversations between bosses and employees	Speaking Discussing and prioritising aspects of working Talking about good and bad employers and work obligations
Part 3 SB page 58	Vocabulary Leisure activities Extend your vocabulary – *play* Grammar *-ing* verb forms Pronunciation /ŋ/	Listening Presentation about *The serious leisure perspective*	Speaking Discussing leisure time Talking about casual and serious leisure activities Writing Students write a paragraph about a leisure activity
Part 4 SB page 60	Grammar Present perfect; *have been / have gone* Pronunciation Past participle vowel sounds	Reading Ten facts about amusement parks	Speaking Talking about amusement parks and personal experiences
Function globally	Turn-taking Discussing meetings; English and work Students analyse and practise turn-taking questions		
Global English	David Crystal text: *All work and no play* Students talk about jargon in language		
Writing	A CV Correcting spelling and punctuation Writing dates		
Global review	Grammar and vocabulary review Extra speaking practice		
Study skills	Students review ways of recording new words and phrases		

Additional resources

eWorkbook	Interactive and printable grammar, vocabulary, listening and pronunciation practice Extra reading and writing practice Additional downloadable listening and audio material
Teacher's Resource CD	Communication activity worksheets to print and photocopy
Go global: ideas for further research	**Work** – Ask students to find examples of Dilbert or other humorous comics **Leisure** – Ask students to make a slide presentation on a favourite leisure activity and upload the slideshow to the internet or share it in class

Work & Leisure

Part 1

Speaking (SB page 54)

TEACH GLOBAL THINK LOCAL Lead-in

Put the quote up on the board, with two key words omitted, as follows: "When you go to work, if your name is on the building, you're rich. If your name is on your desk, you're middle-class. If your name is on your _____, you're _____."
Clarify *middle-class*. Elicit possible alternatives for the gaps, then students check in their books.

1 Students read the quote in pairs.

2 Ask students to work in pairs and check they know the different jobs in the box before speaking. Drill any words you think might cause problems, eg *politician* /pɒləˈtɪʃən/.

Discuss open class how they think the quote describes jobs in the US. (*suggested answer: It may imply that a class system exists for jobs, where people are labelled, and which is hard to break out of*). Ask students if this is similar to their country.

Encourage students to give reasons for their choices of the jobs from the box. Monitor and give feedback as appropriate afterwards.

Vocabulary (SB page 54)

1 Ask students where they might see these mini job-advertisements, eg the job ad section in a newspaper. Students work alone to replace the vocabulary, then check in pairs. In feedback, elicit the word class in each case.

1	give work to: employ (v)
2	money: salary (n)
3	extra money: bonus (n)
4	giving jobs: hiring (v)
5	teaching of the skills: training (n)/ (v)
6	money per hour: wages (n)
7	talk about the job: interview (n)

2 To start students off, let them read the questions, then you provide two separate answers to random questions. Students decide which question you are responding to. Clarify any language at this point, eg *wage, shift, salary*.

Ask students to work in pairs to discuss the questions. Take some whole class feedback on any points of interest. These sentences also contain common job-related collocations. Elicit and record these on the board as collocations, eg *minimum wage, job interview, work night shifts, (a good) starting salary*.

Language note

Wage and *salary* both refer to your income from your job. Your *wage* is the money that you earn per week, often referred to in the plural: *wages*. Your *salary* is per month or year. If you are in a profession, eg a teacher or business person, you will probably use the word *salary*.

Background note

In the UK, the minimum wage is £5.80 (Oct'09); in the US the federal minimum wage is $7.25 (July'09), although different US states also have minimum wage regulations.

Reading and Speaking (SB page 54)

This reading is an interview with an Indian call centre worker, talking about her work.

1 Ask students to look at the photo of the call centre and of Rajeshwari (SB page 55). Read aloud the introduction on SB page 55, then ask the whole class the questions in exercise 1 SB page 54.

Find out if students have had any personal experiences with call centres which were amusing or annoying.

TEACH GLOBAL THINK LOCAL Pre-reading activity

Put the following questions on the board for discussion:
How many call-centre workers do you think there are in India?;
What kind of companies use them and why? What exactly does a call centre worker do?;
What are the positive / negative aspects of this job?

Take feedback on suggestions, then ask them to read the text in the four circles.

2 Focus students on the photo of Rajeshwari again. Point out the glossary, then let students find out about Rajeshwari, answering the questions. After a few minutes, let students compare their answers.

1	She was very happy when she got the job. She misses her parents.
2	She works nights and she gets home from work at five in the morning.
3	She mainly talks to Americans. Sometimes they get angry. Sometimes she talks to Indian people who want her to speak Hindi.

TEACH GLOBAL THINK LOCAL Reading extra

If necessary, to help your students understand the text more fully, dictate these additional questions:

a) *Who is Katie Jones?* b) *Is her salary good?* c) *Why does Rajeshwari need to dress smartly?* d) *Does she like it when an Indian person picks up the phone?* e) *Do you think she regrets taking the job?*

Mixed ability

Stronger students work out the questions that the British journalist must have asked, eg *How did you feel when you first got this job?* (see para 1).

Monitor as students are working. Take whole class feedback.

Extend your vocabulary (SB page 54)

Approach this as a test-teach exercise. Books closed. Write the words *job* and *work* on the board, then read out the five sentences. Students write down the appropriate missing words in each case.

Students read the explanation in this section and amend their answer accordingly, before checking as a whole class.

```
1  job
2  work/job
3  jobs
4  work
5  job
```

3 Students choose their task in pairs. If many / all students choose **B**, brainstorm the words and put them on the board. Students should justify why they have chosen their adjectives, referring to the text.

Grammar (SB page 55)

1 Do the first two examples together, reading out the sentence and asking what 'have' is used for in each one. Check that students understand the metalanguage used here, eg *possessing*, *auxiliary*, etc.

Students complete the matching task in pairs. Try to elicit similar examples when checking answers as a whole class.

```
1  b
2  d
3  e
4  e
5  c
6  a
7  c
8  c
```

Language note

The multiple uses of *have* can be confusing for students. All of these uses are high frequency. In relation to uses a) and b), *have* is considered a little more formal than *have got*, eg *I have several qualifications in this area.*

In American English, *have* is often preferred to *have got*, eg *I have a dog.*

2 First of all read out the **Language note**. Elicit examples or use those from exercise 1 to illustrate, eg sentences 1 and 3: *I've got a job as a call centre operator*; *We'd a small party.*

Exercise 2 focuses on form and pronunciation. When students have finished, they should amend the sentences so that they are true for themselves, then compare their answers in pairs, orally. Monitor, focusing on the target language.

```
1  –
2  I've
3  –
4  I've
5  I've
6  –
```

G Grammar focus

Show students the icon. Write page 140 on the board and ask them to find it. Show students the language summary on *have*.

You can use exercise 1 on page 141 for

a) extra practice now
b) homework
c) review a couple of lessons from now.

The answers are on page 142 of the Teacher's Book.

Homework extra

In class elicit Rajeshwari's feelings about the job – they are clearly mixed. Set the scene: Rajeshwari is feeling homesick. She writes a letter to her best friend (she can't tell her parents the truth). Start:

Dear Bina, I'm so sorry for not writing earlier. It's been a bit difficult since I left home. Please don't tell my family what I'm going to tell you now … . Elicit some suggestions of what she might say. Encourage students to be imaginative and to understand her situation.

Part 2

Listening and Vocabulary (SB page 56)

Lead-in

If appropriate, ask students to talk about their own bosses – past or present – in threes. Find out first if they are willing and able to do so. Then brainstorm onto the board what a 'good' boss does / says.

The listening text involves four different bosses talking to employees on different work-related subjects.

1 Ask students to comment on the cartoon. Then ask what other (humorous) things besides watering plants a new employee might be asked to do: students work in small groups to think of at least three things, eg making coffee and tea, doing photocopying, ordering sandwiches, etc.

2 **1.63–1.66** Students listen and order the topics. In feedback, if there are / were any problems, then play the recording again for students to check.

1	the weekend
2	a dress code
3	the computer
4	a meal

 1.63–1.66

Boss 1: Oh, hello good to see you. Listen, somebody has to work this Saturday morning. Susan has called in sick. Now, I know that you've worked every Saturday this month, but there isn't anyone else. That all right? You can take next Saturday off.

Boss 2: Excuse me? Yes, come here please. Now, I don't know if anybody told you, but we have a dress code here. Employees mustn't wear jeans to work. It's not allowed. You don't have to wear a jacket and tie, but try to be a little bit more formal.

Boss 3: No, no, NO. How many times do I have to say this? You *can't* use the computer to send private emails and you *can't* send personal messages to each other on the computer. You are on company time, and you *must respect* that time. That means *working* everybody, and *not talking*.

Boss 4: It's *okay*, you know. Of course you can go on your lunch break now. You don't have to come in to my office and ask me every time. I like to keep things informal around here, and as long as everyone does their work then I don't see a problem. All right? By the way, I recommend the Italian restaurant on the corner if you don't know where to go. *Very* good pasta.

3 Let students circle the preferred answer in pairs before they listen. Then play the recording. Pause the recording after each line or possibly re-play it.

Write the target phrases on the board to focus students: *call in sick; take (time) off; be on company time; go on a lunch break (or have / take a break).*

1	Someone has called in sick.
1	You can take next Saturday off.
3	You are on company time, and you must respect that time.
4	Of course you can go on your lunch break now.

4 Ask students which of the four bosses they think are bad, and why.

Grammar (SB page 56)

1 Write the heading 'Modal verbs' on the board. Elicit anything they know about these, then let students read the examples.

They work in pairs to explain what the modals (in bold) mean, without looking at the rules (a–d). Clarify the word 'allowed'. Students then do the matching task in pairs. Make sure you give support to less confident learners in this guided discovery task.

Take whole class feedback. Elicit similar, additional examples, using the work context, eg

You can't leave the office before 5 pm.

Extra activity

If students find it hard to distinguish between the modals and your class make-up allows it, get them to translate sentences 1–6 into their mother tongue in pairs. They should underline the word(s) which express modality in their first language. Walk around and see if you are able to identify any patterns (whether you know their L1 or not), asking students questions – this helps students to focus on the concept.

1	have to, must
2	mustn't, can't
3	don't have to
4	can

Language note

Have to and *must* are very similar in meaning but as students tend to overuse *must*, recommend using *have to* if they are unsure. *Must* usually suggests strong obligation, the obligation often coming from the speaker him/herself: *I really must give up chocolate*, or from someone in a position of authority: (mother to child) *Listen! You must stop eating all those sweets!*

In British spoken English, both *have to* and *have got to* express obligation, eg *I've got to be / I have to be in work early tomorrow.*

Whereas *have to* and *must* (affirmative) are similar in meaning, the negative forms are not. *You don't have to wear a suit* = a suit is not necessary. *You must not wear a suit* = wearing a suit is forbidden.

2 Let students first work alone on this fairly challenging task, before checking in pairs.

When checking as a whole class, discuss options, eg in text one *employees must wear a suit* is the first option, but in the second text, they *can't* or *mustn't* send personal email messages. Highlight differences in meaning, eg the contrast between *people don't have to dress so formally* vs. *people must not dress so formally.* Ask: *Can you wear a suit on Friday if you want to?* (Answer: *yes, but it's not necessary.*)

Text 1

must

don't have to

can

Text 2

can

can't / mustn't

mustn't / can't

Text 3

have to

don't have to

can

---

3 Ask students to make sentences about their jobs using the modal verbs. First choose a job together and do an example on the board. Then students work alone.

Monitor and check individuals' work. Early finishers can read and check a partner's work.

Hear some examples as a whole class.

G Grammar focus

Show students the icon. Write page 140 on the board and ask them to find it. Show students the language summary on modal verbs.

You can use exercise 1 on page 141 for:

a) extra practice now

b) homework

c) review a couple of lessons from now.

The answers are on page 142 of the Teacher's Book.

Extra activity

If your students need more practice, ask them to reflect on their class rules and norms of behaviour. Imagine speaking to a new student about the class. Elicit some ideas, then students brainstorm ideas in groups, eg *you can't smoke; you have to come to all the lessons,* etc. Add extra prompts on the board if students dry up, eg *food/drink; homework; behaviour; speaking in English; clothes; dictionaries,* etc. In feedback, one member of each group reports back. Students could then roleplay in pairs: an old student chatting to a new one. Demonstrate first with a stronger student.

Pronunciation (SB page 57)

1 **1.67** Students may want to say these sentences aloud first, so ask some students to read them, then listen to the recording. Elicit from students what they now know about the pronunciation of these modals (see below).

Point out the **Language note** on British English pronunciation.

1.67

1 You can't wear that.
   You can wear that.
2 She can't come to class today.
   She can come to class today.
3 You must use your books.
   You mustn't use your books.

---

2 **1.68** Students listen and compare answers in pairs. After a quick check, students practise saying the sentences in pairs. Go around and help individuals, drilling where necessary.

---

1 mustn't

2 can't

3 must

1.68

1 Workers mustn't use the computers on the first floor.
2 You can't take your lunch break at two o'clock.
3 I really must answer emails more quickly.

Pronunciation note

Pronunciation is a key consideration: *You must wear a suit for work* (boss to new employee) is likely to be unstressed: *You must* /məs/ *wear a suit for work.* Stressing 'must' here could sound rude or dogmatic.

The negative forms, eg *can't* and *mustn't* are stressed, but generally the affirmatives are not, resulting in a schwa, eg *You can't* /kɑːnt/ *go* versus *you can* /kən/ *go.*

Speaking (SB page 57)

1 Give students time to work on their own to read the job characteristics and choose the ones important to them personally.

2 Students first read the example sentences, then work in pairs to share their ideas. Encourage students to give reasons for their choices and remind them to add their own job characteristics if they want.

At the end, ask if anyone changed their mind in the discussion. If so, why?

3 Before joining pairs together, ask students to look in the *Useful language* box, to help them discuss their points more naturally. Take whole class feedback, asking students their final choices of job characteristics, and what they changed from their original list.

TEACH GLOBAL THINK LOCAL Extra activity

If students need more practice, they write secret job descriptions in pairs. Others then guess the mystery job. Provide an oral model, or for **less strong students** a written model:

I have to get up very early at times, or even in the middle of the night. I sometimes have very little to do in a day, I can just read or drink coffee and do a bit of training. Luckily I don't have to sit at a computer all day, but I do have to wear a uniform in my job, and I also work shifts. I sometimes work at weekends too. Finally, for my job I have to stay quite fit.

(a firefighter)

Part 3

TEACH GLOBAL THINK LOCAL Lead-in

Bring in objects connected to your own hobbies, or your family's hobbies, eg trainer (tennis); wool (knitting); wooden spoon (cooking), etc. Show them the objects to elicit from students what your hobbies are. Follow this up by asking students to name one object which gives a clue to one of their hobbies. They could just say the word or draw it on the board, for others to guess their hobby. Encourage students to be a little cryptic!

Vocabulary (SB page 58)

1 Do the first example together. Students work alone first, then check in pairs.

Early finishers can add examples to *do*, *go for* and *collect*. Take feedback.

1	read
2	do
3	go for
4	collect
5	watch
6	play
7	chat
8	cook

2 Use the two examples given to remind students of the position of the adverb: adverbs usually go before the verb, except with *be* when the adverb follows it; longer adverbs go at the end of the clause.

You could elicit and write on the board other adverbs of frequency so that students have them as a reminder as they discuss in pairs if and how often they do the activities.

3 Students close their books. Write up *5.1 hours a day* and tell students this is the average time an American spends on sports and leisure. Ask them to guess the activity which takes up most of the time (*watching TV*).

Students look at the pie chart on page 58 and discuss the questions.

Add an extra question on the board for early finishers: *Would a chart for your own country be very similar to this?*

Listening (SB page 58)

This listening is a formal presentation on *The serious leisure perspective* and the differences between 'serious' and 'casual' leisure.

UNIT 5 Work & Leisure

1 🔵 **1.69** Before listening, write *Casual leisure* and *Serious leisure* on the board. Ask students what these might mean and elicit examples.

Then students listen and put the slides in order.

1 a
2 f
3 b
4 e
5 d
6 c

🔵 **1.69**

Good afternoon. My name is Robert Macarthur, and I'm here to talk to you about the serious leisure perspective.

The serious leisure perspective comes from the expert on leisure, Robert Stebbins, at the University of Calgary in Canada. He has been working on this theory since 1974. According to Stebbins, there are two main forms of leisure: casual leisure and serious leisure.

Casual leisure is just that, casual. Sitting about at home is casual leisure. Doing nothing is casual leisure. Watching television, reading a book. Maybe just going for a walk. Or chatting with friends over dinner. People enjoy doing these activities because they feel good, because they're relaxing, because they're fun.

For many of us here in America, leisure has a bad reputation because it's not work. We live in a society that says work is more important than leisure because leisure is lazy.

But there is another form of leisure, called serious leisure. Serious leisure activities are activities which lead to personal development.

Doing a sport regularly, like cycling, running, skiing, or swimming are examples of serious leisure.

Serious leisure activities can also include making things, or collecting things. Here, for example, is an image of a website for collectors of rubber ducks. This is funny, yes, but an example of serious leisure too.

Finally, serious leisure can mean volunteer work. By volunteer work, I mean unpaid work helping people other than your family. For example, volunteering in a local hospital. Or in a school. Or in a home for old people.

I believe serious leisure is important because it's fun, yes, but it also satisfies a need in us, it can change our lives.

And now, moving on to my own research …

2 Give students time to read the questions. If your students are able, they can discuss the answers in pairs before listening to check.

Students compare answers after listening the second time. Be prepared to replay the recording if necessary.

1 Sitting about at home, doing nothing, watching television, reading a book, going for a walk, chatting with friends over dinner.

2 Because they feel good, because they're relaxing, because they're fun.

3 It has a bad reputation because it's not work. The speaker says we live in a society that says work is more important than leisure because leisure is lazy.

4 Doing a sport regularly, making or collecting things, or doing volunteer work.

5 Because it satisfies a need in people, and changes lives.

3 Ask students to work in pairs to ask and answer the questions. Share any interesting points as a whole class.

Extend your vocabulary – *play*

Students complete the task on their own. Check and ask them if any of the phrases use the equivalent of the verb 'play' in their own language. Take feedback.

1 player
2 played
3 playful

TEACH GLOBAL THINK LOCAL Homework extra

Students make their own pie chart, as in the example. They should consider every day including the weekend, then find the average time spent per day. They then talk through their chart in groups next lesson.

Grammar (SB page 59)

1 You may need to clarify the metalanguage before starting, eg *subject*, *replace*. You could write up an example sentence, eg *I love cheese* and then elicit the words: *verb*, *subject* and *object*.

Students then work in pairs to complete the task. Monitor to see how they are doing. Take whole class feedback and clarify further, as necessary.

a watching television
b preposition
c love, like, hate, detest

Language note

The focus here is on the *-ing* form or the 'gerund'. The verb form changes to make a noun, so it becomes more flexible in sentence construction. Students frequently make mistakes with this, saying sentences like: *People enjoy (to) do leisure activities*, or else they avoid it.

2 Put three columns on the board, with the headings *double consonant + -ing / take off e + -ing / + -ing* eg *hit, bake, cake.*

Let students work out the answers in pairs, then individuals write one verb each up on the board in the correct column. If possible elicit the rules.

cutting	cycling	doing
running	smoking	playing
swimming	taking	watching
stopping	making	working

Language note

If there is a consonant at the end of a one-syllable verb which immediately follows one vowel, then the final consonant doubles before adding the suffix *-ing*. So, *cut* → *cutting*, but not *ruin* → *ruinning*. In words of two or more syllables, this rule also applies, as long as the final consonant is stressed, eg *begin* → *beginning* but not *open* → *openning*.

With verbs ending in *e*, the *e* is dropped before *-ing*.

3 Ask students to write out the phrases in their notebooks, before working in pairs to see if there are any similarities. Monitor and assist.

G Grammar focus

Show students the icon. Write page 140 on the board and ask them to find it. Show students the language summary on *-ing* forms.

You can use exercise 1 on page 141 for:

a) extra practice now
b) homework
c) review a couple of lessons from now.

The answers are on page 142 of the Teacher's Book.

Pronunciation (SB page 59)

1 **1.70** Students listen and repeat.

The most common spelling is 'ng'.
 1.70
1 Relaxi**ng** and watchi**ng** TV are my favourite thi**ng**s.
2 I thi**nk** E**ng**lish is a difficult la**ng**uage.
3 No tha**nk**s, I'm stoppi**ng** smoki**ng**.

2 For fun, ask students to choose just two sentences from exercise 3, in preparation for a pronunciation competition. Give students two minutes to practise. Monitor and give help as necessary, particularly to natural sentence stress, linking and phrasing.

Everyone listens to each student say their sentences (or just select random students in a larger class). The winner is the student who sounds the most natural; he or she gets a round of applause!

Writing (SB page 59)

1 Write an example on the board and ask students to identify which type it is from the list in exercise 1, eg: *I sometimes go cycling, but it's not easy for me. I like going downhill, but when I have to go uphill, I get red, hot and sweaty. I always end up getting off and I'm always the last to finish. However, I feel great after a ride, and I know it's good exercise.* (something you aren't very good at)

Give students a time limit for writing and monitor and assist where necessary.

2 Ask students to work in pairs and swap papers. Before students write the questions, remind them that their questions should relate directly to what the writer has already written. Otherwise, part 3 will not work.

TEACH GLOBAL THINK LOCAL Mixed ability

For **less strong students**, refer back to your example. Elicit two possible questions and write them on at the side, in a different colour. They then do the same with their partner's text. Monitor and assist.

3 Students adjust their mini texts to include the extra information. If your students need help with this, again use the example on the board to show how this might be done first.

This exercise encourages students to include more details in their writing, and possibly to support their points more fully.

TEACH GLOBAL THINK LOCAL Homework extra

Students choose a dangerous or extreme sport that they would like to try (or that they would never try!). Students can do a web search with the key words: *dangerous sports* or *extreme sports* for ideas, or just use one from the lesson. Depending on whether they need speaking or writing practice, students either a) write an interview with a reporter, where the reporter is finding out about their passion or b) prepare to talk about their 'new passion' in the next lesson for two minutes. They should pretend this is genuinely their own sport, so use 'I' when speaking or writing.

Part 4

Reading (SB page 60)

This text details facts about amusement parks: facts about their history; what they contain; the business side.

Lead-in

If you have the facilities, show a video clip of a roller-coaster ride by doing a web search on *roller coaster video*. If not, recount a personal anecdote of a time when you went to an amusement park. Give details about what you did; how you felt; which rides you loved or feared, etc. Try to tell your personal account in an animated way.

1 Let students look at the two pictures and ask for any reactions. Elicit the term *amusement park* and *theme park* and write these on the board.

2 Ask students to close their books. Put the students into teams of 3–5. Write the numbers 1–6 vertically down the side of the board, to represent the questions, and give students a few minutes to read and predict the answers to exercise 2 in their teams. Do not let them read the actual text yet.

Take feedback, writing up very short answers from each team. eg number 1: *USA*. Use different colours to highlight the different teams' answers.

Students read the text to find the answers. In feedback, elicit answers and as you do so correct teams' predictions on the board. Find out which team had the highest number of correct predictions.

1	Russia
2	Copenhagen, Denmark
3	rides, roller coasters, eating areas
4	$11 billion (in the US)
5	Disneyland in Tokyo
6	Someone who invents Disney amusement park rides.

3 Dictate these questions, if appropriate: *What's your favourite park / ride? When did you last go to one? Would you like to visit again? Are these parks just for children?* Students discuss these and the two questions in exercise 3 in threes.

Background note

Walter Elias Disney was born in 1901 and died in 1966. Despite starting his career with nothing, he had a major influence on the field of entertainment. He was a very creative and talented man, a film producer and director, voice actor, animator and screen writer, who won multiple awards throughout his life. The corporation he founded with his brother now makes billions of dollars per year. His studios and theme parks have developed into a multi-billion dollar television, tourist and media corporation.

Grammar (SB page 60)

Students close their books. Write this sentence from the text on the board:

The Disney Corporation _____ 11 theme parks around the world.

Try to elicit the missing words from students, filling in the gaps (*has built*). Ask the following concept questions: *Do you know when they built them?* (Answer: *No*). *Is the time of building important?* (Answer: *No*). *What is important?* (Answer: *the fact that there are now 11 theme parks*).

Add the following sentence to the board, as a follow-on sentence to the one above:
*Disney created the first Disney theme park **in 1955 in California**.*
Highlight the use of the past simple and the time reference. Ask students *Do we know when?* (Answer: *Yes*). So, *what tense do we use?* (Answer: *Past simple*).

Highlight the form: *subj + have/has + past participle* and give a heading: *The present perfect to talk about experiences.* Students then read the examples and notes under **Grammar**.

1 Ask students to look at the two short texts with photos. Do the first example together. Let students work alone, then in pairs. Give students time and monitor carefully, referring back to the example on the board and the notes under **Grammar**.

Take feedback and ask concept questions (see above).

1	has visited	5	have never been
2	has taken	6	had
3	became	7	didn't have
4	took		

2 Depending on how confident your students are, you could ask them to tackle this exercise before clarifying the difference between *been* and *gone*. Then ask students to read the **Language note** under the Grammar box.

1 gone	2 been	3 gone	4 been

Language note

The present perfect causes problems for students even at much higher levels, partly because it is not used in the same way as their first language. When talking about experiences, other languages tend to use a past simple equivalent; there is no subtle distinction made between specific versus non-specific time. At pre-intermediate level, students can be sensitized to the form and meaning, eg the fact that the present perfect is non-specific in terms of time; that it is used with certain adverbs which are connected conceptually to this notion of 'non-specificness', eg *ever* and *never*.

3 Some students will find it hard to think of ideas so at the start, you read one of the dialogues with a strong student. Try to act here, showing emotion, eg in situation 1, pretend that you are a parent who has lost their 5-year-old son at the park. Elicit possible scenarios for your example, then students choose one dialogue to continue in pairs.

Monitor and listen out for one or two nice examples, which can be shown to the whole class at the end.

G Grammar focus

Show students the icon. Write page 140 on the board and ask them to find it. Show students the language summary on the present perfect.

You can use exercises 1–3 on page 141 for:

a) extra practice now
b) homework
c) review a couple of lessons from now.

The answers are on page 143 of the Teacher's Book.

Pronunciation (SB page 61)

TEACH GLOBAL THINK LOCAL **Extra activity**

Put students into 3 or 4 teams and stand the first member of each team at the head of their team line, facing the board. Give a board pen to each of the first players from each team. Call out a random verb (infinitive), eg you say *see* and students write *seen*. The student quickest to write a legible and correctly-spelt past participle gets a point for their team. After one turn, students pass the pen to the next person in their team, and so the game continues. Students can help team members by calling out.

1 Ask students to group the past participles according to the pronunciation, or alternatively you could put these participles on pieces of card or paper, giving a set per group of three for students to then complete the task.

Early finishers could try to add any additional ones while waiting for others.

2 🔊 **1.71** Students listen to check, then repeat after the recording.

🔊 1.71			
/ən/	/ʌm/ or /ʌn/	/ɔːt/	/iːn/
driven	come	bought	been
eaten	done	brought	seen
forgotten	swum	taught	
ridden	won		

Speaking (SB page 61)

1 🔊 **1.72** Play the recording and focus students on the words which are stressed. Students repeat it, as close to the model as possible.

> 🔊 **1.72**
> Have you ever **been** to an **amusement park**?

Pronunciation note

In present perfect questions, the auxiliary *have* or *has* is typically crushed to /həv/ or /həz/. The participle is stressed, although *been* is frequently also reduced to /bɪn/, probably because of its high frequency.

2 Highlight the form of the question, with the inversion of the auxiliary and subject (*Have you ever … ?*)

Ask students to work in pairs to look at the questions on the leisure questionnaire and remind themselves of the past participles, referring back to exercise 1 if necessary. Remind students that the focus is on the question form and on pronunciation, so they should not answer the questions yet.

Students practise saying the questions aloud. Monitor and help with pronunciation or form problems.

3 This exercise focuses on the movement from general, non-specific time to specific time; from present perfect to past simple. This is a very natural progression in everyday speech.

Ask two students to read the sample dialogue aloud. Students say which verb tenses are used and why.

Do two or three more 'yes' examples as a whole class (from the questionnaire), including follow-up questions.

Pairs then do the same. Monitor and assist as necessary. Pick up on any relevant points or nice examples at the end.

Ask students to write down a couple of the examples as a record.

TEACH GLOBAL THINK LOCAL **Extra activity**

For students who need more oral fluency practice, write these discussion points on the board, or dictate them for students to discuss in threes:

Why do you think amusement parks are more popular in certain parts of the world, eg the USA?

Why are these parks more popular nowadays than before?

As a parent, do/would you want your child to go to these parks often? What age would you say they are appropriate for?

Is the future good for amusement parks?

Function globally: turn-taking

These lessons in *Global* are designed to provide students with **immediately** useful functional language. They all follow a similar format.

Warm up (SB page 62)

Aim: to introduce the topic via a quick speaking task or picture work.

Tips:

- Do not over-correct here, especially in speaking activities.
- Encourage students to use what language they can at this stage.

Listening (SB page 62)

Aim: to present the functional language in context via a conversation or series of conversations.

Tips:

- Ask students to read the questions first before listening.
- Play the recording all the way through for each task (there are always two tasks).
- For multiple conversations pause the recording after each one.
- If students find it very difficult, play the recording a final time and allow them to read the audioscript at the back of the book.

---

1 1 c   2 b   3 a

🔘 1.73–1.75

1   A: Right. Hello and thanks again for coming. The purpose of today's meeting is to give you all the information about …
    B: Excuse me. Could I just ask a question?
    A: Yes, Mrs. Davies.
    B: My son doesn't have all the books yet. Is this a problem?
    A: Not at all. We can talk about the books in just a moment.
    C: Can I add that my daughter doesn't have the books either? They haven't arrived.
    A: Thank you Mr Brown. Please don't worry about it now …
2   A: And I think you will find that the starting salary is *very* good.
    C: Yes. Thank you. May I ask about working hours again? I'm not sure that I understood. What time do you expect me to arrive in the morning?
    A: Seven o'clock.
    C: Fine. Seven o'clock. That's early.
    A: We need people early in the morning to talk to our European offices.
    C: Of course.
    B: Is there a problem?
    C: No, not at all. Not at all.
3   A: OK, so the next item on the agenda is …
    B: Can I say something here?

A: Is it about wages?
B: No, it isn't.
A: All right then. Because we aren't talking about wages in this meeting.
B: Can I just say that the dress code we have now is terrible. Terrible.
A: Thank you, David.
B: I *hate* these ties.
A: I know, which is why we are talking about a change in the dress code.
B: Can I also mention that the trousers are so *uncomfortable*.

2 Conversation 1: a   2: b   3: b

Language focus: turn taking

Aim: to draw students' attention to the items of functional language.

Tips:

- Make sure students have time to understand the form and meaning of the phrases, but you needn't translate them word for word.
- Students should be able to pronounce these phrases intelligibly, so drill them.

---

1 1 Excuse me. Could I just ask a question? (**b**)

Can I add that my daughter doesn't have the books either? (**c**)

2 May I ask about working hours again? (**a or b**)

3 Can I say something here? (**b**)

Can I just say that the dress code … (**c**)

Can I also mention that the trousers are so uncomfortable. (**c**)

2 1 Can I just say something?

2 Could I ask a question?

3 May I add something here?

Speaking (SB page 62)

Aim: to allow students an opportunity to use this language in a meaningful, real-world context.

Tips:

- There is sometimes a choice of task. Any task involving reading a script will be easier than a task involving making students' own scripts. This gives you flexibility for mixed ability classes.
- Give students time to prepare this activity, and circulate and monitor carefully.
- Correct sensitively, paying particular attention to the target language.
- If time allows, ask students to repeat the task, but with a new partner.

Global English

These lessons in *Global* have two main goals. The first is to give you and your students interesting information about English and language in general. The second goal is to provide students with practice in different kinds of reading comprehension tasks that they are likely to encounter in future study (for example, exams).

**TEACH GLOBAL
THINK LOCAL Lead-in**

Ask students to work in pairs to match these words / phrases to their equivalents, writing them randomly on the board:

boot up – *start*; cardiac arrest – *heart attack*; cavity – *hole*; apprehend – *catch*; morbidly obese – *very fat*; marinate – *leave in the mixture*; infinitive – *main verb*

In feedback, explain that these are words are all 'jargon' (special words / phrases understood by people who do the same kind of work). Ask students in which field they would see / hear each one (*computer; medical; dental; police; cookery; language*). Discuss why people use jargon and also why some people do not like jargon.

Warm up (SB page 63)

Aim: to engage students with the topic, and highlight potentially difficult vocabulary in the text.

Tips:
- Be generous in helping students here with any unknown words in the first task.
- Ask students to relate this task, wherever possible, to similar events or texts in their own lives. This will help them with the reading.
- You may want to give your students an overview of the text before they read, possibly even in their first language. Make it interesting and involving.

Reading (SB page 63)

Aim: to provide students with interesting information about English, and reading exam practice skills.

Tips:
- Be ready to help less confident readers, explaining words or ideas in simpler terms if necessary.
- Get students to read through the whole text once first before doing the tasks.
- Many of these texts have been graded slightly, or not at all. There is a glossary of difficult words. Get students to read that first and reassure them that you do not expect them to understand every word or idea.
- There are two tasks. The first is an easier task, often focusing on the gist of the passage. The second is a more difficult task, similar to reading exam questions.

1

technical vocabulary

2

1 false (we need a balance between work and play)
2 false (outsiders won't understand it)
3 true
4 true
5 false (it wants specialists to speak clearly)
6 true

Language focus (SB page 63)

Aim: to highlight an interesting or useful aspect of language in the text.

Tips:
- The language focused on here is to raise students' awareness; do not expect them to produce it immediately.
- This language is not tested or reviewed in future units, which means you have more flexibility with this material as to when and where you use it.

1 a balance
2 add precision
3 convenient
4 the public
5 in other words

Speaking (SB page 63)

Aim: for students to relate the material in the reading to their own language, culture and experiences.

Tips:
- This is a short speaking activity and can be done in whole class mode or in small groups.
- Wherever possible, ask students to think of and provide examples in their own language but explain them in English too.

Writing a CV

Reading (SB page 64)

Students look at the photo of Ahmed and predict in pairs the following, making sure they cover up the CV: *his age, nationality, interests, degree (subject); current job*. Students then check their predictions and at the same time fill in the headings. Clarify 'referees' at the end, referring to the relevant place on the CV.

In feedback, find out who was best at predicting. Also ask how their own CVs differ in terms of layout or general content issues.

1	Email address
2	Date of birth
3	Education and qualifications
4	Work Experience
5	Skills
6	Interests
7	Referees

Writing skills: setting out a CV (SB page 64)

Tell students that this CV is for a different person, but there are punctuation and spelling problems. Find the first example together as a whole class. Students check their answers against Ahmed's CV.

Spelling

CURRICULUM VITAE

Email address

Education and qualifications

Work Experience:

Skills

Referees

Punctuation

1) colons to follow:

address

birth

EDF Energy

Referees

2) No capitals on:

birth

qualifications

assistant

3) Underlining or separate headings for:

Education and qualifications

Work Experience

Interests

4) Full points:

B.A. Hons.

Language focus: writing dates (SB page 64)

If you have a multinational class, ask individuals to come up and write today's date in figures and numbers on the board in their first language. Then ask them to write out today's date in English in their notebooks (both in full and in numbers). Go around and monitor to see what they write, before eliciting a correct version to the board. Contrast this with their own countries' versions. Students then read the notes on UK and America and complete the task.

UK	US
	November 22nd 1995
14th Feb 2000	
28 - 05 - 1982	
	10 - 02 - 95

Preparing to write (SB page 64)

Students work in pairs to discuss first what they would write for themselves. Then they write notes.

Writing

Refer students to the notes and phrases for describing skills on this page. If they need a template or further examples, they can do a web search with the key words *writing a CV*. They may find this particular site useful: www.cvtips.com

TEACH GLOBAL THINK LOCAL **Alternative procedure**

If students have already spent time writing their own CVs in English, they could write a CV either for their partner, based on an initial interview (this would extend the task considerably), or for you, the teacher (based on an interview). Give students a blank template of a CV to make notes on in class. Students can type this at home.

Global review

These lessons in *Global* are intended to review some of the language and topics covered in the unit. They follow a similar format.

Grammar and Vocabulary (SB page 65)

Aim: to review the main grammar and vocabulary in the unit.

Tips:

- Students can do these exercises alone or in pairs, in class or at home, depending on their learning style and your teaching situation.
- Ask students to read the questions first to establish the grammar and vocabulary areas which are focused on.
- Encourage students to check their own answers by looking back through the unit.

Grammar 1

1 have you ever been

2 went

3 writing / chatting

4 have never ridden / have seen

Grammar 2

1 have to

2 don't have to

3 mustn't

4 can

Vocabulary

play on the computer

do exercise

go for a walk

chat on the phone

collect stamps

read a magazine

watch television

cook a meal

Speaking (SB page 65)

Aim: to provide extra speaking practice that will review and consolidate language presented in the unit.

Tips:

- Before speaking encourage students to think first about what language they need to focus on from the unit, and a good way to start their conversation.
- Monitor as students are working and note any points for feedback at the end.

Study skills

Recording new words and phrases (SB page 65)

1 First ask students to refer back to a page in their notebooks where they recently wrote down new words. Go around and have a look at their example pages. Show a couple of clear, neat examples to the class.

Students then discuss the questions in exercise 1 in threes. Take class feedback on the more interesting questions, especially the final 'How' question, which focuses on the issue of recycling. If appropriate, write some of students' useful ideas on the board.

2 Students look at the examples. Take feedback on the differences as a whole class.

This activity exposes students to different ways of recording lexis. At this stage, just focus on concrete differences, eg the second approach records pronunciation features; it also gives word class and contextualises the word.

3 Students discuss the three questions in pairs.

In feedback, try to draw out the strengths and weaknesses of each. Stress there is no 'correct' way, but that some are better in terms of clarity and memorability. The first way is likely to be the most common: it is quick and natural, but also limited, eg there may not be an exact translation, and as there is no word class or example, it may prove hard to use later. The third example is visually attractive; it could work well for visual students. However, it might not be possible with all lexical items eg abstract nouns.

4 Ask students to write down which technique they will try out. Ask for and record students' decisions, to formalise this stage. Next time you have new vocabulary in a lesson, remind students to experiment. Remember to take feedback on how the experiment went too!

Science & Technology

Coursebook

Unit 6	Language	Texts	Communicative skills
Part 1 SB page 66	Extend your vocabulary – Metaphors for *happy* Grammar Comparative adjectives and adverbs Pronunciation The schwa /ə/	Reading *The science of happiness* *Fitter happier*	Writing / Speaking Listing and comparing what makes people happy Talking about measuring happiness
Part 2 SB page 68	Vocabulary Noun suffixes Grammar Modifiying comparisions	Listening Conversation about jobs in scientific research Reading *Frankenstein*	Speaking Discussing research jobs Writing A comparisons quiz
Part 3 SB page 70	Vocabulary Compound nouns Grammar Superlatives	Reading *Going, going, gone*	Speaking Discussing online auctions and internet shopping Writing Writing website and email addresses
Part 4 SB page 72	Extend your vocabulary – other ways of saying *yes* Pronunciation Word stress in compounds Grammar Phrasal verbs and objects	Listening Conversations about computer problems Reading *The Luddites*	Speaking Giving opinions about modern technology and the workplace
Function globally	Finding things in common Agreement with *so, too, neither*		
Global voices	Listening to opinions of the most important technological advances Joining clauses with *and, so, because*		
Writing	Describing advantages and disadvantages Students use listing points to sequence ideas and introduce advantages and disadvantages		
Global review	Grammar and vocabulary review Extra speaking practice		
Study skills	Students learn how to personalise their language learning		

Additional resources

eWorkbook	Interactive and printable grammar, vocabulary, listening and pronunciation practice Extra reading and writing practice Additional downloadable listening and audio material
Teacher's Resource CD	Communication activity worksheets to print and photocopy
Go global: ideas for further research	**Science** – Ask students to interview ten people about what makes them happy and make the ideas into a form of word art, for example a 'wordle' **Technology** – Ask students to find a website or book that questions technology or is neo-luddite and bring findings to class

6 Science & Technology

Part 1

TEACH GLOBAL
THINK LOCAL
Lead-in

Mime some examples of what makes you happy: draw a big smiley face on the board ➜ and elicit some ideas about yourself eg *swimming* or *baking a cake*.

Writing and Speaking (SB page 66)

1 Ask students to write five things which make them happy, while you monitor to see if they are using the *-ing* form (from Unit 5) as the subject of the sentence, eg *Being in the countryside makes me happy.* You could comment on this here, or leave it until later. (see *TGTL* Extra activity, below).

2 Ask students to work in pairs. They compare lists and then discuss the questions. Take feedback on any points of interest from this discussion, although be sensitive with the final question: *How happy are you?*

Reading (SB page 66)

This reading text is a factual account about different factors which influence people's level of happiness.

1 First clarify *climate* (n) and *measure* (v). Put the four headings on the board and students predict in pairs what the text will say about each, before reading. Guide students by telling them that for the last question *What makes people happy?* there are three main points which they should try and anticipate too.

After discussing, hear some suggestions, then let students complete the reading task.

Take feedback on anything students find interesting.

1	Measuring happiness
2	Climate and happiness
3	Money and happiness
4	What makes people happy?

2 Students read the text and complete the questions in pairs. If your students are able, they can cover the text and then complete the questions (the questions are not in the text but the verbs and other key words are). They then check in pairs and with the text, if necessary.

Write up *satisfied (with sth.)* (adj) on the board.

1	can / do we measure
2	people are most
3	make people happy
4	make people happy

3 Write the first highlighted word (*calculate*) on the board: *Social scientists usually calculate … people are.*

Encourage students to try to deduce the meaning of the word 'calculate' from context together. Elicit the word class (v), then possible meanings or synonyms. Then students complete exercise 3.

1	valid	4	outlook
2	enjoyable	5	calculate
3	purpose		

4 First students ask the two questions noted in the text in pairs: *How happy are you from 1–10? How satisfied are you with your life?* Ask students if they think these questions are 'valid' for research, without eliciting responses.

Students ask each other the questions in Exercise 4 in groups of three. To expand on the second point, write up: *How well do we know ourselves? Is it better to ask the people we live with? Could mood, age, embarrassment, etc. affect our answers?* Clarify any words as necessary, then students discuss these points in threes.

Take whole class feedback.

Extend your vocabulary – metaphors for *happy*

Do the first expression together, deciding if it is happy or sad (the word *lift* means going upwards). Students draw smiley or sad faces next to each expression 1–6.

After feedback, to follow on from the last Study skills section (recording new words, SB page 65), you could encourage students to store these phrases by drawing, to aid memorisation. Students draw mini pictures of the phrases, eg *I'm on top of the world* could be a picture of stick man on top of a globe.

1	happy	4	happy
2	sad	5	happy
3	sad	6	sad

TEACH GLOBAL
THINK LOCAL
Extra activity

At the end of the text about happiness, there are three naturally occurring examples of the gerund in paragraph four: *having close relationships, believing in something, having objectives.* As a revision task from Unit 5, students close their books and recall the three things, telling their partner. Write them on the board. Students can also look back at their five initial things (see exercise 1, SB page 66) and, where appropriate, rewrite them using the gerund.

Grammar (SB page 67)

Let students read the rules first and then complete the gapped text, after doing the first example together.

Alternatively, if your students are able, adopt a test-teach approach: students do the exercise alone before looking at the rules / examples under **Grammar**.

Monitor closely as students work, to identify any problems. Students compare answers in pairs – refer students (back) to the Grammar rules for guidance.

Take whole class feedback. Encourage students to refer to the rules explicitly, eg *why not 'stressfuler'*? Use the board to clarify further, as necessary.

(Note that this text includes a mixture of comparative forms: irregular (*good*); regular, but requiring knowledge of spelling rules (*healthy*, *late* and *fit*). If students want to know more about spelling rules, refer to the Grammar focus on page 142.)

Ask students to tell their partner which facts in the text they a) already knew b) were new and interesting for them.

You could also put these questions on the board for discussion: *Why do younger (not older) children make people happy? Why do many people become happier as they get older? Why do happier people live longer? How and why do men and women differ in terms of happiness?*

healthier	younger
longer	more stressful
better	more enjoyable
fitter	more content
happier	happier
more satisfied	later

Ⓖ Grammar focus

Show students the icon. Write page 142 on the board and ask them to find it. Show students the language summary on comparative and superlative adjectives.

You can use exercise 1 on page 143 for:

a) extra practice now
b) homework
c) review a couple of lessons from now.

The answers are on page 143 of the Teacher's Book.

For students, it is sometimes difficult to determine what a 'longer' adjective is and whether to use *more* or adj. + *-er*. Students may give a combination of both: ~~more stupider~~. Adjectives of two syllables can often take either form, eg *cleverer* or *more clever*. However, two-syllable adjectives ending in some common suffixes like: *-ing, -ed, -ful, -less,* for example, typically use *more* + adj., eg *more stressful*. If students are unsure, recommend using *more* + adj. Note that even one-syllable adjectives formed from past participles often take *more*, eg *more tired*.

The *than* phrase is often omitted in use, if it is obvious, eg *Sally's cleverer (than Bill).*

Pronunciation and Reading (SB page 67)

1 💿 **2.01** This exercise focuses on the schwa sound /ə/, useful not only to help students sound more natural, but also in terms of listening.

💿 **2.01**		
fitt<u>er</u>	comfort<u>a</u>ble	pati<u>e</u>nt
happi<u>er</u>	regul<u>ar</u> exercise	bett<u>er</u> driv<u>er</u>
more pr<u>o</u>ductive		

2 Students listen and repeat, chorally and individually. Assist further by drilling and responding to individuals, if necessary.

3 If you can get hold of a copy of the song, then play it, though in many ways it is not 'a song' but rather a poem (see note below). Ask students to first say the lyrics quietly to themselves, paying careful attention to the crushed sounds. Then they read in pairs, alternately, as suggested.

Background note

This song is from Radiohead's album *OK Computer* and is a rather bleak comment on the consumerism and modern malaise of the 1990s. The computer-generated voice speaks rather than sings the words in an emotionless voice, to the accompaniment of a piano and other noises. It describes an apparently ideal life, yet one which feels bland and soulless.

4 Some students might find it hard to respond to the irony in the poem. Also ask students if this poem could be about their country now and why / why not.

TEACH GLOBAL THINK LOCAL **Extra activity**

For students who enjoy being creative and / or who need writing practice, they compose a poem about happiness, a useful and imaginative way to recycle ideas / lexis / the *-ing* form. Give the heading: *Happiness is … .* Elicit some ideas for the opening lines, encouraging specific examples. Include examples with 'not' too, eg *staying in bed in the morning / not having to get up in the morning,* etc. Students work on their poem in pairs. After checking their work, they write a final draft and can decorate their work for a class display.

Part 2

Speaking and Listening (SB page 68)

TEACH GLOBAL THINK LOCAL **Lead-in**

Put these genuine but bizarre jobs on the board, without the explanation: *breath sniffer* (to test products such as gums or mouthwash); *egg smeller* (checks broken eggs to see if they are spoiled); *gold getter* (looks through old teeth for fillings to get the gold); *gum scraper* (the person who scrapes off chewing gum from public places); *snail picker* (picks and packs snails for eating). Students talk in threes about what they think the jobs are. Take feedback and clarify what each one involves. Students say which one they would do if they had to, justifying their choice.

This listening involves two people describing two of the jobs from exercise 2.

1 Tell students they are going to read and hear about some other unusual jobs this lesson. Refer them to the *Useful language*, and ask students to discuss the three photos in pairs, without looking (they should cover the text). Hear some suggestions as a whole class.

2 Students complete the matching task and discuss what the jobs involve.

Take some feedback, encouraging them to use the words and phrases in the boxes, where relevant. Help students with the pronunciation of the longer words: *forensic entomologist* /fəˈrenzɪk entəˈmɒlədʒɪst/; *garbologist* /gɑːˈbɒlədʒɪst/. These words are very infrequent, but are fun to try and pronounce!

Picture a – forensic entomologist

Picture b – garbologist

Picture c – Gravity research subject

3 Students listen once to find out which jobs are described. Take feedback.

Gravity research subject, garbologist

 2.02–2.03

I did this last summer. It was an interesting part time job – much more interesting than the other jobs I've had. There were 15 of us in total. The study was in Texas and the scientists were looking at the effects of no gravity on the human body. For the study we had to stay in bed for 15 days. Every day the scientists put us in a special machine that turned us around and around upside down for an hour really quickly. I felt like my brain was in my stomach after the first day.

But … at the end of the project I got $6000 – enough to get me to Los Angeles and to look for work as an actor.

Many people think my work is just disgusting, but I think it's interesting. I spend all day working in people's rubbish.

It's not as bad as you think. Not always, anyway. I often work at a city landfill, you know, the place where they put all the

rubbish. Sometimes I study specific kinds of rubbish. I'm finishing a project at the moment on office rubbish: paper, plastic, that kind of thing. Office rubbish is much less disgusting than restaurant rubbish. That was last year's project.

4 If necessary, before listening again, ask students to share any additional information they may have heard. Give students a minute to read the four points, then they listen.

Students compare their answers in pairs. Replay the recording if necessary, before checking as a whole class.

1 c	3 b
2 a	4 a

5 Students share their views on which job is the worst and why, in pairs.

TEACH GLOBAL THINK LOCAL **Extra activity**

Students who need or enjoy oral fluency can imagine they are taking part in an interview for a radio programme called 'The Strangest Jobs' where they will talk about their strange jobs. Students choose one of the jobs from this page. Give them time to consider the following points: *your hobbies as a child, personality, current hobbies, your family's and friends' attitude to your job, daily routine, best thing about your work, your career and the future.* Students pair up with someone who holds a different job from themselves. One of them is the interviewer, one the interviewee. When they finish, swap roles. For **less strong students**, elicit possible questions first, and how to start the interview.

Grammar (SB page 68)

1 Write the first parts of the example sentences from the Grammar section on the board: *Office rubbish is less disgusting than …*; *It's not as bad …*; *It's a bit more …*; *She works much faster than …* (the first two are from the listening). Elicit how they might finish, and also try to elicit / clarify the meaning of the new language as you go along, eg contrast the modifiers *much* and *a bit*. Students then choose the best alternative in exercise 1.

1 a
2 b

2 Students complete the sentences alone, using the target language. Monitor and assist, focusing on accuracy.

3 Divide half the room into **A** students and the other half into **B** students. **A** students work together initially, as do **B** students, to make their five questions.

Explain that soon they will test their partners' knowledge by asking each question and responding to their partner's suggested answer. Model an example with a student and put the two example questions given for **A** (page 127) and **B** (page 129) on the board.

Monitor and assist as students are writing the questions, then re-group them into mixed A and B pairs for the general knowledge test.

G Grammar focus

Show students the icon. Write page 142 on the board and ask them to find it. Show students the language summary on comparative adjectives with *a bit* etc.

You can use exercise 1 on page 143 for:

a) extra practice now
b) homework
c) review a couple of lessons from now.

The answers are on page 143 of the Teacher's Book.

TEACH GLOBAL THINK LOCAL **Extra activity**

If students need some more practice of comparatives, ask them to think of their past language learning experiences and to compare the following areas: *the classroom; the other students; the way English was taught; the homework; the teacher; the class eg length*, etc. After making a few notes, students discuss their points in pairs. Students could write this up for homework, as it provides you with useful information.

Vocabulary (SB page 69)

1 Ask students to work in pairs. Check and drill the new nouns.

happi**ness**	exist**ence**
scient**ist**	research**er**
relation**ship**	

2 First students guess what the noun ending might be in each case. Refer students back to the choices in exercise 1, if necessary. Monitor to see how students are doing, and let students check in dictionaries at an appropriate point: this also gives practice in searching for word class.

TEACH GLOBAL THINK LOCAL **Mixed ability**

Early finishers can find the adjectives for *economy* and *science*. Take feedback but do not focus on correct pronunciation yet.

Students predict in pairs how the nouns are pronounced, and where the stress is. Again, they can check in a dictionary. Take feedback and drill, as appropriate.

Students close their books. Call out the words from the first column (under Word) of exercise 1 at random, and any of the words from exercise 2. Nominate individuals to call out the new nouns from memory. Then ask about common noun endings for jobs, eliciting them with examples onto the board:

economist	job	silence	
friendship		teacher	job
painter	job	tourist	
nervousness		weakness	

3 Students work alone to complete the gap-fill, making logical guesses as appropriate. Students compare answers.

Take whole class feedback and invite students to comment on Karen's job and whether they would like it. Ask: *What sort of person does a job like this?*

researcher	loneliness
scholarship	silence
existence	

Reading and Speaking (SB page 69)

1 🔊 **2.04** Elicit from students what they already know about the story of Frankenstein. Also ask students if the author is a man or woman. Then get a student to read out the text in the circle about Frankenstein and another to read the notes on Shelley under the picture.

Play the extract aloud, letting students read along with the recording.

Pause at the end and ask students what happens next, how this makes them feel and if they like books of this type. Then ask the question in exercise 1.

He made a monster

Background note

Frankenstein is actually the name of the maker, not the monster. Victor Frankenstein is a scientist who becomes obsessed with discovering the secret of life. He makes a creature, using old, scavenged body parts. This monster is later responsible for numerous deaths, including those of Victor's own wife and brother. As the creator, he is plagued by guilt but the struggle to capture and kill the creature ends in the scientist's own death.

2 Write the words 'dangerous knowledge' on the board but say nothing for half a minute, to focus students. Then add the question underneath: *Do you think scientific knowledge can be dangerous?*

Put students into pairs or groups of three to discuss this and to think of at least two examples. Go around and input any scientific language, as necessary.

Hear suggestions from groups, which might include: *cloning, stem-cell research, eugenics (genetic selection), nuclear / atomic weapons*, or even *evolution* or *the invention of the computer*.

Science & Technology

Part 3

Vocabulary (SB page 70)

Lead-in

To both introduce the topic and revise comparative structures, students compare mobile phones in threes, discussing features, size, weight, age, etc. Let them show and talk about their phones first, then stop them and ask them to make comparisons. If necessary, put some adjectives on the board to help, eg *modern, simple, light, technical, fancy,* etc.

1 Ask students to cover the text with paper or a book and look at the photo for two minutes to focus on the electronic items, including the parts. The person with the most things after the time is up reads out their list.

2 Students match the two halves of the compound nouns and tick off which ones they can see in the picture.

computer screen
headphones
keyboard
laptop
memory stick
mobile phone
mouse pad
text message
website

3 **2.05** Some students may be able to predict the pronunciation, including the stress, in pairs before they listen. Drill the words, as necessary. The compound which is different is *mobile phone* (see **Language note** below).

> 2.05 See Student's Book page 70

Language note

In compound nouns, typically the first part of the compound carries the main stress, eg **memory** *stick*, though the second part has a secondary stress. This is the case in the examples in exercise 2, with the exception of *mobile* **phone**. A compound is formed when two (or more) words are joined together. They may be written as one word, with a hyphen or a space between the words. Compound nouns are usually made up of two nouns, eg *memory stick*, or an adjective and a noun, eg *blackbird*.

Reading (SB page 70)

This reading gives some facts tend figures about the online auction website eBay.

1 Ask students to work in pairs to ask the two questions. You could also add: *How much time do you spend per day / per week?* Take whole class feedback, nominating individuals.

If students seem interested in others' responses, get them to write up on the board their favourite site(s), for further class discussion.

2 Write up on the board a list of goods that you could buy from eBay, eg *sun hat, boots, garden furniture, flooring, a doll's house, dog kennel, buttons, a car, a painting.* Ask students which single place they might buy these things from. Elicit / pre-teach the word *auction* (n) /ˈɔːkʃən/. Elicit from students what they know about eBay.

Pre-teach the words *jet* (n) and *kidney* (n). Put students in pairs to predict the words they will see in exercise 2.

3 **2.06** Before students read, show the headline 'Going, going, gone'. Clarify the context where this appears: this is what the auctioneer says in a live auction just before he / she bangs a small hammer to close the bidding at the highest offer. Give students a short time only to scan for the words.

expensive, kidney, buy, internet, jet, sell

4 Give students about 8–12 minutes to read the text again, and before they start, point out the glossary on page 71.

Let students compare answers before whole class feedback. If appropriate, play the recording here.

1	buy and sell things
2	241,000,000
3	a human kidney, a 50,000 year old mammoth, the meaning of life, the internet and a world war two submarine.

5 Put students in groups of three or four to discuss online buying habits. Encourage them to refer to other people they know who have used eBay too. Take some whole class feedback on points of interest.

Reading extra

If your students would benefit from an additional comprehension task, put the following numbers from the text on the board and see how quickly students can list what each refers to: 50,000, 1999, 1995, $ 4.9 million 4th, £1.81, £61,000, £0 (the last one is a trick one, as the kidney sale was cancelled!) **Stronger students** first see how many answers they know without looking at the text again, before checking.

Grammar (SB page 70)

1 Write the words *Superlatives* and *Comparatives* on the board, eliciting / giving an example for each. Let students tackle exercise 1 before referring to the rules.

Monitor closely as students are working to evaluate their knowledge and to assess if or when to intervene. If students do well, elicit the rules from them, using the examples they have written as a starting point. Write up two examples on the board (remember to highlight the article as part of the superlative form, eg *the strangest things*). Refer students to SB page 142.

1	the strangest	4	the best
2	cheaper	5	the richest
3	safer		

2 Ask students to work in pairs to complete Exercise 2. Monitor and help, referring them back to the examples and rules under **Grammar**.

If some students finish early, they can write at least three more questions.

1	the longest	4	the strangest
2	the funniest	5	the best
3	the coldest		

3 Ask students to choose 3 questions to ask a partner. If appropriate, they can use follow-up questions to get more information, for example (you could model this with a strong student):

What's the longest time you've ever spent on the internet? … Why did you spend that much time?

As students are talking, monitor and take notes for feedback later. Refer students to the third bullet-point under **Grammar** on this page: superlatives are often used with the present perfect; they often also occur with 'ever', to talk about something extreme or momentous in your life.

G Grammar focus

Show students the icon. Write page 142 on the board and ask them to find it. Show students the language summary on superlatives.

You can use exercise 3 on page 143 for:
a) extra practice now
b) homework
c) review a couple of lessons from now.

The answers are on page 143 of the Teacher's Book.

Language note

The same spelling rules apply as for comparatives (see SB page 142). In spoken and written English the noun type and context is omitted, because it is understood, eg *I think broccoli is the healthiest* (vegetable [type]) *in the world* [context]); *I think Sarah is the prettiest* (girl in the class). Students sometimes muddle superlatives with comparatives: *She is the more intelligent*; they frequently forget the article: *She is most intelligent* and they also confuse the long / short adjective rules: *She is the most nice* or *She is the most nicest*.

Listening and Speaking (SB page 71)

1 🔊 **2.07** First get students to try to tell their partner their email address. Then let them read the *Useful phrases*.

Students listen and write down the addresses they hear. This is intensive listening, so ask students if they would like to hear it again and let them compare their answers.

🔊 2.07
1 www.ebay.it, (that's "i-t" for Italy).
2 j324@hotmail.com
3 www.facebook.com
4 www.itt.com/english
5 Jason_17@gmail.com
6 www.myspace.com
7 www.amazon.de, (not com, d-e)
8 sean@yahoo.co.uk, (that's S-E-A-N at y-a-h-o-o dot c-o dot u-k)

2 Give students enough time to write their five addresses down.

3 First dictate your own example to students, at speed. Put the following up on the board, for students to use: *Can you repeat that? What comes after the … ? That's 's' for 'soup', 'p' for Paul … .* Put students in pairs and ensure that those students dictating cannot see what their partner is actually writing.

Once finished, they can compare. If students find this realistic task difficult, make a mental note to practise it further in a later lesson, for example as a warmer.

TEACH GLOBAL THINK LOCAL Extra activity

If your students need further practice in pronouncing numbers, ask them to circle all the numbers in the eBay text, including dates and prices. Students then work alone to say the words to themselves before checking with their partner, and finally you. For fun, drill the long number really quickly, getting students to repeat: 241,000,000. If students enjoy this and find it useful, dictate some additional numbers, for students to note down and check in pairs, eg *257; 5,789; $46, 296; £21,300; 821,360; 20,401.* In feedback, nominate individuals to say the words back to you.

TEACH GLOBAL THINK LOCAL Homework extra

Ask students to collect examples of either comparatives or superlatives from their daily life, eg the supermarket, TV ads, posters, leaflets, etc. If the examples are in their first language, they can translate them. Students should look for at least two examples to bring in for next lesson.

Part 4

Lead-in

Write up the four quotes from exercise 1 in the order below, with number 4 last (as this one is more tricky).

Tell students there are two short sentences in each quote. Students unjumble the quotes in pairs. Be prepared to clarify any words, eg *lack* (n), *fear* (n/v).

1   you Computers answers can only are useless give They

2   think? to us do We computers that for have Why

3   are fear dogs like Computers smell They

4   I of them fear lack computers not do the fear I

Students then check with the SB.

Speaking and Listening (SB page 72)

This listening comprises five conversations between a computer expert and a user with a problem.

1   Put students into different pairs and let them discuss whether they agree with the quotes. Take some feedback as a whole class.

2 **2.08–2.12** Tell students of a problem that you have had in relation to your computer, exaggerated if necessary! Ask students to share any problems or annoyances that they have experienced, either in small groups or as a class.

Let students read the list of phrases first, then they listen and order them. Allow students to compare answers after the first listening.

Conversation 1: internet connection

Conversation 2: printer and printing

Conversation 3: email

Conversation 4: saving work

Conversation 5: password

 2.08–2.12

1
A: OK. Try now.
B: Nope. It's still not working.
A: Nothing? Can you see anything on the screen?
B: Yes. But when I click on the internet button nothing happens.
A: And now?
B: Yes! It's working now. Oh *thank you thank you*. What did you do?
A: The cable was old. I took a new cable and connected it up to the internet again.

2
A: So, tell me the problem again?
B: OK, when I try to print out a document the computer prints out a *different* document.
A: You mean, not the one you want to print?
B: That's right.

A: Have you tried …
B: I've tried everything!

3
A: No, no, it's okay, the computer person is here now. You're here.
A: Yes? What's the problem?
B: Well, I try to open my email … and … I get this.
A: Urg … yuk.
B: Yeah. Disgusting, huh?
A: Yeah … OK. Shut down the computer and leave it.
B: Is it a virus or something?
A: I'm afraid so.

4
A: Oh no. No!
B: What's wrong?
A: The laptop's gone down again.
B: Did you save your work?
A: No.
B: You should really back up all your work. I always do.
A: Great … Thanks for the advice.

5
A: OK, ready to do this?
B: Yep. Definitely.
A: First, click on this button here.
B: OK … done.
A: Now log on to the system.
B: What?
A: Log on. Type in your username and password.
B: Oh.
A: What?
B: I can't remember my password!

3   Give students time to read the questions and see if they can choose any correct answers, then play the recording again. Monitor to see if students need to listen for a third time. Students work in pairs to compare answers.

1 a	4 b
2 c	5 a
3 a	

Extend your vocabulary – other ways of saying *yes*

Ask random students a couple of *yes / no* questions, to which you expect a 'yes' answer, eg *Is it normal to have problems with your computer sometimes?* Write up the word 'yes' or other answers like 'yeah' or 'definitely'.

Read out the information under the heading in the SB. Students then read the audioscript to find examples of the ways of saying *yes*. Give students sufficient time for this task.

| Conversation 1: That's right. |
| Conversation 2: Yeah. I'm afraid so. |
| Conversation 3: – |
| Conversation 4: Yep. Definitely. |

To set up the next mini stages, 2 and 3, first elicit three or four 'yes' questions directed at you, eg a student asks: *Do you come to work by car?* Answer: *That's right.* Students then work in pairs to prepare similar questions for their partner to answer.

TEACH GLOBAL THINK LOCAL **Extra activity**

A fun way to practise this language is to play the *Yes / No* game. Students stand up. Fire *yes / no* questions at individual students, who must not say *yes* or *no*, eg *"Your name's Elena, isn't it?"* *"That's right / It is"*. When a student accidentally says either 'yes' or 'no', they sit down. Try to get all the students out by going as fast as you can! For large classes, choose about 10 students to play and others watch.

Vocabulary and Pronunciation (SB page 72)

1 Students who regularly use the computer will be quite familiar with at least some of these phrasal verbs. Let students work alone, then check in pairs. If the words appear to be new to (some of) them, write them up on the board.

1	on	4	in
2	down	5	out, out
3	down	6	up

2 2.13 Students listen to check their answers.

| 2.13 |
1	Now log on to the system.
2	Shut down the computer and leave it.
3	The laptop's gone down again.
4	Type in your username and password.
5	When I try to print out a document the computer prints out a different document.
6	You should really back up all your work.

3 Students repeat the sentences. In giving attention to the sentence stress, most students will also naturally practise other phonological features of connected speech such as *log on*, *print out*. Highlight these, as necessary.

Pronunciation note

'Grammar words' such as *on*, *off*, *up*, etc. are often crushed in speech. However, when they act as a particle in a phrasal verb, the particle is normally stressed and they retain the full vowel sound.

Grammar (SB page 73)

1 Without reading the Grammar notes, students complete this task in pairs, choosing the correct answer simply by what sounds right.

In feedback, elicit which alternative they selected in each case, but without saying why. Write 'Pick it up' on the board and elicit the terminology: object, pronoun, particle. Students refer to the rules.

Then elicit the relevant rules in each case, eg *In sentence 1, c can't be right because of the fourth rule.* When students have finished, get them to read out the sentences, paying particular attention to the stress and to connected speech again.

1	a and b are correct
2	b and c are correct
3	a and c are correct

Language note

The phrasal verb focus includes both intransitive verbs (verbs with no object) and transitive verbs. The focus avoids prepositional verbs, eg *She looked up the tree*, not ~~She looked the tree up~~. *Tree* can only go after the particle because *up* is a preposition, not an adverb. Contrast this with: *She looked up the word in the dictionary*, where the object can be moved because *up* is an adverb. However, pre-intermediate level students are unlikely to need this information!

2 Students circle the objects in each case. Take whole class feedback and draw attention to sentences 4 and 5, where 'words' occurs both before and after the particle.

1	volume	4	words
2	–	5	words
3	the school system	6	–

3 Focus students on the example given. Remind students to use either *it* or *them* for this task. Students work in pairs. In whole class feedback, as students are reading out the new sentences, encourage them to say them fluidly and naturally, with the stress on the particle.

1	Turn it up	4	look them up
2	–	5	write them down
3	–	6	–

Science & Technology

Ⓖ Grammar focus

Show students the icon. Write page 142 on the board and ask them to find it. Show students the language summary on phrasal verbs and objects.

You can use exercise 1 on page 143 for:

a) extra practice now
b) homework
c) review a couple of lessons from now.

The answers are on page 143 of the Teacher's Book.

**TEACH GLOBAL
THINK LOCAL** **Extra activity**

Ask students to think about themselves in the last 24 hours and write four true sentences and one false sentence, using the verbs from this page and the previous one, eg *at 7 pm last night, I printed out two documents; I logged off my computer at midnight.* Students write their sentences within two minutes, then read them to their partner, who has to guess the false one.

Reading and Speaking (SB page 73)

1 🔊 **2.14** Ask students to focus on the photograph with the text. Ask them what the man is going to do, eliciting the words *hammer* (n) and *destroy* (v) (these are in the text). Elicit why he might be doing this.

Inform students that this man is a 'Luddite', pointing to the heading. Students read and answer the question in exercise 1. Play the recording as appropriate.

People who were against technology

**TEACH GLOBAL
THINK LOCAL** **Reading extra**

If you want to check students' comprehension of the text further, give the following multi-choice task, after explaining *violence* (n):

1 This movement was in the
a) 1700s   b) 1800s   c) 1900s

2 The workers were angry about
a) working conditions   b) poor pay   c) new machines

3 They complained
a) with violence   b) by letter   c) through the law courts

4 A 'luddite' is someone who is
a) anti-government   b) anti-work   c) anti-machinery

Background note

The Luddite movement began in the early 1800s, in northern England, when the working class was already suffering as a result of the Napoleonic Wars. The textile industry was very important in Britain, employing hundreds of workers, many skilled. The introduction of mechanized machinery during the Industrial Revolution threatened their livelihoods. Support grew and many cotton and wool mills were destroyed. The army intervened and many workers and supporters were executed or imprisoned; some were sent off to Australia.

2 Clarify the task and the rating procedure, giving a personalised example. When they have marked their opinion from 1–4, give students time to think of reasons and/or examples to support their opinion. Tell students you will ask them to provide reasons in both pairwork and whole class feedback.

3 Students discuss their opinions in pairs. Monitor for interesting and well-supported points and note these down for later feedback.

Bear in mind that it might be difficult to even consider the negative side of technology, particularly for younger students who have grown up with it!

**TEACH GLOBAL
THINK LOCAL** **Extra activity**

To round off the lesson, you could do a web search using the key words: *luddite cartoons*. Show some amusing examples for your students to comment on or try to explain.

Function globally: finding things in common

These lessons in *Global* are designed to provide students with **immediately** useful functional language. They all follow a similar format.

Warm up (SB page 74)

Aim: to introduce the topic via a quick speaking task or picture work.

Tips:

- Do not over-correct here, especially in speaking activities.
- Encourage students to use what language they can at this stage.

Listening (SB page 74)

Aim: to present the functional language in context via a conversation or series of conversations.

Tips:

- Ask students to read the questions first before listening.
- Play the recording all the way through for each task (there are always two tasks).
- For multiple conversations pause the recording after each one.
- If students find it very difficult, play the recording a final time and allow them to read the audioscript at the back of the book.

1

They are going to a Technology conference.
The man discovers that the woman's husband is his boss.

🔊 **2.15**

A: Hi, excuse me. I noticed your bag. Are you going to the Technology conference?
B: That's right.
A: Me too! Could we share a taxi?
B: Sure.
A: The conference centre please.
C: OK.
A: Have you been to San Francisco before?
B: Err, no. No I haven't.
A: Neither have I. Nice weather.
B: Mm.
A: My name's Frank, by the way.
B: Nice to meet you. Claudia.
A: Hi Claudia.
A: Where are you from Claudia?
B: Frankfurt.
A: Wow. Frankfurt. You don't have a German accent at all.
B: I went to school in England.
A: So did I! Well, I'm English so … I guess that's normal.
B: Yes, I guess.

A: Sooo … do you work for ABT Technology?
B: Yes. I work in the Frankfurt office. This is my first conference.
A: Oh, I've been to lots of conferences. They're very boring you know.
B: Really?
A: Oh yes. The worst part is listening to our president, Lance Thomas.
B: Really?
A: Gosh yes. His talks are so boring. But the evening party is quite good. Do you like parties?
B: No, not really.
A: Ah. Me neither. Not really.
B: Thanks Frank.
A: You're welcome. Are you staying in the conference hotel?
B: No, I'm not.
A: Ha. Neither am I. It's horrible. Where's your hotel?
B: I err … I don't know. Oh look, here's my husband.
A; Oh. Oh.
B: Lance, this is Frank. Frank, this is my husband Lance.
A: Oh … Er …
D: Nice to meet you, Frank. Glad you could be here.
A: Hi.

2

| 1 ✓ | 2 no | 3 no | 4 ✓ | 5 ✓ | 6 no | 7 no |

Language focus: finding things in common (SB page 74)

Aim: to draw students' attention to the items of functional language.

Tips:

- Make sure students have time to understand the form and meaning of the phrases, but you needn't translate them word for word.
- Students should be able to pronounce these phrases intelligibly, so drill them.

| 1 so | 3 too | 2 neither | 4 neither |

Speaking (SB page 74)

Aim: to allow students an opportunity to use this language in a meaningful, real-world context.

Tips:

- There is sometimes a choice of task. Any task involving reading a script will be easier than a task involving making students' own scripts. This gives you flexibility for mixed ability classes.
- Give students time to prepare this activity, and circulate and monitor carefully.
- Correct sensitively, paying particular attention to the target language.
- If time allows, ask students to repeat the task, but with a new partner.

Science & Technology

Global voices

These lessons in *Global* are designed to provide students with exposure to authentic speakers of English from both native and non-native English backgrounds. They all follow a similar format.

Warm up (SB page 75)

Aim: to introduce the topic and highlight potentially difficult vocabulary the students will encounter.

Tips:

- Be generous in helping students with the vocabulary here, but let them try and work it out first.
- Circulate and monitor any speaking task, but be careful not to overcorrect.
- Follow up any short discussion pairwork with an open class discussion, asking students to report back what they said.

> **1**
>
> internet   television   mobile phone   computer   plane

Listening (SB page 75)

Aim: to expose students to English spoken with a variety of accents.

Tips:

- The first time they listen, tell them you don't expect them to understand every word; some of it will be hard. This is because the text has not been scripted or graded in any way. It's what they would hear in "the real world".
- Pause after each speaker on the second listening, and don't be afraid to replay the whole thing if students appear to need it.
- Students can read the audioscript at the back of the book if you / they wish.
- Try to avoid hunting for specific pronunciation or language errors. In real world communication not everyone speaks perfect English all the time, not even native speakers.

> 💿 **2.16–2.22**
>
> 1 Honor, England: I think that the most useful technical advance for me has been **the internet**, yes, because I can do things like bookings tickets and so forth.
>
> 2 Arthur, France: **Television** is very important for the information and for entertainment.
>
> 3 Sara, Italy: The most important useful technological advance is, we could say now is a **computer**. It's very important. I think that nobody could really live or work without a computer.
>
> 4 Antonis, Greece: I think the **plane**. The aeroplanes, yeah.

> 5 Maxim, Russia: I think that most important technological advance for me is SMS services, of course so **mobile phone**, but especially **SMS services**.
>
> 6 Starla, England: For me the most technological advance I'd say is **the internet** because it's convenient and quick and saves you a lot of time.
>
> 7 William, Ghana: Well, I think **the internet** is the most important, especially when you are looking for information.

> **2**
>
> Honor – says the internet because she can do things like book tickets; Arthur – says television is important for information and entertainment; Sara – says a computer because nobody could live or work without it; Starla – says the internet because it is convenient, quick and saves time; William – says the internet is important for looking for information.

Language focus: *and, so, because*

Aim: to raise students' awareness of a particular piece of language present in the listening.

Tips:

- This language is not included in tests or reviews, it is here to help students understand international English.
- Don't expect students to produce this language in an exercise or in conversation immediately.

> **1**
>
> 1 because   3 and   5 and   7 so
> 2 and   4 so   6 so
>
> 💿 **2.23**
>
> Guy Jackson, England: I think the most important technological advance – well for me personally recently has been a hard disk recorder for recording TV programmes because it means I can record everything very easily and I can see exactly what I have recorded by looking at everything on the screen and I don't have to find lots of video tapes and different things like that so it's much easier now to record TV programmes than it was in the past and because of digital television we have lots more programmes to choose from so there's much more variety and choice so that means you need to record even more programmes than in the past.

Speaking (SB page 75)

Aim: for students to discuss the same or similar questions as the speakers in the listening.

Tips:

- The speaking tasks here are slightly more open to allow for students to explore the subject. Give them time to do this.
- If students are working in pairs, circulate and monitor. Make notes of incorrect language use to correct afterwards (or in a future class).

Writing: describing advantages and disadvantages

Reading (SB page 76)

1 Elicit who in the class has used the internet in the last 24 hours, and what for. Write headings on the board, in two columns: *The advantages (of the internet)* and *The disadvantages.* Give students two minutes to brainstorm ideas on the board, and leave the room. (This can have a galvanizing effect!)

Students read the essay to find out if Mohammed has listed any different ideas, and to respond to the task in 1.

> He thinks there are more advantages than disadvantages.

2 Invite feedback on Mohammed's ideas.

Language focus: listing points (SB page 76)

1 Ask students what the problem is with Mohammed's essay, then they read the corrected version of paragraph two to find the differences. Students should underline any key differences in choice of words, before comparing answers. Take feedback, putting the 'organisational' phrases on the board.

> Instead of bullet points, the sentences start with the following expressions:
>
> *First of all, In addition, Another important advantage is that …*

2 Students change paragraph three in the same way. Refer them to the useful phrases in the *Listing points* box. Monitor and assist as students are writing. If necessary, allow them to work in pairs or write the paragraph as a whole class activity.

Writing skills: getting ideas (SB page 76)

Students discuss the bullet points alone for two minutes, before talking in small groups. Take whole class feedback on any techniques they use, including ones not mentioned: this helps to raise awareness of different sub-stages in the process of writing and exposes them to new ideas. You can refer them to the Student's book page 8 for an example of a word map.

Preparing to write (SB page 76)

1 Tell students they are going to write an essay like Mohammed's. Students in pairs choose a topic from the list, or another of their choice (but make sure it has both pros and cons).

2 Pairs brainstorm the advantages and disadvantages of their topic in two columns. If possible, mix students with another pair focusing on the same topic, to share ideas further.

Students discuss in their pairs precisely which disadvantages and advantages from the brainstorm they will mention in the central two paragraphs, and in which order.

3 Draw students' attention to Mohammed's essay as a model. Elicit some suggestions for the introductory paragraph as a whole class. Students then write out a first draft of the introduction with their partner. Monitor and hear some examples when ready.

4 Read Mohammed's conclusion. In the same way, students draw up their own conclusion. Monitor, assist and choose two good examples from the class. Ask the writers to put the paragraphs up on the board for others to read.

TEACH GLOBAL THINK LOCAL **Mixed ability**

For **less strong students**, provide more support throughout. If the class chooses the same topic together at the start, this will make the writing process easier. The brainstorm can then be done as a class effort. You can also put this organisational overview of the essay on the board:

Introductory paragraph
Discussion of advantages
Discussion of disadvantages
Concluding paragraph

Writing

Draw students' attention to the ways of introducing advantages and disadvantages at the bottom of the page (SB page 76). Point out that these phrases occur in the central part of the essay, not the introduction. Students write their essays at home. Remind them that they can get more ideas by using some of the techniques mentioned in the previous stage, eg reading, using the internet, speaking to others, etc.

Global review

These lessons in *Global* are intended to review some of the language and topics covered in the unit. They follow a similar format.

Grammar and Vocabulary (SB page 77)

Aim: to review the main grammar and vocabulary in the unit.

Tips:

• Students can do these exercises alone or in pairs, in class or at home, depending on their learning style and your teaching situation.

• Ask students to read the questions first to establish the grammar and vocabulary areas which are focused on.

• Encourage students to check their own answers by looking back through the unit.

Grammar	Vocabulary
1 plug in the computer / plug the computer in	1 keyboard
2 back them up	2 memory stick
3 much better	3 laptop
4 harder / less hard	4 headphones
5 more convenient	5 shut down
6 the longest	6 friendship
7 as well-paid as	7 happiness
8 faster	8 researcher
9 a bit less cold	

Speaking (SB page 77)

Aim: to provide extra speaking practice that will review and consolidate language presented in the unit.

Tips:

• Before speaking encourage students to think first about what language they need to focus on from the unit, and a good way to start their conversation.

• Monitor as students are working and note any points for feedback at the end.

Study skills

Personalising language learning (SB page 77)

1 First see if students can recall the different ways of storing vocabulary from the end of the previous unit (page 65), eg direct translation, etc. Different students read out Atsuko's four examples: *nervous, outlook, back up* and *comparatives*. Elicit what all the examples have in common, i.e. Atsuko personalises the language in each case.

Read the suggestion at the end of exercise 1 yourself. Ask students if they do this. Give two minutes to find similarly personalised examples in their notebooks and hear some examples.

2 Give students time to look through their notes or the student's book to find relevant words or phrases. This is also useful revision.

Read students' examples, checking that they have used the language appropriately and accurately, before the next stage.

3 Give an amusing example yourself first, eg *I used to be much fatter before I became a teacher. Now I don't have time to eat!* Students then do the same with the two target structures.

4 Put students in pairs to share and discuss their sentences. Hear a mixture of examples from exercises 2 and 3 as a whole class. Ask students to listen to each sentence and after each one, they should say what the new (Unit 6) word, phrase or structure was, eg *The inside of my car is <u>disgusting</u> because I haven't cleaned it for months!* (*disgusting*).

To finish off the class, ask students if they liked this idea of personalizing, and if they intend to use it in the future. Make a mental note to consciously personalize relevant vocabulary and structures, particularly in the next few lessons.

UNIT 7 Time & Money

Coursebook

Unit 7	Language	Texts	Communicative skills
Part 1 SB page 78	Vocabulary Prepositions of time Grammar Present perfect with *for* and *since*	Reading *A brief history of time zones*	Speaking Discussing the best times to do things
Part 2 SB page 80	Vocabulary Time expressions Pronunciation Spellings and sounds /eɪ/ and /aɪ/	Listening Talk on the concept of time Reading *A Tale of Two Cities*	Speaking Talking about time-saving inventions Discussing times in history
Part 3 SB page 82	Vocabulary Money; verb phrases Grammar Present perfect with *yet* and *already* Pronunciation /ʌ/	Reading *A lifetime of financial concerns*	Speaking Discussing questions about money issues and concerns Writing Writing a *to do* list and comparing with a partner
Part 4 SB page 84	Extend your vocabulary – *borrow* and *lend* Vocabulary Facilities in learning institutions	Reading *A different kind of bank*	Speaking Describing and comparing pictures Budgeting for equipment with a bank loan
Function globally	Shopping in a market Buying and selling Students practise selling		
Global English	David Crystal text: *The English language and the number four* Students talk about the history of their language and influences on it		
Writing	Giving your opinion Organising ideas in an essay		
Global review	Grammar and vocabulary review Extra speaking practice		
Study skills	Students learn how to manage their study time and make a study plan		

Additional resources

eWorkbook	Interactive and printable grammar, vocabulary, listening and pronunciation practice Extra reading and writing practice Additional downloadable listening and audio material
Teacher's Resource CD	Communication activity worksheets to print and photocopy
Go global: ideas for further research	**Time** – Ask students to explore the Royal Observatory at Greenwich (www.nmm.ac.uk) and prepare a short presentation **Money** – Ask students to find out more information about the Grameen Bank and other micro-credit organisations

Part 1

TEACH GLOBAL THINK LOCAL **Lead-in**

Students write down the answers <u>only</u> to these questions, which you read aloud.

How much time do you spend:

1 doing English homework every week?
2 cleaning/tidying your home?
3 getting ready each morning (from waking up to leaving the house)?
4 shopping (food, clothes, etc.) on average per week?
5 doing your hair each morning?
6 cleaning your teeth?

Amend / add any questions to suit your students' daily routines. Students work in pairs to recall the initial questions and compare answers (if they cannot remember, put word prompts on the board). Take whole class feedback on any areas of interest or amusement.

Vocabulary and Speaking (SB page 78)

1 Tell students that the topic is 'time'. Write the first line of the puzzle silently on the board. Elicit what *h* and *d* mean. Students complete the puzzle alone, then check their answers in pairs.

Monitor to see if students need to have whole class feedback too.

1	hours in a day
2	days in a year
3	days in February every four years
4	seconds in a minute
5	days in a week

2 Students work in pairs. After 2–3 minutes, hear some suggestions as a whole class. Read out the text in the circle and ask students if they have ever tried an IQ test, and if so, why.

suggested answers:	
1	60 m in an h, 60 minutes in an hour / 60 s in a m, 60 seconds in a minute
2	12 m in a y, 12 months in a year
3	52 w in a y, 52 weeks in a year

Background note

IQ tests have been used since 1912 when German psychologist Willliam Stern created them to measure children's intelligence. Nowadays, they are often used by employers during the recruitment process. During an IQ test, people solve different problems within a limited time.

3 Ask students to look at the expressions. Elicit the answer to the first gap. Students complete the task alone, checking in pairs.

Write the answers on the board for students to check.

1	seasons and years
2	dates
3	specific times

Language note

Students typically confuse prepositions with time phrases, eg *in the 4th November.* This may be due to the influence of their mother tongue, or because these 'little grammar words' are seen as less important in communication. To prevent errors becoming ingrained, it is worth focusing on this area as these expressions are often high frequency.

4 Students choose five questions and write down the answers independently.

TEACH GLOBAL THINK LOCAL **Mixed ability**

Early finishers complete all seven questions, and can even think up an additional, colourful example of their own.

5 Prepare students to give clear reasons with their statement: students look at the example, and give another reason, eg *people like to get married in June because it's the holiday season and most guests can come.* Tell students they need to give at least one reason for each answer.

During pair work, monitor and if there are any interesting answers – perhaps from a personal or cultural perspective – share these in whole class feedback.

Reading (SB page 78)

This reading gives interesting facts about time zones, including the history and time differences.

TEACH GLOBAL THINK LOCAL **Mixed ability**

Ask students to look at the clocks on page 79, and ask quick questions:

What's the time in London? And in Moscow? Sydney? etc. So how many hours ahead of London is Moscow, and Sydney? Does anyone know what the <u>actual</u> time is in London right now? So, what's the time difference between here and there? Does anyone have any relatives or friends that live in another time zone? Where, and what are they probably doing now?

1 Students read the three questions in pairs. Hear some suggestions as a whole class, to raise interest. Do not tell students if they are right or wrong at this point.

Then refer students to the mini time-zone map on page 79 and the clocks, to find the answers. Do not let students read the text yet. Take quick feedback.

2 🔘 **2.24** Students first read the statements 1–5 and then the text to find the answers. Students compare their answers in pairs, before checking as a whole class.

1	F (less than 200 years)
2	T
3	F (China used to have 5 time zones)
4	T
5	F (Greenwich has its own internet time)

3 For classes where students have little experience of travelling, select task **A**. Students do this task individually, writing the three points down. Encourage confident students to try and write the points down with the book closed.

Students compare answers in pairs.

For both **A** and **B** tasks, monitor and listen out for any points of interest for whole class feedback.

Possible ways of coping with jet lag might include: staying awake until 'bed-time' in the new time zone (not the previous one); not eating at all during the flight; avoiding alcohol; taking melatonin tablets.

TEACH GLOBAL THINK LOCAL **Extra activity**

Students often need further practice of prepositions with time. Ask them to write three columns headed *in*, *on* and *at*.

Dictate random time phrases, eg *Saturday,14th October, June, 1989, 5 pm, weekend, Thursday, night, 7.39 am, the afternoon, the summer,* etc. Students write them in the appropriate column. Students compare their answers in pairs. Alternatively, do a similar activity using cards: cut up about 12–15 time expressions, giving one set per three students to categorize into 'in', 'at', 'on' groups.

Grammar (SB page 79)

1 Write up the two example sentences on the board, unfinished:

We have had standard time for less than _____ .
Greenwich internet time has existed since _____ .
See if students can complete, referring to the text if necessary.

Then focus students on the prepositions *for* and *since*. Try to elicit the difference. Refer them to the grammar explanation. If necessary, provide mini prompts before they do exercise 1, eg *Sunday, two months, 7 am, 10 minutes,* etc. Students decide if these are 'points' or 'periods'.

Students complete the exercise independently, then compare answers in pairs. When checking as a whole class, ask students to say why they made their choice of preposition, using the language from the grammar

section. Note that this exercise focuses on the prepositions, not the present perfect yet.

for
In
since
in
since
for

Language note

Some students confuse *for* and *since* even at much higher levels, though conceptually it is not very difficult. A *How long?* question connecting the past and the present requires a *for* and *since* answer, though the preposition may be omitted in speech, eg *How long have you been sitting here? 20 minutes.*

To explain *for* and *since*, show this:

POINT	PERIOD
since 8 this morning (starting point)	*for* the whole morning (length of time)

2 With books closed, elicit the following to the board, miming it: *I've had my watch since I was 21.* Students may not give you the present perfect here: if not, when the rest of the sentence is on the board, ask them to try and improve it.

When completed, draw a time-line and ask relevant concept questions: *When did I buy my watch? Do I still have it?*

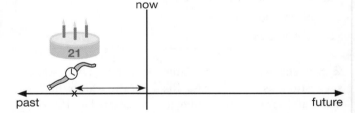

I've had my watch since I was 21.

Write the heading *The Present perfect* on the board. Tell students that because the present perfect links past and present, it is often used with *how long* and *for* or *since*.

Students complete exercise 2. Monitor and assist as students are writing.

1	I've lived, for
2	I've studied, since
3	I've been, since
4	I've known, for
5	I've had, since
6	I've known, since

3 Remind students that the auxiliary *have* is contracted: *I've lived* … . Drill the first example. Students then write out the complete sentences in their notebooks.

When ready, they compare sentences, saying them aloud.

TEACH GLOBAL THINK LOCAL Mixed ability

Stronger students could make three more *How long* questions, to ask other students at the end of the lesson, eg *How long have you had that jumper?* Be sure to monitor closely and to focus on accuracy of the target language. If students are still having problems discriminating between *for* and *since*, they can transform four of their sentences from exercise 3, using the other preposition, eg *I've studied English since I was 12* → *I've studied English for 14 years.*

G Grammar focus

Show students the icon. Write page 144 on the board and ask them to find it. Show students the language summary on Present perfect with *for* and *since*.

You can use exercise 1 on page 145 for:

a) extra practice now
b) homework
c) review a couple of lessons from now.

The answers are on page 143 of the Teacher's Book.

Language note

Students studied the present perfect to describe events and experiences at a non-specific time in Unit 5, so are familiar with the form. Conceptually, the unfinished past use is often the easiest to grasp. It is used here to show the link between past and present; the situation started in the past and remains true until now. In students' L1, this may be replicated by a present simple equivalent, so translation can be used to show the differences, eg students translate the first two examples of exercise 1.

Part 2

TEACH GLOBAL THINK LOCAL Lead-in

Copy and cut out each cartoon on page 80, blowing them up if you can for ease of visibility. Stick each one separately around the room, with a very large empty speech / thought bubble coming out of the relevant person's mouth in each one. Students then go around the room and in threes, fill in two bubbles each. Let students read or hear the suggestions and at the end choose the best caption for each picture.

Vocabulary (SB page 80)

1 Students complete exercise 1 in pairs, then check open class.

As you are going through each one, concept-check as appropriate and also personalise the questions, so that students can demonstrate understanding, eg *What do you spend too much time / waste time doing? What saves you time in the morning?* Write the words on the board, clarifying the part of speech too, eg *waste time* (v); *a waste of time* (n).

1	c
2	e
3	a
4	b
5	d

2 Students translate the sentences in pairs where appropriate. Take class feedback on similarities or differences between expressions used in students' mother tongue(s) and English.

Listening (SB page 80)

This listening is an excerpt from a lecture about the concept of time in the English language.

1 🎧 **2.25** Although this is fairly short, the ideas and language used are quite complex. Pre-teach or check *currency* (n), *spare time* (n), *convert* (v), *connected* (adj), before playing the recording. Students may need to listen again.

TEACH GLOBAL THINK LOCAL Mixed ability

For less strong students, you could facilitate the task by writing up these three alternatives on the board. Students select the most appropriate:

Time is different from money; Time is very similar to money; Time is money.

> Time is money.
>
> 🔊 **2.25**
>
> The concept of time in the English language, and in western culture in general, is very much linked to money. Time can be seen as a form of currency. You can spend time and money, or save it. Time can be wasted. You can give someone your time, just like you can give them money. We have free time, extra time, spare time and overtime. We can convert time into money, and money into time. Time, money and work are intimately connected.

2 🔊 **2.26** Clarify *concept* (v).Students match the two halves in pairs, then listen to check. If necessary, pause the recording when checking.

This exercise encourages students to look at verbs which collocate with both time and money, eg *spend*, *give*, *save*. In addition the verbs *have* and *waste* are also mentioned in the listening. Write these on the board:

VERBS	NOUNS
spend	*money/time*
give	
waste	
have	
save	

> 1   b
> 2   d
> 3   c
> 4   a
>
> 🔊 **2.26**
>
> 1   The concept of time in the English language is connected to money.
> 2   You can spend time and money or save it.
> 3   You can give someone your time, just like you can give them money.
> 4   We can convert time into money and money into time.

3 Ask students to translate these sentences: *It saves money, it saves time; it wastes money; it wastes time*. See if the same verb is used with both nouns, *time* and *money*, in their first language, as in English. Take feedback on points of interest.

Pronunciation (SB page 80)

1 🔊 **2.27** This exercise focuses students on the diphthongs /eɪ/ and /aɪ/. Elicit the sounds first, then quickly drill the sounds from the CD, if necessary.

> 🔊 **2.27**
>
> /aɪ/ time
> /eɪ/ save

2 🔊 **2.28** Let students work in pairs to try and predict which word is different, without referring to a dictionary. Then students listen to check and repeat the words after the recording. Aim for accurate pronunciation of the target sounds at this point. Different nationality groups may find particular diphthongs difficult.

> 🔊 **2.28**
>
> | | | | |
> |---|---|---|---|
> | 1 | fly | **gym** | why | eye |
> | 2 | time | smile | life | **machine** |
> | 3 | mobile | might | **friend** | height |
> | 4 | save | waste | mail | **money** |
> | 5 | great | break | **meat** | paper |

3 Give students a moment to try and find any regularities in spelling and sound. Then elicit some suggestions, putting correct ones on the board.

> /aɪ/: i + consonant + e, as in *time*, *smile*, *life* (compare *bit / bite*, *Tim / time*, *mill / mile*).
>
> Also *igh* as in: *light*, *might*, *fight*.
>
> /eɪ/: a + consonant + e, as in *save*, *paper*, *male*, and *ai* as in: *mail*, *sail*, *daily*. Also *ea* as in *break*, *great*, *steak*.

4 🔊 **2.29** Students in threes look at the four proverbs and try to explain what they mean to each other, either through definition or a situation.

Students then reflect on their own language for similar proverbs. If you have a multilingual class, consider how to group students at this stage. Hear some proverbs from students' first language as a whole class.

Finally, students listen to and repeat the English proverbs.

> 🔊 **2.29**
>
> 1   Time flies when you're having fun.
> 2   Time waits for no man.
> 3   So many things, so little time.
> 4   Life is short and time is swift.

 Extra activity

For more imaginative students, they could put their chosen proverb into a context. Give this example: *My daughter was at a friend's house. When I arrived to take her home at bedtime, she burst out crying, saying she had only just arrived. I replied:* (Pause and elicit) *Time flies …* Students choose one of the proverbs in pairs and do the same. Monitor and assist as students are writing. Students then read their situations out, pausing at the end for their classmates to supply the appropriate proverb.

Speaking (SB page 81)

1 Tell students they are going to read about the top ten time savers. Ask students in pairs to predict five things that will be on the list, eliciting one or two examples. Students then compare with the list in exercise 1.

Students rank the top five most important inventions from the list and try to give reasons, eg *I think X is a bigger time-saver than X because … .* As they are discussing, students should both write the list with reasons. Monitor so that you can see which pairs have different ideas, in preparation for exercise 2.

2 Try to put pairs together who have different ideas. Refer them to the *Useful phrases* box and model the task with a strong student, using some of the phrases given. Students compare and discuss their rankings, then negotiate a new list. Take whole class feedback on any points of interest, particularly disagreements.

3 Ask students if there are any additional time savers not mentioned in the Student's book.

TEACH GLOBAL THINK LOCAL **Speaking extra**

Give out a copy of these quiz questions, to discover how effective your students are at time-keeping and time-management (A= always; S= sometimes / usually; N= never):

1   How often are you on time for class and other appointments?

2   How often do you catch trains, flights, etc with lots of time to spare?

3   Do you get your assignments or homework in on time?

4   How often do you submit these at least a day early?

5   Do you wear a watch when you are in bed?

6   If you are going on holiday, do you give extra hours to your work, so as to get the work done before you travel?

7   Do your friends or colleagues ever comment on your good time-keeping?

8   Is it impossible to distract you when you are in the middle of work?

9   Do you believe good time-keeping is important always, sometimes or never?

Students compare their answers in pairs. Then they add up their totals: *each A answer = 3 points; each S answer = 2 points; each N answer = 1 point.* Then give out the results:

24–27: Time-keeping and time-management are extremely important in your life. You live life by the clock and do not like surprises. Try being a little more relaxed about it!

15–23: Overall, you have a healthy attitude towards time-keeping and time-management. You are realistic about it and you know when work stops and pleasure begins.

9–14:   Your attitude to time-keeping and time-management is relaxed, but probably too relaxed! It may be a problem for your work or studies, and even relationships. Try to respect time – it could make your life easier.

Reading and speaking (SB page 81)

1 **2.30** Students look at the photo of Dickens and read the short summary of his life. Ask students if they have heard of him; if they can name any of his novels; if anyone has read any, either in English or in translation?

TEACH GLOBAL THINK LOCAL **Extra activity**

You could do an image search and bring in pictures of various aspects of Victorian England. Ask if students can say anything about life in those times with regard to: *education, money, jobs and industry, men and women, health care* and *disease?*

Tell students they will hear an extract from one of Dickens' novels. Students read the glossary before hearing and reading the text. Tell students that in Victorian times parts of novels would be read out at the theatre. Students read the same extract like an actor, in pairs, one at time (in this case, it helps to give an awareness of the balance of opposites in the text).

At the end, ask students what they think the opening phrases mean.

2.30 See Student's Book page 81

2 This task asks students to think broadly and critically about the positive and negative aspects of our current times: *it is the best of times, but also the worst … .* Elicit two examples of 'best' things, eg *freedom, easier lives* and two examples of 'worst', eg *the fear of terrorism, environmental problems.*

Students work in pairs or threes to discuss the best and worst things, giving reasons for their choice. They do not write at this point.

3 Let students work alone here on the two sentences. Monitor and assist, as appropriate.

4 Students compare their ideas. Manage whole class feedback, focusing in on interesting ideas and putting new, high frequency lexis on the board.

Background note

Charles Dickens' novels were very popular in his own lifetime. Dickens himself often read extracts from his novels at the theatre. His most famous works include: *Great Expectations, Oliver Twist, A Christmas Carol, Hard Times and David Copperfield. A Tale of Two Cities* (1789) is a historical novel and romance, set around the time of The French Revolution, a bloody period when the class system changed and the poor rose up against the aristocracy. The opening and closing lines of the novel are very famous in English literature.

Part 3

Lead-in

Bring in some foreign coins / notes to show students. Do a mini general knowledge quiz of currencies, with students in pairs. Name 6 different currencies (choose ones they might know) and they write down the country, eg *yen* ➜ *Japan*. To raise the challenge, give the countries first and students name the currency. Invite any students to add an extra currency question, to test their peers.

Vocabulary (SB page 82)

1 Students complete the matching task alone and then in pairs. You could also bring in the real objects to elicit the words instead. Check students understand that *cash* is both notes and coins; *wallet* usually belongs to a man; whereas a *purse* is for a woman.

cash c
cheque d
coins a
credit card e
notes b
purse g
wallet f

2 Do the first one together and introduce or remind students of the word 'collocation'. Students work initially alone and then in pairs.

When checking the answers as a whole class, focus on any relevant prepositions, eg *spend on sth.*, *owe money to someone*, and the phrasal verb *take out a loan*, putting these on the board.

Drill any new words, giving attention to the vowel sounds in: *earn* (v) /ɜː/, *loan* (n) /əʊ/, *owe* (v) /əʊ/. Ask concept questions to clarify meaning as appropriate, eg *owe: If you owe money, what did you do before?* (Answer: *you took out a loan / borrowed it*); *bill: What other bills do people pay? How often do you pay an electricity bill?* (Answer: *gas, every month / every quarter / twice a year*)

1	you earn money, a salary – not c
2	you can spend money on clothes, on food – not c
3	you can take out a loan from a bank, for a car – not b
4	you owe money to a friend, to the bank – not c
5	people pay electricity bills, water bills – not c

3 Students first work alone, putting a cross (X) by the ones they would not ask, and a question mark (?) by those they are unsure of. Students then compare answers in pairs.

Questions 2 and 6 are the only acceptable ones, as they are not asking personal questions.

4 After checking, students can ask each other the questions in pairs, but first elicit / input a response to questions that are inappropriate, eg *If you don't mind, I won't answer that*. This is a polite way of saying: *Mind your own business!*

Background note

Asking personal details about money issues is generally seen to be taboo in the UK, Australia and the US, except in certain circumstances, eg a bank clerk might ask you questions 1 or 8 if you were trying to get a new loan.

Reading (SB page 82)

This reading discusses typical financial concerns at different stages in people's lives.

1 Write up the title of the text on the board and elicit some ideas of what the text might be about, writing students' ideas on the board. Use prompt questions to steer them towards the text, eg *Have you got the same concerns as a 70 year old person?* Be prepared to clarify *financial* and *concerns*, using the synonyms *money* and *worries*.

Pre-teach *mortgage* (n) /ˈmɔːgɪdʒ/, *inheritance* (n) /ɪnˈherɪtəns/, and *heir* (n) /eə/, using concept questions, as appropriate, eg *mortgage: Where do you get a mortgage from? What do you want to buy?*

2 Allow students just two minutes to gist read to check their predictions from Exercise 1.

3 Students read the text again to scan for the answers. They compare answers in pairs before whole class feedback. Early finishers can write two more questions about the text, which they can ask the rest of the class at the end.

1	5 Euros
2	No
3	At the end of the month
4	In the city centre
5	Paid for her house and a new car
6	No

4 Ask students which of these people in the text has the greatest financial concerns, in their view. Then students talk about common concerns for their age group. If you have a multicultural class, put them in different nationality groups as they may find there are interesting differences, eg perhaps fewer students go to college, etc.

Time & Money

Extra activity

To expand your students' lexical range, focus on the high frequency collocations in this text, eg *start / stop work; pay money back; leave someone money; a bank account; a difficult situation; have a child; pocket money; a student loan.* Read out example sentences, either from the text or about the text, and stop before the second part of the collocation. Elicit it from students, if possible, and put the collocation on the board, eg *The heir said her uncle _____ her some money when he died; She's going to put money in a _____.*

Grammar (SB page 82)

Put up the two example sentences under **Grammar** on the board. Ask students who said each one in the text. Focus students on *already* and *yet*.

They discuss the difference between the two words (students can do this in their first language in a monolingual class). Then refer students to the two bullet-point rules.

1 Students search for examples in the text, writing them in their notebooks. They then complete the rules and compare notes in pairs.

> present perfect
>
> already
>
> yet

2 To motivate students, show a picture of a busy-looking woman and elicit some ideas about her first, eg why does she look a bit stressed? Then show the *to do* list and read out the first two examples.

Students make sentences with the target language, taking it in turns to read an example each.

If this tense is unfamiliar to students, it would benefit them to write all the examples down. Monitor as they do so to check for accuracy.

> She hasn't called work about a day off yet.
>
> She has already done her English homework.
>
> She has already been to the bank.
>
> She hasn't phoned her parents yet.

3 Give your own pre-prepared list here, eg *I haven't marked all my homework yet; I haven't prepared tomorrow's lessons yet*, etc. Students then write their own lists.

4 First ask two students to read out the mini dialogue aloud. Focus students on the follow-up question: *When are you going to visit them?* and remind students that they should do the same. Students then compare lists.

Help students with the follow-up questions and responses, and monitor students as they practise.

G Grammar focus

Show students the icon. Write page 145 on the board and ask them to find it. Show students the language summary on present perfect with *yet* and *already*.

You can use exercises 1 and 2 on page 145 for:

a) extra practice now

b) homework

c) review a couple of lessons from now.

The answers are on page 143 of the Teacher's Book.

Extra activity

Students change partners, then read out their *to do* lists again. Their new partner responds by declaring the opposite in each case, eg:

Student A: *I've already done my shopping.*

Student B: *Oh, I haven't done that yet.*

Student A: *I haven't washed my car yet.*

Student B: *Oh, I've already done that.*

This activity gives very controlled manipulation of form.

Language note

Already usually goes before the verb (or past participle) but it can also come at the end of the sentence, for emphasis, eg *I've already seen him; I've seen him already!*

Draw students' attention to the fact that these two adverbs, *already* and *yet*, are very frequently used with the present perfect in British English, as they are both strongly connected to 'now' and there is no specific time reference given. In American English, the past simple is often used, eg *I already spoke to him.*

Pronunciation (SB page 83)

1 🎵 **2.31** Students listen and repeat.

> 🎵 **2.31**
>
> /ʌ/
>
> sun
>
> mother

2 🎵 **2.32** Students work in pairs to first find the words with /ʌ/ then listen to check. Ask if anyone can think of other examples, particularly with *o*, eg *done, come, London, love, none, honey*, etc.

brother, bus, money, some

🔊 **2.32**

brother

bus

buy

cost

home

money

some

3 Give students a moment to read the poem to themselves, to think about what it actually means. Then they listen and read.

🔊 **2.33** See Student's Book page 83

4 Students work in pairs and read the poem out, alternating with the lines. Then swap.

For fun, the whole class could recite the poem together. Nominate a 'maestro' and leave the room for five minutes for students to practise, then return for them to give you their recital. Give ideas before leaving: perhaps they could start soft and gradually get louder; different students say different words or lines, etc. Allow students to decide as much as possible on their own, where appropriate.

TEACH GLOBAL THINK LOCAL Speaking extra

Students who enjoy or would benefit from further oral fluency on the topic can discuss the following in groups:

Does having lots of money always bring happiness?

Do people buy things to please themselves, or to look good for other people?

Would you prefer to work harder for more money, or work less and simply have less?

How do you keep a healthy attitude to money?

Part 4

Speaking (SB page 84)

TEACH GLOBAL THINK LOCAL Lead-in

Ask students the names of any banks they know in the area. Students close their eyes for a minute and imagine they are in a bank they are familiar with. Ask: *What does it look like? What colours / pieces of furniture are there? How many cashiers and desks? What sort of machines? Is the style modern?* Pairs compare and discuss their own banks or ones they know about.

Students look at the pictures on page 84. Ask: *Which bank looks more like yours?* Students prepare to describe the pictures, looking at the language in the *Useful language* and *Useful phrases* boxes. Students find as many differences as possible, taking it in turn to say one difference each, eg *In the first picture, all the customers are women.*

Reading (SB page 84)

This reading describes an unusual bank, the Grameen Bank, set up in Bangladesh to cater for poor customers.

1 🔊 **2.34** First elicit some differences between the two banks: (*there are no computers, it's outside, it seems to be giving money to groups, not individuals,* etc.). Pre-teach the words *borrow* (v), *borrower* (n) and *(make a) profit* (n). Remind students of the word *loan* (SB page 82).

Students read and listen to find two differences between this and a normal bank.

This bank lends money to poor people instead of rich people; The bank workers go to visit the customers, not the other way around.

🔊 **2.34** See Student's Book page 84

2 Refer students to the glossary. Read out the text in the orange circle, then the text in green. Ask students to quickly discuss in pairs: *Why was Yunus shocked and what did he do? What kind of man is Yunus?* Take whole class feedback.

Students re-read the text and answer the comprehension questions. Monitor to assess the level of difficulty and to determine how much time is needed.

Students compare answers in pairs. Take whole class feedback.

1	b
2	a
3	a
4	c
5	b

3 Put students in groups of three to discuss the two questions. For early finishers, put these extra ones on the board: *What are the risks? If you were rich, would you be like Yunus? Why do you think most of the borrowers are women?* Take feedback on points of interest, including linguistic ones.

Background note

Grameen means 'of the village' in Bangla. Yunus himself is Bangladeshi and is an economist. He won the Nobel Peace Prize for this project in 2006. The Grameen Bank has loaned nearly $8 billion since it was founded. There is no legal contract between the bank and borrowers; the system is based on trust. In 2003 it set up a scheme specifically to help Bangladeshi street beggars.

Extend your vocabulary – *borrow* and *lend* (SB page 85)

Write this example on the board:
A: I've forgotten my wallet. Can I _____ some money?
B: I'm sorry. I can't _____ you any. I've forgotten mine too!

Elicit the correct words and the difference between the two. Say the sentences, this time with gestures of giving and taking (see Language note below). Students repeat the sentences after you. They read the examples on page 85 and complete the exercise alone, before checking in pairs.

1	borrow
2	lent
3	lend
4	borrowed

Language note

Students and even native English speakers confuse *borrow* and *lend*. Use your voice to emphasize key differences in the pronouns and use gestures to show lending (move your hand away) and borrowing (bring your hand towards you). *I borrow money from the bank. The bank lends **me** money.*

This mnemonic might help students: *I borrowed a book from Bob, and I lent my lighter to Len* or to think of 'lend' as something **l**eaving you (away), and 'borrow' as **b**ringing something towards you.

TEACH GLOBAL THINK LOCAL Extra activity

You could focus on verbs with two objects, such as *give*, *ask* and *lend*, particularly **for stronger students**. Write these two examples from the text on the board:
It gives very small loans to groups of individuals / The bank often lends money to groups of women.

Label the direct object (*small loans*) and the indirect object (*to groups of individuals*). The indirect object is usually a person, the direct object a thing. Elicit a different way of saying each example, changing the objects around and deleting the preposition eg *It gives groups of individuals very small loans.*

Students find the other example in the text: *The Nobel Committee gave Yunus the Nobel Peace Prize.* Students make 4–6 sentences to describe what they did on friends' / relatives' last birthdays using: *send, give, buy,* eg *I bought my mum some lovely flowers.*

Speaking (SB page 85)

1 Students close their books. Read out the situation in exercise 1. Students work in groups of three to brainstorm suggestions in two minutes.

Encourage them to look around the room, and possibly to consider areas outside the classroom too at this point, eg the entrance, the café, toilets, car park, etc. In feedback, students say what the problem is, eg *it's shabby; it doesn't make a good impression; it's difficult to study here because … ,* etc.

2 Students open their books and read the list and costs. Check students understand the items and let them read through the *Useful phrases* box. Give students 10 minutes to discuss and come to a decision. Monitor and ensure students are giving reasons.

3 Each group chooses a spokesperson who will briefly present their ideas to the others. Give the group a final two minutes to prepare, (this will help raise the profile of the 'presentation').

Invite the spokespeople to change places so that they are with different groups, or invite them to the front in turn. If necessary, they just note the top four things. The audience listens and notes down the main differences, and ask a couple of students to specifically check the maths too!

Function globally: shopping in a market

These lessons in *Global* are designed to provide students with **immediately** useful functional language. They all follow a similar format.

Warm up (SB page 86)

Aim: to introduce the topic via a quick speaking task or picture work.

Tips:

* Do not over-correct here, especially in speaking activities.
* Encourage students to use what language they can at this stage.

Listening (SB page 86)

Aim: to present the functional language in context via a conversation or series of conversations.

Tips:

* Ask students to read the questions first before listening.
* Play the recording all the way through for each task (there are always two tasks).
* For multiple conversations pause the recording after each one.
* If students find it very difficult, play the recording a final time and allow them to read the audioscript at the back of the book.

🔊 **2.35–2.37**

1 A: Do you speak English?
   B: A little.
   A: How much is the shirt?
   B: This one?
   A: No. The checked one.
   B: Hundred and fifty.
   A: A hundred and fifty? That's expensive.
   B: You can have it for a hundred and twenty-five.
   A: A hundred and ten?
   B: Sorry, no. A hundred and twenty-five.
   A: No thanks. I'll leave it.
   B: OK! OK! A hundred and ten. (**photo b**)

2 A: Hello. Can I help you?
   B: Can I have some of these please?
   A: Which ones, love?
   B: The red and white ones. They'll look nice in the living room.
   A: Right. Here you are. Three pounds.
   B: Thank you.
   A: Would you like one of these small plants? They're lovely at this time of year.
   B: Oh. All right. How much is it?
   A: Only 75p.
   B: I'll take it. Here you are.
   A: Here's your change.
   B: Goodbye now.
   A: Bye. (**photo a**)

---

3 A: Puedo ayudarte?
   B: Sorry, I don't speak Spanish.
   A: Can I help you?
   B: No, I'm just looking thanks.
   A: OK.
   B: Sorry, yes. How much is this book?
   A: Two euros.
   B: Only two euros. That's cheap.
   A: Yes. I put the price at ten euros. Nobody wants to buy it. At five euros. Nobody wants to buy it. So I made it cheap. Two euros. Do you want to buy it?
   B: Oh.
   A: What's wrong?
   B: I'm the author.
   A: The author?
   B: Yes. I wrote it. I'll take it. For two euros. (**photo d**)

2 1: The man wants a shirt.
     A hundred and ten.
   2: Flowers and plants.
   3: She wants to know the price of a book.
     She is sad because she is the author and nobody wants to buy the book, which is why it's so cheap.

Language focus: shopping (SB page 86)

Aim: to draw students' attention to the items of functional language.

Tips:

* Make sure students have time to understand the form and meaning of the phrases, but you needn't translate them word for word.
* Students should be able to pronounce these phrases intelligibly, so drill them.

---

1 and 2 🔊 **2.38**

1 How much is it?   2 Can I help you?   3 I'm just looking thanks.   4 Have you got a red shirt?   5 You can have it for a hundred and twenty-five.   6 I'll take it.   7 No, thanks. I'll leave it.   8 That's very expensive.

Speaking (SB page 86)

Aim: to allow students an opportunity to use this language in a meaningful, real-world context.

Tips:

* There is sometimes a choice of task. Any task involving reading a script will be easier than a task involving making students' own scripts. This gives you flexibility for mixed ability classes.
* Give students time to prepare this activity, and circulate and monitor carefully.
* Correct sensitively, paying particular attention to the target language.
* If time allows, ask students to repeat the task, but with a new partner.

Time & Money

Global English

These lessons in *Global* have two main goals. The first is to give you and your students interesting information about English and language in general. The second goal is to provide students with practice in different kinds of reading comprehension tasks that they are likely to encounter in future study (for example, exams).

TEACH GLOBAL THINK LOCAL **Lead-in**

Write up a huge number four on the board. Tell students that this number is important for the English language. Elicit how many people speak the English language (point to the number on the board to show that it is connected in some way). Also clarify who Chaucer is (if possible show them *The Canterbury Tales*) and elicit what students know about Shakespeare. Write these two writers' names up.

Warm up (SB page 87)

Aim: to engage students with the topic, and highlight potentially difficult vocabulary in the text.

Tips:

- Be generous in helping students here with any unknown words in the first task.
- Ask students to relate this task, wherever possible, to similar events or texts in their own lives. This will help them with the reading.
- You may want to give your students an overview of the text before they read, possibly even in their first language. Make it interesting and involving.

Reading (SB page 87)

Aim: to provide students with interesting information about English, and reading exam practice skills.

Tips:

- Be ready to help less confident readers, explaining words or ideas in simpler terms if necessary.
- Get students to read through the whole text once first before doing the tasks.
- Many of these texts have been graded slightly, or not at all. There is a glossary of difficult words. Get students to read that first and reassure them that you do not expect them to understand every word or idea.
- There are two tasks. The first is an easier task, often focusing on the gist of the passage. The second is a more difficult task, similar to reading exam questions.

1

Three reasons why the number 4 is important: In 1600 4 million people spoke English in Britain; today 400 million people speak it as mother-tongue and 4 times as many speak it as a second language.

2

449 AD: Angles, Saxons and Jutes arrived in the British Isles.

849 AD: King Alfred the Great was born.

1400: Chaucer died.

1400s–1500s: 'Great vowel shift' began.

1600: 4 million people spoke English (at the time Shakespeare was writing).

2000: 400 million people speak English as their mother-tongue and 4 times as many speak it as a second language.

Language focus (SB page 87)

Aim: to highlight an interesting or useful aspect of language in the text.

Tips:

- The language focused on here is to raise students' awareness; do not expect them to produce it immediately.
- This language is not tested or reviewed in future units, which means you have more flexibility with this material as to when and where you use it.

1	a
2	b
3	b
4	b

Speaking (SB page 87)

Aim: for students to relate the material in the reading to their own language, culture and experiences.

Tips:

- This is a short speaking activity and can be done in whole class mode or in small groups.
- Wherever possible, ask students to think of and provide examples in their own language but explain them in English too.

TEACH GLOBAL THINK LOCAL **Extra activity**

If your students are confident, ask those in a multi-lingual class situation to research and give mini-presentations about the history and development of their own language. They should support their talk with a timeline similar to the one given here. In a monolingual class, you could select two or three interested students to do a joint presentation on their language.

Writing: giving your opinion

Reading (SB page 88)

Pre-reading activity

Exploit the photo, eliciting where they are; what the situation is; what it says about our world today. Dictate the title of the essay to students. Put up the following paragraph starters from Tayse's essay on the board:

People have too many ...
We worry about ... and ...
We should spend more time ...

Tell students that these are opening sentences from the three paragraphs of an essay on this topic. Students work in pairs to discuss and complete the three sentences. Hear some possibilities as a whole class.

1 Students read and find out if Tayse agrees with the statement, and also if her ideas are similar to their own (if you did the pre-reading activity).

> Yes, she agrees.

2 Students re-read the essay and add the sentences in. These sentences act as topic sentences, introducing and clarifying what comes next. Let students compare answers in pairs.

> Paragraph 1 – c
> Paragraph 2 – b
> Paragraph 3 – a

3 Let students discuss Tayse's opinions in groups of three. Encourage students to support their own views with examples or reasons. Hear some different opinions as a whole class.

Writing skills: organising your ideas (SB page 88)

1 Focus students' attention on the fact that Tayse wrote a detailed plan. This task also requires students to re-read the essay more closely. Do the first paragraph together, reminding students to consider the first sentence of each paragraph too.

> 1 b, a, c
> 2 d, c, b, a
> 3 d, a, c, b

Language focus: giving your opinion (SB page 88)

Students complete the sentences.

1 I believe it is important to	3 We need to
2 We should	4 We can't

Language note

Interestingly, three of the four ways given here use modality (*need to* is viewed as a 'semi' modal). However, teach these as functional units of language and avoid going into great detail about form and meaning at this point.

These exponents allow the writer to show their point of view throughout the essay. Unlike some essay sub-genres, the writer does not withhold her opinion until the final paragraph.

Preparing to write (SB page 88)

1 Students in pairs select their title, (or you could provide an alternative title specific to your students and context). If necessary, give more support throughout the preparatory stage. You could brainstorm ideas in small groups and then as a class onto the board.

2 Students continue to work in pairs. Monitor and assist directly. Ensure that they have two or three points under each heading (refer them to Tayse's essay plan) and that the organisation is transparent. You could highlight on the board how to group similar ideas from the brainstorm. Elicit possible paragraph headings.

Writing (SB page 88)

Refer students to the language under **Saying what you think** and the **Language focus** section. Point out that the phrase *I personally believe*, is usually placed in the final paragraph. Depending on your students, you could elicit an opening sentence for the essay, putting it on the board.

Students could write this in class or at home. For students needing more support, one option is to let them continue to work in pairs in class, at least for part of the essay. Be on hand to help with any questions or problems.

Global review

These lessons in *Global* are intended to review some of the language and topics covered in the unit. They follow a similar format.

Grammar and Vocabulary (SB page 89)

Aim: to review the main grammar and vocabulary in the unit.

Tips:

- Students can do these exercises alone or in pairs, in class or at home, depending on their learning style and your teaching situation.
- Ask students to read the questions first to establish the grammar and vocabulary areas which are focused on.
- Encourage students to check their own answers by looking back through the unit.

Grammar 1	Grammar 2
1 on	1 Have you paid the electricity bill yet?
2 at	2 The bank gave me a loan.
3 in	3 I have already saved three euros.
4 for	4 Time flies when you're having fun.
5 since	
6 since	
Vocabulary 1	
jet lag	student loan
pocket money	overtime
traffic jam	cash machine
wristwatch	
Vocabulary 2	
1 lend	
2 borrow	
3 owe	

Speaking (SB page 89)

Aim: to provide extra speaking practice that will review and consolidate language presented in the unit.

Tips:

- Before speaking encourage students to think first about what language they need to focus on from the unit, and a good way to start their conversation.
- Monitor as students are working and note any points for feedback at the end.

Study skills

Managing your study time (SB page 89)

1 Students cover the *Top Tips* on this page, then answer the quiz on their own, before comparing answers in pairs.

Tell students you want to collect some 'top tips for study time'. Students in threes brainstorm at least three tips from their group, either stemming from questions 1–4 in exercise 1 or from their own ideas. Elicit an example, then students work together. After a few minutes, write their tips on the board.

As the board fills up, this should promote useful discussion about managing study time and differences between people. Students compare their own suggestions with the ones in the Student's book: **Top tips for study time.**

2 Students consider their study plans. Give an example. Encourage students to write at least two suggestions in relation to their time-management, and to make them concrete, eg *I am going to re-read my notes on the bus home on Tuesdays and Thursdays.* Tell students you will ask them next week about their study plan. Don't forget to do so!

TEACH GLOBAL THINK LOCAL Extra activity

Get students to imagine a perfect study area for themselves. If necessary, give an example for yourself (either a very spartan room or the opposite). Write up the following or give mini sketches as prompts, if you are artistic.

The room – spacious or small; with windows or windowless; comfortable furniture or hard furniture (a bed / cushions?); a computer; music (headphones?); plants; photos; access to food and drink etc.

Ask students what kind of study area they work best in. Allow a few minutes to consider their preferences and reasons independently. Then students work in threes to discuss and compare their ideas.

Home & Away

Coursebook

Unit 8	Language	Texts	Communicative skills
Part 1 SB page 90	Vocabulary The home Pronunciation /h/ Extend your vocabulary – *house* and *home* Grammar The passive voice	Listening Conversation about famous homes Reading Bram Stoker's *Dracula*	Speaking Describing your home Talking about famous homes Writing Writing a scene from a film
Part 2 SB page 92	Vocabulary Animals Prepositions of movement	Reading *The cat came back*	Speaking Discussing animal and pet preferences Retelling pet stories
Part 3 SB page 94	Extend your vocabulary – words that mean *trip* Grammar First conditional	Reading *A quick guide to the world's most famous guidebooks* *The Beach* Listening Conversations with tourists and travel guides	Speaking Discussing guidebooks, travel and tourism
Part 4 SB page 96	Vocabulary Adjectives and prepositions Grammar Second conditional Pronunciation Sentence stress	Reading *New kinds of tourism*	Speaking Describing places and kinds of tourism Asking and talking about unlikely situations
Function globally	Speaking on the telephone Telephone English for different situations Students prepare and practise a phone conversation		
Global voices	Listening to people talking about local homes and buildings Describing and comparing pictures		
Writing	Writing a description of a town *It* vs *there* Students extend clauses to develop ideas and make their writing interesting		
Global review	Grammar and vocabulary review Extra speaking practice		
Study skills	Students study how to record and learn words with prepositions		

Additional resources

eWorkbook	Interactive & printable grammar, vocabulary, listening and pronunciation practice Extra reading and writing practice Additional downloadable listening and audio material
Teacher's Resource CD	Communication activity worksheets to print and photocopy
Go global: ideas for further research	**Home** – Ask students to find another famous house of a famous or infamous person and bring in pictures and information **Away** – Ask students to research Web 2.0 sites for travellers, for example TripAdvisor, or Dopplr. What is interesting about them? Are they useful?

Home & Away

Part 1

  Lead-in

Draw a sketch of the layout of your house / flat on the board and then give 'a tour', to both raise interest in the topic and serve as a model. Use some of the phrases in the *Useful phrases* box, eg *Over here there's a X … .* Alternatively, you could give a tour of the school.

Speaking (SB page 90)

Give students two or three minutes to draw the sketch of their home, then focus attention on the *Useful language* and *Useful phrases*. Students then work in pairs, starting, 'This is the front door …'.

Pronunciation (SB page 90)

1 🔊 **2.39** Books closed. Students listen and repeat.

> 🔊 **2.39**
>
> /h/ home

Language note

Most nationalities will not find the /h/ sound too difficult, in which case focus more on the diphthong /əʊ/.

2 🔊 **2.40** Write *Home is where ＿＿＿ ＿＿＿ ＿＿＿* in large writing on the left of the board. Elicit how this might finish (*the heart is*), using hints or mime.

Students work in pairs and suggest how to complete these sentences:
Home is where you hang ＿＿＿ ＿＿＿ and *Home is where your ＿＿＿ are.* before listening to the recording and referring to the exercise to check. Students underline the words with /h/.

> Home, heart, happy, hang, hat, hard, hopes
>
> 🔊 **2.40** See Student's Book page 90

3 After listening and repeating, pairs discuss which saying they like and, if possible, why.

Take some whole class feedback. The first one: 'Home is where the heart is', is a fixed expression. Ask students what it means and if they have a similar saying in their first language.

Listening (SB page 90)

This listening consists of three different extracts in which people talk about the three houses in turn.

1 Students look at the three pictures and try to answer the questions with a partner. Ask students if there are any words they are unsure of and respond accordingly (these words are all nouns except *haunted* (adj)).

Ask concept questions, eg *If a house is haunted, who lives there besides people?* Drill the words, drawing attention to the silent letters in *ghost* and *castle*: /gəʊst/, /ˈkɑːsl/; the diphthongs or long vowel sounds in *haunted* and *tower*: /ˈhɔːntɪd/, /ˈtaʊə/, and the schwa at the end of *prisoner*, *tower*, and *Dracula*.

Students use the language to discuss the questions in exercise 1. Elicit some possible answers at the end.

2 🔊 **2.41–2.43** Clarify the task for students here. They should listen to find out if they were right: *Where are the houses* and *Who lived there?* Students compare their answers before whole class feedback.

> 🔊 **2.41–2.43**
>
> 1
> The Tower of London was originally built in 1078. It was used as a home for the kings and queens of England for almost six hundred years, but also served as a prison. Two of the most famous prisoners in the Tower were the young princes Edward and Richard. In 1483, Richard the Third, their uncle and king of England, put them in the tower. They were never seen again. The princes were ten and thirteen years old. Today, people say the tower is haunted by their ghosts.
>
> 2
> A: Look, look.
> B: Oh, I recognise this place. It's from a film.
> A: Yes, it's the house from some scary movie.
> B: Right! It was used in the film *Psycho*.
> A: Hold on, the guide says … this is probably one of the most well-known film set houses in Hollywood history. The old house and motel next to it were built originally for the Hitchcock film *Psycho* in the 1960s.
> B: Mmm.
> A: Sometimes, at Halloween, the house and motel are opened for the public to come and stay.
> B: Brrr. Staying at this place on Halloween? No thank you.
>
> 3
> Well, welcome to Bran Castle, one of the most famous castles in Romania. The castle was occupied by the government in communist times, but was returned to its owners in 2006. Of course, as many of you know, the castle is known as Dracula's castle. People believe that Vlad Tepes – the original Dracula – lived here. This isn't exactly true, however, but he *was* kept as a prisoner here for some time.
>
> The castle is now a famous tourist attraction, and it is visited every year by thousands of people.

3 Give students time to read the statements first, before playing the CD.

Let students compare answers before feedback.

1:	a	T
	b	T
2:	a	T
	b	F
3:	a	F
	b	F

4 Find out about students' own experience of famous homes open class, asking the questions given. Also find out which of the three houses described they would like to visit and why. Ask students which one they would / would not like to stay in!

Extend your vocabulary – *house and home* (SB page 90)

Put the following two sentences on the board and see if students can fill in the gap. If necessary, give the two options: *home* or *house*.
I'm going _____ *after the lesson.*
My _____ *was built about 30 years ago.*

Pairs discuss the difference in meaning between the two words. Elicit ideas and clarify. Ask students to translate the two examples, to see if one or two words are used in their own language.

You could elicit other places that people can call 'home' – places which are not necessarily a house or a building, eg an igloo, a tent, a caravan, a boat, a cave, etc.

Students read the rules in the Student's Book, and complete the sentences.

1	home
2	home
3	house
4	house
5	home

Grammar (SB page 91)

Students read the two examples given. If possible, elicit the structure: *the passive*, writing it up on the board.

Students turn to their partner and try and explain what the passive is, if necessary in their first language. They read the information about use. Meanwhile, write up the two examples given on the board.

Ask students to complete the 'active' version for the first sentence: *People say …* (*a ghost haunts the tower*). Write this on the board underneath, as a contrast. Elicit the difference between active and passive, referring to the rules given. Do the same with the second example.

Analyse the form on the board for students. Show with colours how the object of an active sentence moves to subject position in a passive sentence:

A ghost haunts the tower. (present simple)

The tower is haunted.

Subject + *be* (or *get*) + past participle

Emphasise that the verb *be* remains in the same tense.

Language note

In writing, we can change the sentence syntax to show where the focus is (in speaking, we can use intonation and stress). So, in the passive voice, the object of the active sentence is placed at the start of the passive one.

Placing the agent in end-position can provide a dual focus on both the subject of the sentence and the agent: eg *The Sistine Chapel was painted by Michelangelo.*

Many languages have similar constructions to the English passive, though they may be used differently. Students may have problems with both concept and form. Students may omit the *be* part of the construction: *Her bag taken*; they might forget to make the subject and auxiliary agree: *the grapes is picked by local workers*; or they may simply avoid it, sounding unnatural: *The fall injured her.*

1 Students complete the recognition task, after doing the first example together.

Let students check their answers in pairs, before feedback. Ask students to circle the *be* auxiliary and the past participle in each case, where appropriate.

1	P
2	A
3	P
4	A
5	P

2 First of all, ask students to scan the names of these official residences and to tell the class if they know anything about them. Students then complete the task with a partner. This task simply focuses students on the tense – both options are in the passive. Check the answers as a whole class.

Palacio de la Moncloa:	was, was
Abdeen Palace:	was, is
The Lodge:	was, was
Mariyinsky Palace:	was, was
The Zhongnanhai:	was, are

Ⓖ Grammar focus

Show students the icon. Write page 146 on the board and ask them to find it. Show students the language summary on the passive voice.

You can use exercises 1 and 2 on page 147 for:

a) extra practice now
b) homework
c) review a couple of lessons from now.

The answers are on page 143 of the Teacher's Book.

TEACH GLOBAL THINK LOCAL Extra activity

Give students two minutes to re-read these mini texts; they should try and remember at least two facts for each one. Write the names of the buildings on the board. With books closed, students try to recall the information in pairs. Monitor to see if students are using examples with the passive. Give feedback: if students avoided the passive, ask them how to change their examples, so that they sound more natural in this context, where the focus is on the buildings, not the people.

TEACH GLOBAL THINK LOCAL Homework extra

If your students need further practice of the passive in context, students can choose a building (local or famous) they admire and write a description. They find information using the internet, etc. and include: *when it was built; its purpose; what makes it unusual or special; any additional points of interest.*

Reading and Writing (SB page 91)

1 If your students are likely to be familiar with this character, write the word *Dracula* in red on the board. Brainstorm associations, eg blood, killing, teeth (fangs), etc. Ask students: *Is the author of Dracula a man or a woman? What's the author's nationality? Was the story written about 200, 100 or 50 years ago?* Encourage students to guess, then to read the information in red about the novel, SB page 91.

Nominate two students to read Dracula's and Harker's lines and you read the narrator's part (if possible, choose a male student with a deep voice for Dracula!)

2 Elicit from students what might happen next. Students in pairs write the next three lines, though early finishers could write more. Make sure that all students 'perform' to at least one other pair and if students enjoy it, watch some examples as a whole class.

Background note

Bram Stoker's classic is probably the most famous vampire story of all times. Dracula lives in the Carpathian mountains, in Transylvania. A young British lawyer, Jonathan Harker, visits him to carry out some legal business but is imprisoned in Dracula's castle. The vampire goes to England to begin his reign of terror, but is eventually forced to flee back to his castle, where his pursuers find and kill him. The book consists of diary entries, letters, telegrams and newspaper cuttings, for authenticity. It was received well when first published in 1897, and later film versions increased its popularity even more.

Part 2

TEACH GLOBAL
THINK LOCAL **Lead-in**

Tell students that you are going to name some different animals. For each one they write two or three word associations. Emphasise that students do not write the name of the animal. Do an example with 'spider', eliciting suggestions, eg *black, hairy*. Then say the following, allowing 30 seconds for each one: *dog, cat, horse, mouse, snake, goldfish.* Students work in pairs to first recall the animal and then compare associations.

Vocabulary and Speaking (SB page 92)

1 Ask students to look at the animal photos and identify any they know. Quickly clarify any new animal words to students, eg 'budgie' (short for 'budgerigar') and 'hamster'. Then students respond to the two questions, giving reasons. Take whole class feedback.

2 Check students understand *tail, fur, fin, wing*, using gestures to clarify. Drill any words that are new, in particular *fur* /fɜː/. Students work in pairs to ask and answer the questions in turn. Monitor and respond to any problems.

> a tail – cat, dog, horse, mouse, rabbit
>
> eight legs – spider
>
> fur – cat, dog, mouse, rabbit
>
> big ears – cat, dog, horse, mouse, rabbit
>
> fins – goldfish
>
> wings – budgie

3 Students work in pairs to ask the questions. You could add more questions on the board, depending on your class, or discuss open class: *How important is it for children to grow up with animals? Why do people keep pets? Is keeping pets common in your country? If not, why not? What sort of people keep pets in your country?*

Take feedback on any points of interest.

TEACH GLOBAL
THINK LOCAL **Extra activity**

For students who need to consolidate or extend animal-related lexis, and who need extra writing practice, ask them to guess the animal, after you have read this text aloud:

This animal lives in the sea, but it is not a fish. It swims large distances and is often loved by people, although in some countries, people consider its meat to be a delicacy. This animal can grow to be very large, depending on the species. Certain types can grow to be over 100 years old.

Add two extra 'clues' if necessary, eg *It lays eggs; it has a hard shell.* Answer: *(sea) turtle.*

Students write two descriptions in the same way, in pairs. In the end, others read / listen and guess the animals described.

Reading (SB page 92)

This reading tells of four separate cats who travelled very long distances to reach home.

1 Tell students that in Britain, people are often either dog lovers or cat lovers! Students then talk about their own preferences, answering the questions in pairs. This task also revises comparative structures.

2 Students read just the introduction to the text. Ask students if they find the information surprising. Students discuss the questions in Exercise 2 in pairs.

Hear any interesting comments in feedback. You could introduce the idea of a 'black cat' to see if there are similar superstitions in other countries (in Britain, a black cat crossing your path is considered to be good luck).

3 Students first read the choice of titles. This is a skim reading task, so tell students they will only have two minutes to read the text. Take whole class feedback.

> b

4 🔘 **2.44** This second reading task is more challenging. Let students read and listen and then do the task in exercise 4.

Monitor and towards the end, let students work in pairs. Do not let students use their dictionaries (see exercise 5).

> | 1 | Ernie |
> |---|-------|
> | 2 | Minosch |
> | 3 | Ernie, Gringo |
> | 4 | Gringo |
> | 5 | Howie |

5 This is an intensive reading task. It also practises an important sub-skill of reading: deducing words from context (unless, of course, the students know the words already). Make sure that students do not refer to their dictionaries yet. Allow time for them to work alone, writing down all four possible answers before comparing ideas in pairs.

Students then look the words up in a monolingual dictionary to check.

> | 1 | sacred | 3 | filthy |
> |---|--------|---|--------|
> | 2 | border | 4 | purring |

6 Let students discuss these two questions in threes. As usual, they should try to justify their choice. If anyone has an unusual pet story, they can share it with the whole class.

If appropriate, you could input words to describe their reactions to the story, eg *That's incredible / amazing / unbelievable / remarkable!* Drill these, as they are very common in spoken English.

Vocabulary (SB page 93)

1 Students complete the pictures with the appropriate preposition. Do the first picture together, then students carry on in pairs. Some students could try to complete the exercise without looking at the options, covering the prepositions. When they have finished, they can look and amend any of their answers.

> 1 out of, across
> 2 across, through
> 3 along, in
> 4 past
> 5 up, down
> 6 into

Language note

In English we can say *to go / drive / walk up / down* or *along* a road and there is little difference between them. Obviously, if the road is not flat, then the preposition *up* or *down* is used, depending on the incline.

2 **2.45** Students will enjoy listening to the complete story, even if they are sure of their answers. Students then cover the text (they could use their pens to cover the writing!) and retell the story, first in their heads, then to their partner.

To make the pairwork more fun, partner A closes their books and B elicits each sentence in turn about Ernie using noises, mime, hand gestures, etc. This technique is also a good way for you to elicit the story, perhaps as a warmer, next lesson.

> **2.45**
> 1 Ernie jumped out of the truck and walked across the highway.
> 2 He went across a bridge, and through some fields.
> 3 He walked along the river, but fell in by accident.
> 4 He ran past some sleeping dogs.
> 5 He climbed up a tree to sleep and climbed down again the next morning.
> 6 He walked into the family home one week later.

TEACH GLOBAL THINK LOCAL Extra activity

There are some useful geographical phrases in the text: *in the south of France; in northern France / Germany; at the border; (on) the coast.* Elicit these, eg ask where Gringo travelled from / to, using a sketch of France. Build up the other compass points: *(in the) north (of) France, south, west* and *east.* Elicit the adjectives: *north + ern ➔ northern,* etc. Ask students to describe where their town is, and then in pairs test their partner's knowledge, eg *Where's London? It's in the south of England.*

Part 3

TEACH GLOBAL THINK LOCAL Lead-in

Show students some guidebooks and ask them to write the introductory paragraph to their town in pairs, as a guidebook entry. Elicit a few suggestions, eg *location, size, age, characteristics, famous for …*etc. Help students with the first sentence, eg _____ *is a small, historic town situated in the north-east … .* Let students read others' descriptions.

Alternatively, get a guidebook of the local area / country and read or copy out five mystery destinations, omitting the place names. Students listen and guess the place. If it is too obvious, disguise it a little!

Reading (SB page 94)

Show students some different guidebooks and ask which series they have heard of. Students complete the first exercise alone, before comparing in pairs. This exercise also revises the passives in context (sentences 2 and 4). You could quickly point this out to students, asking what the focus is in these examples: (*the book*).

> 1 Michelin
> 2 Frommer's Europe on 5 dollars a day
> 3 Baedeker's
> 4 Lonely Planet and Frommer's

Listening (SB page 94)

This listening is three extracts involving tourists or potential tourists.

1 **2.46–2.48** Students look at the four options, then listen to the three conversations for the situation.

> Conversation 1: travel office
> Conversation 2: city centre
> Conversation 3: market
> **2.46–2.48**
> 1
> A: Well, now is really the time to visit the United States.
> B: Really?
> A: Oh *yes*. The dollar is not very strong, so things are really cheap.
> B: Oh. I wanted to go to France. But, cheap is good.
> A: Listen, if you travel this month you'll get an extra twenty percent discount.
> B: This month isn't possible.
> A: Really?
> B: Yes. I have a week's holiday next month. Are there any specials then?
> A: I'll ask if you like.
> B: Yes, please.

2

A: And here is the main square and the tower. The tower is more than five hundred years old, and it's the tallest building in the city. The view from the top of the tower is truly amazing. Today, with this beautiful sunshine, if you go up the tower, you won't regret it.

B: Excuse me, does it cost anything to go up the tower?

A: I'm afraid so. It costs eight euros.

3

A: These are the carpets. I thought you were going to show me the food part. And have some lunch.

B: Yes, yes. The food is on the other end of the market. Do not worry, my friend. We'll go there later if you want. As your guide, though I have to show you everything. Look, isn't this amazing.

A: Mmm.

B: Some of these carpets take more than two months to make. They are all made by hand.

A: I'm just hungry, that's all.

B: Are you sure? If you buy one of these carpets now, I can get a good price for you.

A: Oh. Well …

B: She says if you buy two she will give you a *big* discount.

A: OK, then. How much …?

2 Give students a minute to read through the options first. Students listen again. At the end, ask if they heard any additional facts in each conversation.

> Conversation 1: c
> Conversation 2: b
> Conversation 3: a

Extra activity

For students who need to have more fluency practice, or simply to change the focus in the lesson, put students in pairs and allocate roles of tourist and guide / agent. Students choose either conversation 1 or 3 and have an impromptu dialogue. If they enjoy it, let them change roles.

Extend your vocabulary – words that mean *trip* (SB page 94)

Put the target words on the board: *trip, drive, flight, journey, tour* and *ride*. Ask students if they know the difference between these words and to discuss this in pairs.

Elicit some suggestions, but do not comment. Ask students to complete sentences 1–4, referring to the definitions given, if necessary.

Tell students that sometimes more than one answer is possible.

> 1 drive / ride
> 2 flight
> 3 drive
> 4 journey

Language note

In British English, when you offer to take someone in your car, instead of giving them a *ride*, you give them a 'lift'.

Grammar (SB page 95)

Elicit what the guide might have said to the tourist in conversation 2, writing this on the board:

If you _____ the tower, you _____ a great view.

Ask students concept questions, such as: *Are they talking about the past, present or future? (future); Is it sure to happen? (no, but it **can** happen)*, etc. Refer to the form too: *Is there a 'will' in the 'if' clause? (no).*

Highlight relevant parts of the example on the board:

If you go up the tower, you'll get …

If + subj + present,	subj + *will* + inf.
If clause	main clause

Refer students to the rules and other examples under Grammar, SB page 95, and also draw attention to the negative contraction: *won't*.

Mixed ability

Stronger students could complete exercise 1 without being reminded of the rules at the start, in a test-teach approach. Monitor as they work, to see if they are having any difficulties. Let them compare answers and then tell you the rules in feedback.

1 Students complete the exercise alone, then with a partner. Take whole class feedback. Highlight the fact that in sentence 3, the *if* clause comes second.

> 1 travel, you'll
> 2 go up, won't
> 3 We'll, want
> 4 buy, will give

2 This exercise focuses on the difference between the modals. Students work in pairs to try and explain the difference, if necessary using their first language.

In whole class feedback, ask concept questions, eg for 'might': *Are you definitely going to buy an English guidebook? (no); Which is more sure, might or will? (will).* To check 'can', you could ask: *What else can I buy in London? (souvenirs, a map) Do I have to buy a guide book? (no).*

Home & Away

a	probable
b	less probable
c	possible

3 Give an additional example to start: *If we get no homework tonight* … Elicit suggestions, focusing on accuracy of the target language, then students work on the exercise in pairs, writing the language down. Monitor as students work, and guide them. Encourage students to use other modals besides *will*. Take some whole class feedback.

Language note

When using the so-called 'first conditional', many students attempt to make the first clause more obviously future in form: *If you will go up the tower, you will get a great view*.

The two clauses in the first conditional can swap position, and if you put the subordinate *if* clause second, the comma is not necessary (unless it's a very long clause): *You won't regret it if you go up the tower.*

Drill the complete clauses or sentences, paying particular attention to the modals and contractions: *I can* /kən/ *buy an English guidebook; I'll* /aɪl/ *buy one.*

Ⓖ Grammar focus

Show students the icon. Write page 146 on the board and ask them to find it. Show students the language summary on the first conditional.

You can use exercise 1 on page 147 for:
a) extra practice now
b) homework
c) review a couple of lessons from now.

The answers are on page 143 of the Teacher's Book.

Reading and Speaking (SB page 95)

1 Draw some 'beach' images on the board, eg an umbrella, an ice cream, a shell. Ask students where you find these. Perhaps let one or two students add any other related images! Students answer the questions in exercise 1 – do this directly as a whole class.

You may want to clarify *resort*: *a place that many people go to for a holiday eg a ski, mountain, seaside resort.*

2 🔊 **2.49** Introduce the text and ask a strong student to read the text in the blue circle. Ask questions to check comprehension: *Where does it take place? What's special about the beach? Who's Sal?* Play the recording. Students listen and read, then respond to the questions. Take feedback on the first question, which checks their comprehension, before letting students discuss the more general second and third points in groups of three.

TEACH GLOBAL THINK LOCAL Extra activity

For students who like discussing more 'adult' topics, they can brainstorm the negative / positive aspects of tourism in threes. Positives might include: *money, great facilities (eg hotels, shops), blending of cultures, interest value*. Negatives could include: *can damage cultures and languages, might destroy or damage wildlife, (eg water sports can destroy sea-life etc.), the locals do not benefit, possible increase in crime*, etc.

Background note

This frightening novel describes a young traveller, Richard, who finds an idyllic, secret island resort in Thailand with two friends. Visitors are not welcomed and very few are allowed to stay by the founders. Richard and his friends do integrate into the community, but soon distrust grows, leading to several deaths and grisly events. Ultimately, Richard escapes to civilization and safety. The novel touches on the quest for mystery and experience in today's world, and the expansion of tourism.

Part 4

Lead-in

Show students the photo of the beach on SB page 95. Ask students to write down the top eight essentials they would take for a two-week-long beach holiday in Thailand. Give students 90 seconds only, then they compare in pairs, amending their list to make one improved one between them. Monitor throughout and help with any necessary lexis. Listen to and discuss students' lists as a whole class.

Speaking (SB page 96)

Tell students they are going to discuss the photos on page 96, referring them to the *Useful language* and *Useful phrases*. Check their understanding of: *ancient* (adj), *operating theatre* (n), *storm* (n) and *disaster area* (n). Tell students they need to find the link between these photos. Students discuss them in pairs. Take whole class feedback on comparisons and suggestions. Do not tell them what the link is yet.

Vocabulary (SB page 96)

1 Let students work on their own, before comparing answers in pairs. Give out monolingual dictionaries, if possible, and let students look up any items they are unsure of. Give guidance on how to use the dictionary here if necessary. This is a strategy they may find useful when writing.

1	in
2	with
3	about
4	of
5	at
6	of

2 Students work in pairs. This exercise encourages students to read the target phrases again.

1	d
2	b
3	a
4	b
5	c
6	d

3 Give an example of the task yourself, giving your own ideas after each preposition, eg *I'm not good at horse riding, but I'd like to learn*. Remind students that they can finish the sentences how they choose but they should keep to the holiday theme where possible.

Students write down the answers and then compare answers in pairs. Monitor to assist and to focus students on accuracy of the target lexis.

Reading (SB page 96)

This reading describes four unusual types of tourism that have recently emerged.

1 Tell students they will now discover the link between the photos (if they haven't already identified it). Point out the glossary, checking the words further if necessary, and ask them to match a picture from page 96 with a kind of tourism. After reading, students compare their answers.

Briefly elicit some reactions to the four types of tourism, but keep this brief (see exercise 3).

a	disaster tourism
c	culinary tourism
d	literary tourism
e	medical tourism

2 Students read and add the missing sentences. Let students compare their answers, before taking whole class feedback.

Paragraph 1 c
Paragraph 2 a
Paragraph 3 d
Paragraph 4 e
Paragraph 5 b

3 Students give their opinions on the different types of tourism. First check students' understanding of *acceptable* (adj) and *unacceptable* /ˌʌnəkˈseptəb(ə)l/; also drill them. Students complete the task alone, before discussing in groups of three. They can also comment on which one they would like to try, or perhaps have already tried.

Grammar (SB page 97)

This lesson introduces the second conditional. The contrast with the first conditional can be helpful to students in terms of the concept.

For students likely to be unfamiliar with the second conditional, put the examples below on the board. Students match the two jumbled halves in pairs; this can give them a sense of the form and meaning on a receptive level.

If I went to Morocco,	I'd learn how to prepare Italian dishes.
If we were in New Orleans,	I'd visit the market in Medina.
I love cooking, so if I had the choice	I wouldn't visit the disaster area.

Focus on the form and concept, analysing one example on the board:

If I went to Morocco,   *I'd visit the market in Medina.*
If + subj + past,   *subj + would + inf.*
If clause   **main clause**

Ask concept questions: *Is it possible that I will go to Morocco? (Yes). Do I think there's a big or a small chance of my going? (small).*

1 Students look at the sentences and complete the questions (questions a and b relate to form and c to meaning). They discuss their answers, if necessary in their first language.

> a   past tense
> b   infinitive
> c   unreal situations

2 Students complete exercise 2 in pairs. This task encourages students to consider the difference in meaning between the first and second conditional.

> 1   b
> 2   a
> 3   a

G Grammar focus

Show students the icon. Write page 146 on the board and ask them to find it. Show students the language summary on the second conditional.

You can use exercises 1 and 2 on page 147 for:

a) extra practice now
b) homework
c) review a couple of lessons from now.

The answers are on page 143 of the Teacher's Book.

Language note

The second conditional is more challenging than the first: firstly, knowledge of the first conditional can interfere; secondly, the second conditional confusingly uses a past form to show hypotheticality of a present/future situation; thirdly, the perception of the speaker/reader is integral to the choice of conditional, which can be hard to grasp, eg a Botswanan who regularly goes on safari, might say: *If I go on safari this summer, I'll take my son.* Others outside Africa, with no such trip likely, would probably say: *If I went … , I would … .* Concept questions can focus learners on the likely versus unlikely nature (see above).

Students typically overuse the first conditional: *If I have the chance, I'll try space travel* ; they confuse the clauses: *If I would have the money, I went to Paris* ; they might use *would* in both clauses: *If I would have the opportunity, I would visit all the museums there.*

Note that the past form need not be past simple, eg *If I was wearing a swimming costume and my teacher saw me, I'd be embarrassed.* Also, other past modals can replace 'would', eg *If I had enough money, I might/could go.*

Pronunciation and Speaking (SB page 97)

1 **2.50** Students may be able to complete the question before listening so provide this opportunity by giving a little time and by eliciting. This exercise focuses on natural word stress. Typically, most of the grammar words, eg prepositions, some pronouns, auxiliary verb, articles, are not stressed.

> **2.50**
>
> If **you** could **go anywhere** in the **world**, **where** would you **go?**

2 Drill students on this question, using either the recording or yourself as a model. If necessary, break up the sentence into smaller, more manageable chunks first.

Draw students' attention to the pronunciation of 'would you' in the question form (see language note in SB page 97). Also focus on the contraction in the reply: *I would go* → *I'd go.* Get several students to ask and answer this question across the class, so that everyone can hear.

3 First let students spend three minutes quietly thinking about these situations.

Before pairwork, focus on how to say these sentences naturally. Model the sentences and ask students to underline the stressed words. If necessary, repeat these and check them. Drill one or two examples chorally and individually. Ask students to use the complete sentence when answering, eg *If I … , I would …* but tell them that we often start the reply with just *I'd …* in practice.

Monitor as students are talking and give feedback on accuracy, either on the spot to individuals, if appropriate, or at the end. Remember to give feedback on the content of what they say, not just the language, so elicit some interesting answers too.

TEACH GLOBAL THINK LOCAL **Extra activity**

Your students may need more practice of this form. Elicit possible holiday nightmares, eg *lose your passport, get bitten by a snake, plane crash in the desert*, etc. Remind students these are unlikely. Elicit an example question and response: *What would you do if you lost your passport on the first day? I'd go to the police.* Students work in threes to make three questions, then move to mixed new groups to ask their questions. Monitor and ensure that they refer to unlikely events only.

Function globally: speaking on the telephone

These lessons in *Global* are designed to provide students with **immediately** useful functional language. They all follow a similar format.

Warm up (SB page 98)

Aim: to introduce the topic via a quick speaking task or picture work.

Tips:

- Do not over-correct here, especially in speaking activities.
- Encourage students to use what language they can at this stage.

Listening (SB page 98)

Aim: to present the functional language in context via a conversation or series of conversations.

Tips:

- Ask students to read the questions first before listening.
- Play the recording all the way through for each task (there are always two tasks).
- For multiple conversations pause the recording after each one.
- If students find it very difficult, play the recording a final time and allow them to read the audioscript at the back of the book.

Pablo Alonso is trying to find information about an English-learning holiday. At the end he talks to the person who has the information he wants.

💿 2.51–2.54

1   A: Hello, Greenway Holidays.
    B: Hi, my name's Pablo Alonso. I'm calling about the English learning holiday.
    A: You need to speak to Mrs. Knight. I'll put you through.
    B: Thank you.
    A: Just a moment, please.
2   B: Hello?
    A: I'm sorry, but the line's busy. Do you want to hold?
    B: OK, I'll hold.
3   A: Hello?
    B: Hello, is that Mrs Knight?
    A: No, I'm afraid she isn't here.
    B: Can't you give me information about the English learning holiday?
    A: I'm sorry, I can't. Can I take a message?
    B: No, that's all right. I'll call back.
4   A: Hello, Greenway Holidays.
    B: Hello, this is Pablo Alonso again. Can I speak to Mrs Knight?

A: I'll put you through …
C: Sandra Knight speaking. Sorry to keep you waiting.
B: Oh, hello. My name's Pablo Alonso. I'm calling about the English learning holiday.
C: What would you like to know?
B: Well, I've looked on your website and I have a few questions about the cost.
C: Right, of course Mr Alonso. Our prices, I think you'll find, are very competitive …

Language focus: telephone English (SB page 98)

Aim: to draw students' attention to the items of functional language.

Tips:

- Make sure students have time to understand the form and meaning of the phrases, but you needn't translate them word for word.
- Students should be able to pronounce these phrases intelligibly, so drill them.

---

1 and 2

💿 2.55

1   I'm calling about the English learning holiday.
2   Can I speak to Mrs Knight?
3   Just a moment, please.
4   I'll call back.
5   Can I take a message?
6   Hello, Greenway Holidays.
7   Hello, this is Pablo Alonso.
8   I'll put you through.

3

a 6	c 1	e 8	g 5
b 7	d 3	f 2	h 4

Speaking (SB page 98)

Aim: to allow students an opportunity to use this language in a meaningful, real-world context.

Tips:

- There is sometimes a choice of task. Any task involving reading a script will be easier than a task involving making students' own scripts. This gives you flexibility for mixed ability classes.
- Give students time to prepare this activity, and circulate and monitor carefully.
- Correct sensitively, paying particular attention to the target language.
- If time allows, ask students to repeat the task, but with a new partner.

Global voices

These lessons in *Global* are designed to provide students with exposure to authentic speakers of English from both native and non-native English backgrounds. They all follow a similar format.

Warm up (SB page 99)

Aim: to introduce the topic and highlight potentially difficult vocabulary the students will encounter.

Tips:

- Be generous in helping students with the vocabulary here, but let them try and work it out first.
- Circulate and monitor any speaking task, but be careful not to overcorrect.
- Follow up any short discussion pairwork with an open class discussion, asking students to report back what they said.

Listening (SB page 99)

Aim: to expose students to English spoken with a variety of accents.

Tips:

- The first time they listen, tell them you don't expect them to understand every word; some of it will be hard. This is because the text has not been scripted or graded in any way. It's what they would hear in "the real world".
- Pause after each speaker on the second listening, and don't be afraid to replay the whole thing if students appear to need it.
- Students can read the audioscript at the back of the book if you / they wish.
- Try to avoid hunting for specific pronunciation or language errors. In real world communication not everyone speaks perfect English all the time, not even native speakers.

2.56–2.60

1 David, Georgia: So homes in Georgia are very big – some big ones and so we have two kind of homes. There are block of flats – there are many of them and we also have houses and houses are usually are in the outside of the country – in the villages. (**c not mentioned**)

2 Elena, Russia: In my country we have different homes, like in England, because in England many people live in cottages, yes, but in my country we have very big houses. Many flats, but not so big, but good, and mostly Russian families have a cottage – it's not a cottage, it's maybe a little house in the countryside where we can grow fruit and vegetables but we don't live these cottages, but what I can say more. Maybe prices – if you buy – if you sell your flat in Moscow you can buy three houses in Great Britain. (**c not mentioned**)

3 Valeria, Bolivia: I would say homes in Bolivia are much more coloured. Here, above all in Oxford all the homes are looks very similar I would say and in Bolivia you can find a red house just besides a yellow house and it is a pretty nice combination of colours. (**a not mentioned**)

4 Katie, Northern Ireland: Where I live in Belfast homes are … they're quite varied. In inner city Belfast you have very small red brick terraced houses. Two up and two down houses and they're – I think they date from the 1800s – they sort of typify whenever you think of the city you think of red brick terraced houses. (**b not mentioned**)

5 Bea, England: Homes where I live are quite large. In my street in particular the houses have four or five bedrooms. They are usually shared between lots of different house mates. I personally live with two people I didn't know before and now one of them is a very good friend. The houses have kitchens and separate living rooms and dining rooms and the best thing about my house is that it has a large garden. (**a not mentioned**)

Language focus: adverbs of degree

Aim: to raise students' awareness of a particular piece of language present in the listening.

Tips:

- This language is not included in tests or reviews, it is here to help students understand international English.
- Don't expect students to produce this language in an exercise or in conversation immediately.

1

+ a bit, slightly   ++ fairly, quite   +++ extremely, very

2

1 b   2 d   3 a   4 e   5 c

Speaking (SB page 99)

Aim: for students to discuss the same or similar questions as the speakers in the listening.

Tips:

- The speaking tasks here are slightly more open to allow for students to explore the subject. Give them time to do this.
- If students are working in pairs, circulate and monitor. Make notes of incorrect language use to correct afterwards (or in a future class).

Writing a description of a town

Reading (SB page 100)

This is a student's description of her home town Rajec, in Slovakia.

Students read Aneta's description, then in pairs compare their answers to the questions. Take whole class feedback. Ask students if they would like to go to Rajec. They should give reasons.

> 1 The 16th century Town Hall, a medieval square, lots of historical buildings, thermal baths, a golf course, and tennis courts.
>
> 2 Likes: the countryside around the town. Dislikes: it is a bit quiet and there isn't much to do at night. There is no cinema, and there are not many bars and restaurants.

Language focus: *it* and *there* (SB page 100)

TEACH GLOBAL THINK LOCAL **Mixed ability**

For less strong students, clarify the rules beforehand. Write on the board: *Let me tell you a bit about my town. Is called Rajec* and ask students what is missing. Then ask: *What does it refer to?* (*my town*), which is talked about in the previous sentence. Write up: ____ *is also a medieval square.* Elicit the missing word and ask: *Has the square been mentioned before?* (*No, this is the first time*).

1 Do the first two or three examples together (the first example: *it will be great …* is actually a slightly different use. Let students work alone, before checking in pairs. Check answers as a whole class, if possible projecting the letter onto the board.

> **Paragraph 1: It** will be great to see you again.
>
> **Paragraph 2: It** is called Rajec and **it** is in the north of Slovakia, near the Mala Fatra mountains.
>
> **It** is not a large town (**there** are about 7,000 inhabitants) but **it** is very old and beautiful.
>
> **There** is also a medieval square … … **there** are also thermal baths,…
>
> **Paragraph 3:** The worst thing about Rajec is that **it** is a bit quiet and **there** isn't much to do at night. **There** is no cinema, and **there** are not many bars and restaurants. **It** is wonderful to go … . **There** are mountains nearby …

2 Students complete the rules in pairs. Take whole class feedback and ask students how this works in their own language. Students translate the two example sentences a and b, if possible with a student who shares the same first language.

> a there   b it

Language note

In some languages, there is no need to use the equivalent of 'there' or 'it' in the sentence, eg *It's a very large building* → ~~is very large building~~. *There* is used in English before a form of the verb *be*, to say that something exists, and is followed by a noun phrase: *There is a big castle just outside the town.*

The pronoun *it* is used in discourse to mention something that is already mentioned. *It* is also used when referring to the weather, temperature or time, eg *It's 3.30*. *It* also adds a subject, eg *It will be great to see you again*.

Writing skills: giving more information (SB page 100)

This exercise focuses on relative clauses starting with *where* and is a useful way to make language more sophisticated, helping students at this level to produce longer sentences.

Do the first example together, highlighting the comma: *There are mountains nearby, where people go skiing in winter.*

Then students work alone to complete 2, 3 and 4, writing the sentences. Show on a screen or OHP in feedback.

> 1 There are mountains nearby, where people go skiing in the winter.
>
> 2 But what I like best is the countryside around the town, where you can go for a day trip.
>
> 3 … as well as a small lake, where you can go fishing.
>
> 4 Outside the town there are also thermal baths, where you can enjoy the natural hot water all year round, …

Preparing to write (SB page 100)

Students look at the language under *Describing a town* and spend two minutes in silence considering the questions. Be on hand to respond to any questions at this point. Students then describe their town to their partner.

Writing (SB page 100)

Ask students to send you an email or letter, similar to Aneta's, which they can either write at home or in class time. Tell students that you will collect all the descriptions for a class display entitled 'Our hometowns'; students can also provide visuals for the display. It is up to you whether you correct students' writing before displaying it, though focusing on any problems with 'it' or 'there' would be appropriate. Consider whether their message is clear and be sensitive to individuals' abilities and personalities.

Global review

These lessons in *Global* are intended to review some of the language and topics covered in the unit. They follow a similar format.

Grammar and Vocabulary
(SB page 101)

Aim: to review the main grammar and vocabulary in the unit.

Tips:

- Students can do these exercises alone or in pairs, in class or at home, depending on their learning style and your teaching situation.
- Ask students to read the questions first to establish the grammar and vocabulary areas which are focused on.
- Encourage students to check their own answers by looking back through the unit.

Grammar	
1	was built
2	is visited
3	are not permitted
4	with
5	don't
6	had
7	don't
8	could

Vocabulary 1		Vocabulary 2	
1	giraffe	1	along/down/up
2	whale	2	across
3	bee	3	past
4	guidebook		
5	suitcase		

Speaking (SB page 101)

Aim: to provide extra speaking practice that will review and consolidate language presented in the unit.

Tips:

- Before speaking encourage students to think first about what language they need to focus on from the unit, and a good way to start their conversation.
- Monitor as students are working and note any points for feedback at the end.

Study skills

Learning words with prepositions
(SB page 101)

1 Students complete the exercise. Early finishers come and write the answers up on the board.

Highlight the preposition and ask students how the preposition is shown in a dictionary. Dictionaries use different devices – sometimes it is simply shown by example sentences – so check this before the lesson, where possible.

2 Monitor as students are doing this, to check they are noting down the appropriate example sentences.

Students then underline the adjective and the preposition within the sentence in two different ways, eg *He's <u>keen</u> <u>on</u> adventure holidays.*

3 Students work in pairs to try and predict the answers. Elicit which part they look up to check: *the noun or the verb?* (Answer: *noun*). Students then check in the dictionary.

After checking, ask students if there are any similarities in meaning between expressions sharing the same preposition, eg *to* = in the direction of a place; *on* = a holiday, cruise, picnic (something leisure-related and pleasant) etc; *for* = for the purpose of eg a drive, a ride, a drink.

1	on	6	on
2	for	7	on
3	to	8	to
4	for	9	to/for
5	on	10	on

Health & Fitness

Coursebook

Unit 9	Language	Texts	Communicative skills
Part 1 SB page 102	Vocabulary Feeling ill The common cold Pronunciation *ch* and *gh* sounds Grammar Modal verbs of advice	Listening Giving advice on treatments for colds	Speaking Discussing the common cold and giving advice Writing Writing sick notes and giving advice
Part 2 SB page 104	Vocabulary Medical treatment Pronunciation Word stress Grammar *Could / couldn't, had to / didn't have to*	Reading *Arab influences on medicine* *Milestones of modern medicine*	Speaking Asking about health and treatment experiences Talking about important developments in medicine
Part 3 SB page 106	Vocabulary Sport Extend your vocabulary – *win* and *beat* Grammar Past perfect	Reading *Olympic losers*	Speaking Describing sports Talking about the Olympic Games Speculating Taking part in a sports questionnaire
Part 4 SB page 108	Grammar Reported statements Vocabulary *Say*, *tell* and *ask*	Reading / Listening Conversation between doctor and patient	Speaking Preparing a dialogue Discussing health, exercise and keeping fit
Function globally	Describing an illness How to read a drug label Students practise describing symptoms and recommending treatment		
Global English	David Crystal text: *Sports English* Students talk about sports commentating		
Writing	Writing an online post to give advice and suggest alternatives Giving examples		
Global review	Grammar and vocabulary review Extra speaking and writing practice		
Study skills	Students learn how to use a dictionary to explore collocations		

Additional resources

eWorkbook	Interactive and printable grammar, vocabulary, listening and pronunciation practice Extra reading and writing practice Additional downloadable listening and audio material
Teacher's Resource CD	Communication activity worksheets to print and photocopy
Go global: ideas for further research	**Health** – Ask students to find museums about medicine in different places. Which sites are most interesting? Do any of them have a virtual tour? Find images of old medical tools. **Fitness** – Ask students to find the official Olympic site. Make a quiz about the Olympics for others in the class.

Health & Fitness

Part 1

Lead-in

Start by miming a sneeze and cough. Elicit what your problem might be and maybe what the symptoms are: *runny or blocked nose* (n), *cough* (n)/(v), *sneeze* (n)/(v), *sore throat* (n). Don't write these on the board as some of them come up in Vocabulary exercise 1. Ask open class: *When was the last time you got a cold? What did you do / take?*

Speaking and Listening (SB page 102)

1 Students discuss the three questions in pairs.

For early finishers, put the following questions on the board: *Do you see yourself as a healthy person? What do you do to stop catching colds (if anything?) What known remedies are there in your country for colds? What facts do you know about colds?* Take whole class feedback on any points of interest.

Write up any relevant words or collocations not in the Vocabulary exercise (SB page 102), eg *catch / get / have a cold*.

2 Pre-teach the words *average* (adj/n) and *symptom* (n). Students complete the information on the common cold, first working alone, then in pairs. More confident students could discuss the significance of the numbers before looking at the text. If students need help, go around and underline the key words, such as time, number and cost in the text, to guide them to the answer.

```
1  200
2  2–5
3  6–10
4  24–48 hours
5  2–3 years
6  $3.5 billion
```

3 **2.61** Students listen and check their answers. You could check the answers as a whole class if your students would benefit from saying the numbers aloud.

2.61

The common cold can be caused by more than 200 different viruses.

An adult gets between two and five colds a year, while for children or babies the number is higher; between 6 and 10 colds a year.

From the moment you get a cold to the moment you feel the symptoms is between 24 and 48 hours. The total time in your life that you will have a cold is two to three years.

The common cold is not a deadly disease, but it is expensive. In the US alone, experts estimate that it costs the economy $3.5 billion dollars in lost time at work and school.

Vocabulary (SB page 102)

1 Elicit from students what you say to someone who looks ill, then do the first one together. Students work alone, then check in pairs.

When checking the answers as a whole class, put the target lexis on the board, as follows: *be / feel tired, have a headache, hurt* (v), *a sore throat* (n), *a blocked nose* (n), *sneeze* (v) / (n). Elicit from students the word class in each case. Drill students in response to any pronounciation problems they have, eg *ache* /eɪk/, *hurt* /hɜːt/, *blocked* /blɒkt/ and *sneeze* /sniːz/.

```
1  What's
2  feel
3  got
4  sore
5  hurts
6  blocked
7  I'm
```

Language note

Focusing on the word class can help students distinguish between words with similar meanings, eg *pain* (n) *sore* (adj) and *hurt* (v). Note that in sentence 7, the adverb 'always' is used with the present continuous, where students might expect the present simple. The continuous is used here to express the speaker's slight annoyance with this habit: it's something she can't stop.

2 Model the task, eliciting which sentence from exercise 1 you could put *cough* into (3). Students complete this task in pairs. When checking answers, you could highlight that in American English 'a sore head' is 'a headache' in British English.

```
1  wrong
2  sick
3  stomach ache, toothache, fever, cough
4  head, leg
5  head, leg
6  –
7  coughing, sick
```

3 Do an example to start with, miming a sore throat. Then put students into pairs, **A** and **B**, referring them to pages 127 and 129. Ask students to give a full sentence, starting with *You* or *Your / You're*.

Pronunciation (SB page 102)

1 **2.62** Give students two minutes just to try and read the words themselves. Allow students to check the meaning of any of the words with you first, eg *technique* (n): *we looked at different techniques or ways to remember vocabulary in Unit 5 (SB page 65)* or *tough* (adj): *meat can be tough, if it is not soft* (mime chewing tough meat) or *character*: *in the story of Dracula, Dracula and Harker are two of the main characters.*

Students listen to the recording.

Mixed ability

Stronger students can attempt to find the word with the different sound before listening, in pairs. Then they listen to check.

🔊 **2.62**
1   cheap chicken choose **machine**
2   character **catch** technique headache
3   tough enough **ought** cough

---

2 Students fill in the columns in pairs. You could let students use a dictionary to double-check.

/f/ eno<u>ugh</u>, co<u>ugh</u>, to<u>ugh</u>

/k/ <u>ch</u>aracter, te<u>ch</u>nique, heada<u>ch</u>e

/tʃ/ <u>ch</u>eap, <u>ch</u>icken, <u>ch</u>oose, cat<u>ch</u>

/ʃ/ ma<u>ch</u>ine

silent: ou<u>gh</u>t

Pronunciation note

In English, the most common pronunciation of ch is /tʃ/, though there are a few exceptions as exercise 1 shows. Also consider words such as *choir* /kw/, *Christmas* /kr/, *champagne* /ʃ/. Words spelt with *ough* can have a variety of pronunciations, as illustrated in the poem in exercise 4.

3 🔊 **2.63** Ask students to read the sentences to themselves, then repeat aloud after the recording.

For students who do not have problems with the specific sounds, use the sentences to focus on features of connected speech and sentence stress:

*I /ə/ **think** I … **caught** it from /frəm/ **Charles**.*

🔊 **2.63** See Student's Book page102

---

4 🔊 **2.64** Play the recording and tell students to listen and read along silently. Afterwards, explain any words that students request, eg *bough* (main branch of a tree) and *slough* (to remove a layer of skin). Drill individual words, as appropriate.

8

---

5 If students seem motivated, they should prepare to read the poem aloud. First, listen to the poem again, then students mumble it quietly to themselves. Then ask students in pairs to read it together, to each other.

One or two students can read out the poem to the class – applaud them if successful. Finally, all students read along with the recording.

🔊 **2.64** See Student's Book page102

Listening (SB page 103)

This listening gives different speakers' remedies and advice for the common cold.

1 Write 'the common cold' on the board and then read out the quote. Students close their books. Elicit some common treatments or remedies, and general advice. This prepares them for the listening.

2 🔊 **2.65** Students look at the pictures first. Tell them that there are fewer pictures than suggestions. Less strong students work in pairs to discuss what each picture shows before listening. Clarify any words you think may be necessary before listening, eg *honey*, *garlic*, *soup*. Students listen and order the pictures.

2, 5, 8, 4, 1/8, 3, 7, 6, 9

🔊 **2.65**
1   You should eat hot chicken soup as soon as you feel ill.
2   Just drink water. Lots of water.
3   Drink orange juice and lots of vitamin C.
4   I think you should eat foods with vitamin A, like carrots.
5   Drink hot water with lemon and honey in it.
6   I think you should drink water with a spoonful of salt.
7   Breathing hot steam works. Go for a sauna.
8   You should eat garlic. It works, I promise!
9   Just take two aspirin and stay in bed.
10 Cold medicine. Take cold medicine.
11 You shouldn't do any exercise. You should stay in bed. Don't go out.
12 I don't think you should stay in bed. Be active. Go out.
13 What you should do, what you really *ought to* do, is to wash your hands regularly.
14 You should stay dry. Don't wash your hair or go out in the rain.

---

3 This listening task gives students practice in listening for specific information, potentially useful when listening to medical advice in real life. Encourage students in pairs to choose different verbs. Stronger students may be able to listen out for two or three verbs.

Be prepared to pause the recording and just replay relevant sections.

4 Students compare their answers, then read the audioscript to check.

Grammar (SB page 103)

Alternative procedure

You could adopt a more task-based approach here, if it would suit your group. Students complete the sick-note Writing task exercises 1 and 2 (SB page 103) first. Take in the reply, which gives advice, and use it to analyse the kind of language that students are using for this function. Take out both good examples and also weaker examples of the target language, eg ~~you must take vitamin C~~ (arguably a little strong), or ~~Stay in bed!~~ (this imperative is acceptable, but if used solely throughout, it might suggest that the writer's repertoire is limited). Put good and weaker examples on a worksheet, asking students to comment on and improve the weaker ones.

1 Students read the examples given under **Grammar**. Elicit an example using the pictures. For less confident students, ask them to write down at least four example sentences with the target language, in pairs. Monitor as students are doing this, referring them back to the examples as appropriate.

2 Tell students that you have a problem: *you sometimes cannot sleep*. Elicit the name of the problem: *insomnia* and the person who suffers from this: *insomniac*. Give each student a slip of paper and ask them to write down a good piece of advice. Take these in and read some of them out, eliciting class opinions about the advice as you do so.

Students do the controlled practice exercise in the book in pairs. As students read out their answers in class feedback, highlight the fact that the modal auxiliary is unstressed in affirmative statements, eg *You should* /ʃʊd/ *take a warm bath*.

1	You should take a warm bath before bed
2	You should sleep on a good bed
3	You ought to see a doctor if the problem continues
4	You shouldn't smoke before bed
5	You should get some exercise during the day

G Grammar focus

Show students the icon. Write page 148 on the board and ask them to find it. Show students the language summary on modal verbs of advice.

You can use exercise 1 on page 149 for:

a) extra practice now
b) homework
c) review a couple of lessons from now.

The answers are on page 144 of the Teacher's Book.

Language note

Learners tend to overuse 'must' and it is worth highlighting this fact to your students. In the example given under **Grammar**, *You must stay in bed,* the speaker is likely to be in a position of authority, eg someone in the medical profession, or a parent. If *must* is stressed, this makes it even stronger, and might suggest frustration on the speaker's part. Typically, the modals are unstressed in affirmative statements:

You should **eat garlic**.   *You must* **stay** in **bed**.

Consider banning the use of *must* when speaking, in preference for *have to*!

Writing (SB page 103)

1 Tell students that they are going to write a sick-note, eliciting when people write these and why. Ask students if this happens in their culture, and what sort of things they might say.

Students read and choose a situation. Focus students on the *Useful language*. Elicit how to start and end the note.

2 Read out one of the students' notes and elicit some possible replies, again referring them to the *Useful language*. Students swap letters and reply. Give a minimum word limit of 60 words. Take the letters in for analysis and correction.

Part 2

TEACH GLOBAL THINK LOCAL **Lead-in**

Give each student a mini health problem on a piece of paper, eg *headache, back ache, sore feet, can't concentrate, can't stop eating, insomnia,* etc. Students mingle and approach at least four others to get advice. Model the task with a strong student:

A: *(groan and pained expression)*
B: *What's the matter? You don't look too good.*
A: *(state the problem)*
B: *(give some advice)*

Join in the mingle, noting any problems with health-related vocabulary or functional phrases. In feedback, highlight any language difficulties and also any good advice received.

Vocabulary (SB page 104)

1 Students complete the task in pairs. Do an initial example together.

had	go for	having
stayed	visit	going
broken	take	becoming

2 Students ask each other at least one question from each box. For early finishers, ask them to use follow-up questions to find out more, eg *When did you have an operation? Which bone did you break?* though bear in mind that this could be a sensitive topic.

The exercise focuses on collocations. When students have asked their questions, they close their books. For each of the nine lexical items, say the noun and elicit the verb, eg *a bone (break), an injection (have).* Put these collocations on the board for students to record, if they are new to them.

Pronunciation (SB page 104)

TEACH GLOBAL THINK LOCAL **Pre-reading activity**

Particularly **for less strong students**, check their understanding of the reading text first before they read / listen to it for pronunciation purposes. Put this question on the board: *How did the Arab world help medicine develop? Find at least 3 ways.* Students read and give whole class feedback. In feedback, the students will probably have difficulties saying some of the long words, linking neatly to the pronunciation focus.

1 Students work in threes to check and explain the words to each other, using dictionaries if appropriate. Check their understanding of some of the words as a whole class, eg *operation: What might you have an operation for or on?*

Students then complete the word-stress categorisation task. To help students, you could tell them that one category has only one example.

Alcohol = 3	**Med**ical = 3	**Phar**macy = 3
Arabic = 3	Ope**ra**tion = 4	Preser**va**tion = 4
Hospital = 3	O**ri**ginally = 5	Trans**la**tion = 3

2 **2.66** Students read the mini text silently to find and underline the words from exercise 1. Play the recording. After listening, elicit the correct pronunciation of the target words and drill the students on them, paying particular attention to the word stress and to the schwa sounds.

Point out that in words ending *-tion* or *-sion*, the stress lands on the previous syllable, eg ope**ra**tion, preser**va**tion. The last syllable is unstressed.

3 Students listen and repeat the words from exercise 1.

2.67 See Student's Book page 104 Pronunciation ex 1

4 Students practise reading this alone, muttering it quietly. Then pairs read alternate lines. Monitor and assist, where appropriate, with pronunciation.

Reading (SB page 104)

This reading summarises a survey given to doctors and nurses about the most important discoveries in modern medicine.

1 Let pairs work together to discuss the five lexical items, bearing in mind that they are quite difficult to explain. Clarify and check with concept questions, eg *Can you give me an example of a disease? Do you know what vaccines are given to babies in your country? When does someone get antibiotics and who gives them?*

To prepare students for this challenging text, ask students how these things have helped in medicine, eg *Why are antibiotics so important? How do you think DNA has helped in medicine?*

2 Students predict in pairs what the text will be about. Hear some suggestions, inviting students to give reasons, where possible.

a

3 **2.68** Students read and listen to the text to check their answers.

4 Allow students to read through the sentences first, pairing stronger and weaker students together to help with vocabulary.

Check understanding of the following verbs: *identify, reduce, treat;* the nouns *infection, rabies;* the adverbial, *by accident* (the latter could be misleading here, given the topic). Note that *infection* and *identify* are in the Glossary. Refer students to this.

Give students several minutes to read the text and complete the task. Have dictionaries on hand in this lesson as this text is lexically dense, but only let students look up three words each. Students compare answers in pairs. Take whole class feedback.

1	(the discovery of) DNA
2	sanitation
3	germ theory (washing hands)
4	anaesthesia
5	vaccines (the first vaccine)
6	antibiotics

5 Read the title of the text: *Milestones of Modern Medicine*. Ask students what they think 'milestone' means, now they have read and listened to the text (*it is used to talk about an important, life-changing historical event, often with reference to an invention, such as the wheel*).

Ask students to discuss in pairs the most important milestone and why. Hear some suggestions, before telling students what doctors themselves voted for.

Doctors chose sanitation.

Grammar (SB page 105)

Language note

Students generally find *could* and *couldn't* relatively easy to conceptualise as the past of *can* and *can't*.

Remind students that *do / did not have to* means that *it is / was not necessary*, eg *Doctors did not have to wash their hands before 1947*: it was not necessary (by law) for doctors to wash their hands before 1947.

1 Students read through the examples and rules under **Grammar**. They complete the texts alone, using the rules to help, before checking with their partner.

Take whole class feedback. Ask probing questions in relation to the target language where relevant, eg *if doctors wanted to know what was inside a body, they <u>had to</u> open it*. Ask: *is 'must' also OK here? Why not?* (Answer: *It's not OK because it needs to be past, and the past of 'must' (in this sense) is 'had to'*).

The x-ray:	had to	could
Risks of smoking:	didn't have to	could

2 Write the first word, 'ambulance' on the board. Elicit what happened before this was invented, in the same way as the X-ray. Ensure that students use modals at this point. Students look at the other inventions in the box and discuss them in pairs.

Monitor as students are talking and assist with problems with the target language. Students can write 1–2 examples down, as consolidation.

Mixed ability

Stronger students can think of an additional invention, which they describe to their classmates at the end. They should not identify the item itself, but let their peers guess it from their description.

(suggested answers)
1 ambulance – people had to go to hospital by car, they couldn't be picked up at their house
2 anaesthesia – patients had to be awake during operations, people could feel pain during operations
3 wheelchair – patients couldn't move around so easily, people had to stay in bed
4 eye glasses – people couldn't see properly; they had to use a magnifying glass to read
5 thermometer – people couldn't judge temperature – they had to use their hands or guess
6 microscope – people didn't know about the structure of animal and plant material – they couldn't see cells, for example

G Grammar focus

Show students the icon. Write page 148 on the board and ask them to find it. Show students the language summary on *could* and *had to*.

You can use exercise 1 on page 149 for:

a) extra practice now

b) homework

c) review a couple of lessons from now.

The answers are on page 144 of the Teacher's Book.

Extra activity

To revise the passive, ask students to find three examples in the paragraphs *Anaesthesia*, *Antibiotics* and *DNA*. They record these in their notebooks: *drugs were developed … ; antibiotics were first produced … ; DNA was discovered … .* Students tell their partner why the passive is used here. Hear suggestions. These particular verbs are, understandably, often used in the passive: the focus is on the thing, rather than the agent.

Part 3

Lead-in

Give students ninety seconds (in threes) to think of as many sports as possible. The group with the longest list reads theirs out. Alternatively, with a sporty group, bring in photos from the sports sections of local or national newspapers. Students name the sports and tell you what they know about them or the players.

Vocabulary (SB page 106)

1 Elicit three pieces of equipment that a footballer (or other popular sportsperson) needs. Students look at the pictures and identify the sports in pairs.

a	Martial art, eg karate	d	baseball	g	cycling
b	football	e	boxing	h	basketball
c	swimming	f	golf	i	skiing

2 In pairs, students fill in the table with the sports from the previous exercise. In whole class feedback, try to elicit what the generalisations are regarding the choice of verb (see **Language note** below), asking students to notice similarities within the sports in each column.

Play – football, baseball, basketball, golf

Go – swimming, skiing, cycling

Do – martial arts, boxing

Language note

Play is usually used for sports which use a ball and competitive team sports, eg *football*. *Do* is used if the sport is played indoors, eg *judo*. *Go* is usually used if the sport is played outside in a bigger area, eg *go waterskiing*. Sport nouns ending *-ing* also take *go*, eg *go fishing*. These are useful guidelines, though there are exceptions.

3 Ask a confident student to read out the text. Elicit the sport described.

football

4 Using the model in exercise 3, students write a description of a sport from this page (or of their own choice), in pairs. Ask students to use at least two different modals. Early finishers should write an additional description. Make dictionaries available.

Students swap their texts with others to see if they can guess the sport described. Take in these texts as they provide evidence of whether students are using, misusing or avoiding modals and could be used as a basis for feedback.

Reading (SB page 106)

This reading gives details of four past Olympic athletes who are not remembered for winning!

1 Instruct students to look at you, not their books. Elicit what the Olympic flag looks like. You could also do an image search, using the key words: *Olympic games* and use these images to introduce the topic. Focus students on the questions in exercise 1, which they discuss in pairs.

Add the following points on the board as they are talking; refer students to them once they have finished, eg *What can you remember about the last Olympics? What for you is the most a) interesting b) boring c) dangerous d) beautiful Olympic sport?*

2 Make sure that students understand the four choices a–d. Pre-teach or check *gold medal* and *marathon* and also point out the Glossary. Tell students they have 2–4 minutes to skim read the text, depending on your group.

losers

3 This exercise demands more intensive reading, so allow sufficient time. Before starting, highlight the missing final line at the end of each story, and ask students to complete it. Remind them to look at the headings too. As students are writing the sentences alone, monitor and note the verb forms that they are using. Then students compare sentences with their partner.

Hear suggestions in whole class feedback, but focus on the ideas rather than accuracy of tenses.

Mixed ability

For **less strong students**, to facilitate this reading do one or a mixture of the following: a) students complete only two or three of the four texts; b) students write the concluding sentences in pairs, not individually c) you read aloud each story, with expression and gestures to help clarify what happened d) put the four closing sentences randomly on the board at the start of exercise 2, for students to simply select, rather than trying to write their own.

4 Students compare their lines with the original ones on SB page 130. Invite their reactions, finding out which story they find the funniest or even the saddest.

5 Handle this as a whole class, exploiting any student stories where possible.

Extend your vocabulary – *win* and *beat* (SB page 106)

Students frequently confuse these two verbs: there may be just one verb covering both meanings in their first language. Write *win* and *beat* on the board, and elicit what they mean. Try to elicit an example sentence for each.

Students read the explanation and examples on SB page 106, before completing the sentences. They check in pairs. Ask an early finisher to come and write the answers on the board.

Mixed ability

Stronger students should immediately tackle the exercise (sentences 1–6), without looking at the examples or explanations. They then check their answers against the examples and explanations. Monitor to confirm they have the right answers.

1	beats	4	beat
2	won	5	beaten
3	beat		

Grammar (SB page 107)

Focus clearly on the meaning and form of the past perfect. Break down the form on the board, eliciting components:

The officials found that he had travelled by car!

(subj + *had* + past participle)

Ask concept questions, eg *When did Lorz take the short-cut?* (*Before* he finished); *Which did he do first – cross the line or cheat?* (*cheat*). *Which does the story talk about first?* (*crossing the line*).

A time-line can help more visual students:

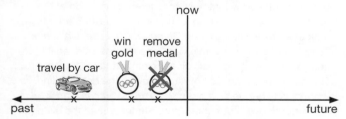

The officials found that Lorz had travelled 11 miles by car.

If events are described chronologically, this can be written in the past simple: *He started running but he cheated by getting a lift. Then he crossed the line and won the gold medal. They took the medal away.*

If not chronological, the past perfect can be used to show that one significant event / action happened earlier or to show that one action is dependent on the other, eg *They took the medal away from him because he'd cheated (earlier).*

1 Students fill in the missing gaps of the two mini texts in pairs.

Take feedback and ask further concept questions, if appropriate.

Text 1:	told, couldn't go, had lost
Text 2:	lost, had thrown, had fallen

2 Students read the example and reasons given. Try to elicit some additional reasons. Encourage students to be imaginative. Then students complete the other three examples in pairs. However, also be prepared to deal with examples that do not require this structure, eg *the match was cancelled because it was raining; maybe he had a headache.* (These are not single, completed events or states for which the speaker wants to emphasise the 'earlier' aspect).

1	Maybe it had started to snow.
2	Maybe he hadn't trained.
3	Maybe he had failed a drugs test.

Ⓖ Grammar focus

Show students the icon. Write page 148 on the board and ask them to find it. Show students the language summary on the past perfect.

You can use exercise 1 on page 149 for:

a) extra practice now
b) homework
c) review a couple of lessons from now.

The answers are on page 144 of the Teacher's Book.

Speaking (SB page 107)

1 Students read the questionnaire and add the last follow-up question in pairs.

2 This is a *Find someone who …* mingle exercise. Students first work in pairs to convert each question orally to a direct question, as well as the follow up question, (as in the example). Students just check their questions here and do not supply answers. Check random ones as a whole class.

Students stand up, mingle, ask the questions and write a different name next to each question asked, but only if they get a 'yes' answer. With a large class, you could have two mingling circles. Remind students that they need to ask a follow-up question, modelling at least two examples with two confident students. If you mingle too, this allows you to monitor effectively.

Reading extra

To extend students' knowledge of phrasal verbs, students read through the text *A Helping Hand*. They find and circle any phrasal verbs, eg *fall down, get up, run over (to someone), pick someone / something up, take someone / something away.* Elicit these onto the board. Books closed, choose three confident students to enact the story, whilst you narrate it. Students work in groups of three to do the same (runner, official, narrator).

Part 4

Speaking (SB page 108)

Put the following points on the board for students to discuss in threes:

Which of these, diet (eg meat, coffee, alcohol), exercise and work are problems for

a   *you? your country / culture?*

b   *Do you think such problems will get larger or smaller?*

c   *Is being a doctor a high-status profession in your country?*

Listen and take feedback on any interesting points.

1 Elicit from students where the people are and what is happening. Invite any other reactions, eg *Do you think she looks ill? What is he saying?*

2 Tell students they have five minutes to choose a picture and prepare a dialogue that they are going to perform to another pair. They should not write anything, or look at the dialogue on the page.

3 Students perform their dialogues to others. If one is particularly strong or amusing, then let the whole class hear it.

Reading and Listening (SB page 108)

This text is an amusing dialogue between a doctor and a patient who has not been taking care of himself.

1 🔊 **2.69** Before listening, elicit what they think the good news and the bad news might be. Encourage imaginative answers here. Stronger students could just listen, with their books closed.

> The bad news is that he isn't very fit and needs to change his eating habits.
> The good news is that he's healthy enough to go back to work.
> 🔊 **2.69** See Student's Book page 108

2 Students work in pairs to recall what the doctor said about the five areas given from memory. Monitor and see how they are doing.

If your students are struggling, let them read it a second time. (They need to be familiar with the initial conversation, in order to do exercise 3). Take feedback.

3 🔊 **2.70** Draw a rough sketch of Mr Cartwright talking to Mrs Cartwright on the board, with speech bubbles coming out of their mouths. Students listen and compare the first and second dialogues, checking in pairs. Students should focus on the content of the dialogues, not accuracy of language.

Let students listen again if they need to, and take whole class feedback. Sum up the differences in note form on one side of the board, in preparation for the grammar focus later.

> 🔊 **2.70**
> (The differences are shown in bold)
> A: Harry, is that you?
> B: Yes, yes … I'm home.
> A: Well, what did the doctor say?
> B: Err. Nothing much. **She said I was healthy**. No serious problems.
> A: Oh, that's wonderful. Did she say anything about a diet?
> B: A what?
> A: A diet.
> B: Oh, oh yes. She said, **she said … I could eat *some* red meat**. Just once a week.
> A: That's good. You do eat a lot of meat. What about salt and sugar? Shouldn't you cut down on those?
> B: Um. No, no **she didn't say anything about salt or sugar**.
> A: Oh. That's strange. What about coffee?
> B: Oh coffee, yes, coffee.
> A: You drink five cups of coffee a day. Isn't that too much?
> B: Oh yes. She told me that I could drink only … **two cups a day**.
> A: OK. And can you go back to work?
> B: Yes. I start tomorrow.

If your students need to be sensitised to intonation features, elicit how Mr Cartwright feels at different stages, eg at the start: fairly calm, not taking it very seriously; etc. Students look at phrases with 'Oh', eg *Oh good, Oh, I see, Oh, Oh no*. They listen to note how this word or phrase is said, eg if it shows surprise, happiness disappointment, acceptance, etc. Drill students on the 'Oh' phrases, saying the doctor's line immediately before as a prompt, eg You: *You can start work again tomorrow!* Students: *Oh no*. Students read the dialogue in pairs, paying attention to intonation. Students swap roles.

Grammar (SB page 109)

Refer back to the sketch on the board from exercise 3. Students finish these two sentences with the prompts (in writing), as if they were Mr Cartwright, talking to his wife: *The doctor said that I … (healthy); She told me that I … (red meat)*. Read what students are writing to see if they are familiar with the focus. Write the heading *Reported speech* up and elicit what students know about it, if anything. Refer them to the grammar section on SB page 109. Ask a strong student to read out the examples and explanatory comments.

Students go back to their own sentences and upgrade them. Elicit a few more examples based on the conversation, using the notes taken in exercise 3.

Health & Fitness

Language note

We can report someone's words directly, using quotation marks, eg *The doctor said: "Mr Cartwright, you have to stop eating so much meat"* or by using indirect speech, where tenses typically move one tense back, as shown under **Grammar**. To report things that are still true or precisely as were said, the tenses can also remain the same, even if the reporting verb is past. So, it is also possible and natural for Mr Cartwright to say: *"The doctor told me that I have to stop eating red meat and she said that I am getting too fat"*. The doctor's instructions remain valid; by keeping the same tenses, there is a sense of relevance and immediacy.

At this level, avoid indirect questions and more complicated reporting verbs, such as suggest, explain, etc.

1 First look at the example given together and highlight the use of quotation marks in direct speech, as well as the change of pronoun. Students do an additional example: *She told me that I had to stop smoking* ➔ *"You have to stop smoking"*.

Students work alone to change the examples into direct speech, before checking in pairs and then with the conversation on SB page 108.

1 "I'm fine."
2 "You aren't very fit."
3 "You can't eat any more red meat."
4 "You also need to do some exercise."

2 Tell students this time they do the opposite, changing the examples from direct to reported speech. Students read the example. Do another example together to further clarify and remind students to use the pronouns 'he' or 'she'. Students work in pairs. Take whole class feedback.

1 The doctor said I didn't have a fever.
2 The doctor said she had ordered some more tests.
3 The patient said he wasn't feeling very well at the moment.
4 The doctor said going to work wasn't a good idea.
5 The doctor said she could give me a sick note.
6 The patient said he had a bad headache.

G Grammar focus

Show students the icon. Write page 148 on the board and ask them to find it. Show students the language summary on reported statements.

You can use exercise 1 on page 149 for:

a) extra practice now
b) homework
c) review a couple of lessons from now.

The answers are on page 144 of the Teacher's Book.

Vocabulary (SB page 109)

1 Students complete the gaps with the appropriate reporting verb. Approach this as a test-teach exercise, allowing the students to work alone and then in pairs to complete the gap-fill.

asked	told	told	said	said	asked	told

2 🔵 **2.71** Students listen to check their answers. Students re-tell you what the man's problem is and the doctor's solution.

🔵 **2.71** See Student's Book page 109

3 Students refer back to the text to help them complete the rules of use for these three verbs. Students work in pairs. Check their conclusions. When they have finished, get students to re-read the joke in pairs. One of the students reads the main part of the story, and the other reads just the direct speech.

After practising, ask students to try to remember the joke without looking.

a tell b say c ask

Speaking (SB page 109)

1 Students work alone to read and choose just four of the seven questions. In pairs they ask and answer. Students take very brief notes on their partner's responses. To make this language practice more authentic, if it suits your situation, you could ask students to keep this information and wait for one or two days, thus making the backshift in tenses a more natural choice.

Ask students to work with a new partner to report what their partner said, using *say* or *tell*, having elicited a couple of examples.

TEACH GLOBAL THINK LOCAL   Extra activity

For students needing further practice of reported speech and 'say' and 'tell', give out slips of paper with 'secrets' on. Write a mixture of secrets that might appeal to your group, using genuinely secret-like examples, eg *I actually already speak fluent English; I've been married three times; I hope to have at least 6 children; I'm not going to do my homework this week,* etc. Students work in groups of four. They memorise their own secrets, then whisper them to their neighbour, who passes it on to the next group member, and so on. Students try to remember all their friends' secrets, then report them, in a 'secret diary', writing them down, eg *Jan said / told me that … They* compare notes at the end.

Function globally: describing illness

These lessons in *Global* are designed to provide students with **immediately** useful functional language. They all follow a similar format.

Warm up (SB page 110)

Aim: to introduce the topic via a quick speaking task or picture work.

Tips:

- Do not over-correct here, especially in speaking activities.
- Encourage students to use what language they can at this stage.

1	temporarily relieves minor pains
2	pregnant
3	consult
4	keep out of reach of children
5	may cause drowsiness

Listening (SB page 110)

Aim: to present the functional language in context via a conversation or series of conversations.

Tips:

- Ask students to read the questions first before listening.
- Play the recording all the way through for each task (there are always two tasks).
- For multiple conversations pause the recording after each one.
- If students find it very difficult, play the recording a final time and allow them to read the audioscript at the back of the book.

> He has a sore throat. He buys tablets for it.
>
> 🎧 **2.72**
>
> A: Hello, can I help?
> B: Yes, I erm, need something for a sore throat … It really hurts.
> A: Well, we have this syrup or these tablets.
> B: Which is better?
> A: They're both good. The syrup is more expensive.
> B: Oh, well … I'll take the tablets then. How many do I take?
> A: Just one …
> B: Sorry. I'm sorry. And how often should I take it?
> A: Just one every four to six hours. Take it before mealtimes. Are you allergic to any medicine?
> B: No.
> A: Then you'll be fine with this.
> B: Can I get some antibiotics too?
> A: I'm afraid you need a prescription for that.

> B: Oh.
> A: You know, you should really see a doctor if that cough continues.
> B: I know. I know
> A: Anything else?
> B: No thanks.
> A: That'll be 4.50 then please.

Language focus: talking about illness (SB page 110)

Aim: to draw students' attention to the items of functional language.

Tips:

- Make sure students have time to understand the form and meaning of the phrases, but you needn't translate them word for word.
- Students should be able to pronounce these phrases intelligibly, so drill them.

1	need something
2	have
3	Which is
4	do I take
5	should I take it
6	Take it
7	Are you … medicine?
8	you need
9	should really see … that cough continues

Speaking (SB page 110)

Aim: to allow students an opportunity to use this language in a meaningful, real-world context.

Tips:

- There is sometimes a choice of task. Any task involving reading a script will be easier than a task involving making students' own scripts. This gives you flexibility for mixed ability classes.
- Give students time to prepare this activity, and circulate and monitor carefully.
- Correct sensitively, paying particular attention to the target language.
- If time allows, ask students to repeat the task, but with a new partner.

Health & Fitness

Global English

These lessons in *Global* have two main goals. The first is to give you and your students interesting information about English and language in general. The second goal is to provide students with practice in different kinds of reading comprehension tasks that they are likely to encounter in future study (for example, exams).

TEACH GLOBAL THINK LOCAL Lead-in

Play an example of a sports commentary, from the TV or radio or other source. (If possible, show / play two different sports commentaries, e.g. tennis and football). Elicit the job: *sports commentator* and what the example is: *sports commentary*. Discuss with students: *Do you think this is an easy job? What skills do you need? Which is more difficult to commentate on: football, horse-racing or snooker? Why?*

Warm up (SB page 111)

Aim: to engage students with the topic, and highlight potentially difficult vocabulary in the text.

Tips:

- Be generous in helping students here with any unknown words in the first task.
- Ask students to relate this task, wherever possible, to similar events or texts in their own lives. This will help them with the reading.
- You may want to give your students an overview of the text before they read, possibly even in their first language. Make it interesting and involving.

Reading (SB page 111)

Aim: to provide students with interesting information about English, and reading exam practice skills.

Tips:

- Be ready to help less confident readers, explaining words or ideas in simpler terms if necessary.
- Get students to read through the whole text once first before doing the tasks.
- Many of these texts have been graded slightly, or not at all. There is a glossary of difficult words. Get students to read that first and reassure them that you do not expect them to understand every word or idea.
- There are two tasks. The first is an easier task, often focusing on the gist of the passage. The second is a more difficult task, similar to reading exam questions.

1

Topics mentioned: sports commentary; style of speaking; English grammar; new vocabulary

2

1 Detailed knowledge of the sport, keen observational skills, the ability to think on your feet, and above-average linguistic skills

2 They're off!; in the lead; into the straight they come.

3 Beckham to Kaka ... back to Beckham ...

4 yoga; pilates; yogalates

5 *exertainment*; *exergaming*

Language focus (SB page 111)

Aim: to highlight an interesting or useful aspect of language in the text.

Tips:

- The language focused on here is to raise students' awareness; do not expect them to produce it immediately.
- This language is not tested or reviewed in future units, which means you have more flexibility with this material as to when and where you use it.

1

1 b	2 a

Speaking (SB page 111)

Aim: for students to relate the material in the reading to their own language, culture and experiences.

Tips:

- This is a short speaking activity and can be done in whole class mode or in small groups.
- Wherever possible, ask students to think of and provide examples in their own language but explain them in English too.

TEACH GLOBAL THINK LOCAL Extra activity

Put these fictitious sports / activities on the board, and ask students to guess what they might be in groups of three:

multi-golf (golf played in a team?)

water tennis (tennis played in pool or with a ball filled with water?)

weightwalking (walking with weights on your arms and legs?)

yogabathe (yoga in the sun?)

Early finishers could make up a couple of their own, for others to guess.

Writing an online post

Reading (SB page 112)

1 Put Carla's written question on the board. Explain this is from an online forum, and check students know what this is. Students in pairs brainstorm at least four possible suggestions for Carla, without reading the suggestions in the Student's book. Then they read the response and tick off the suggestions.

walk or cycle to work	take exercise at home
go for a walk	have an exercise plan
take up a new hobby / sport	

2 Students discuss the best and the weakest suggestion from Darina, giving reasons. Take whole class feedback on their views.

Writing skills: giving examples (SB page 112)

1 Students find three places where they can add the three phrases, initially alone and then in pairs. In whole class feedback, put the posting up on the board / screen so that you can add in the missing words visually, if possible.

> (suggested answers)
>
> If you don't have much time, just try to be more active in your daily life. <u>For example,</u> you could walk or cycle to work instead of taking the bus or driving.
>
> If you have free time in the evening, consider joining an evening class. You could take up yoga, martial arts or dancing, <u>for instance.</u>
>
> Alternatively, you could buy exercise equipment <u>like a</u> rowing machine or an exercise bike.

2 Students add the correct phrases into the gaps.

> 1 for instance / for example
> 2 like
> 3 For instance / For example

Language note

For instance and *for example* are essentially interchangeable. These phrases need a comma before or after them, depending on their position in the sentence. See sentences 1 and 3 in exercise 2, where these phrases occur at the beginning and end.

In contrast, *like* does not take a comma after it, as shown in sentence 2. It is possible to put in a comma <u>before</u> *like* here (to match a short pause and drop in intonation in spoken English). *Like* is not used at the start or end of the sentence and is used in the same way as *such as*. It tends to be used in informal speech and writing.

Language focus: giving advice (SB page 112)

1 Students should search the response to find and underline advice language. Elicit examples, writing them on the board, eg *you should + verb*. You could write up any new, unfamiliar ways of giving advice in a different colour.

> <u>try to</u> be more active
>
> <u>You could</u> walk or cycle
>
> <u>why not</u> get off one stop early
>
> <u>try to</u> go for a walk
>
> <u>consider</u> join<u>ing</u> an evening class. <u>You could</u> take up yoga
>
> <u>you could</u> buy exercise equipment
>
> <u>you should</u> have a clear plan
>
> <u>you should</u> exercise for a short time, but regularly.
>
> <u>don't</u> give up!

2 Students correct the sentences on their own, using the board as a reference. Take whole class feedback. Note that 'why don't you …?' is not used in Darina's letter.

> 1 Why don't you see a doctor?
> 2 Consider going for a long walk.
> 3 You could start a sport.
> 4 Just try to be positive.
> 5 You should watch less TV.

Preparing to write (SB page 112)

1 Students in pairs choose a problem from the list. Add some problems relevant to your group if possible (be sensitive though!), eg *I'm worried about my exams and it is affecting my health; I can't stop smoking; I feel stressed at work and I find it hard to relax*, etc. Students think of at least three different suggestions, with examples, for their problem.

2 Re-group the students with another pair so that they can compare and share ideas. This activity provides further material for the writing.

Writing (SB page 112)

Students work independently on this task, either in class or at home. Remind them of the new language for giving advice and refer them to the *Suggesting alternatives* section, if necessary showing how these phrases work in a sentence using the context of Darina's letter.

Depending on your students, remind them how to organise their work, referring to the example: there are three paragraphs, one for each main idea. Monitor and assist as students are writing. For homework, students type this up, together with the initial problem, for authenticity and clarity. Students read each others' responses next lesson.

Global review

These lessons in *Global* are intended to review some of the language and topics covered in the unit. They follow a similar format.

Grammar and Vocabulary (SB page 113)

Aim: to review the main grammar and vocabulary in the unit.

Tips:

- Students can do these exercises alone or in pairs, in class or at home, depending on their learning style and your teaching situation.
- Ask students to read the questions first to establish the grammar and vocabulary areas which are focused on.
- Encourage students to check their own answers by looking back through the unit.

Grammar 1	Grammar 2
1 had to, couldn't	1 developed, had founded
2 didn't have to	2 felt sick, had eaten
Grammar 3	
1 was working too hard and didn't take enough exercise	
2 would give up my job and take up jogging	
Vocabulary	

1 matter	6 have
2 feel	7 hurts
3 sore	8 take
4 see	9 beat
5 have	10 won

Speaking and Writing (SB page 113)

Aim: to provide extra speaking and writing practice that will review and consolidate language presented in the unit.

Tips:

- Before speaking encourage students to think first about what language they need to focus on from the unit, and a good way to start their conversation.
- Before they do the writing practice, ask students to either make notes or discuss ideas with a partner to activate useful language.
- Monitor as students are working and note any points for feedback at the end.

Study skills

Using your dictionary: exploring collocations (SB page 113)

1 Put the following example on the board: *He's feeling terrible. He has a ___ fever.* Elicit the possibilities and then give the answer: *high*. Elicit the word 'collocation'. Ask students to try and find other words for *very* that go with *ill*: *He's very ill*, eg *seriously*. Students then read the examples and Exercise 1.

2 Check your own class dictionaries before the lesson to see if the answers are provided there or use the Macmillan online dictionary: www.macmillandictionary.com

Students predict the verb that does not collocate, then check in pairs. Students should initially look up the noun or adjective, not the verb.

3 Students work in pairs to choose the collocation which sounds right, then check in the dictionary. Advise students to first look up the part which is not in italics. At the end, put the collocations on the board. Leave these on the board for later (see end of lesson).

4 Put the four words: *catch, diet, sore, recover from* on different parts of the board, circled. Students look up collocations and add them to the appropriate place on the board (maximum of six per word). See SB page 8 for an example of a word map.

To round off the lesson, rub out the collocates from the board record (in exercise 3 the part in italics in the SB; in exercise 4 the newly added words). Students in pairs recall the missing words, eg *be violently _____; a _____ diet*. Check answers orally.

UNIT 10 New & Old

Coursebook

Unit 10	Language	Texts	Communicative skills
Part 1 SB page 114	Vocabulary New words in context Grammar Defining relative clauses	Reading / Listening *Brave new words*	Speaking Describing new words in language Guessing meanings of words in context Writing Writing definitions for new words
Part 2 SB page 116	Vocabulary Places Extend your vocabulary – words that mean *new* Grammar Definite article *(the)*	Reading *New places in a new world*	Speaking Making a word quiz for places Talking about place names with *New* Discussing ideas for quotes about America
Part 3 SB page 118	Vocabulary Transport Pronunciation Consonant clusters Grammar Verb form review	Reading *Old but loved; the Trabant* *The Model T*	Speaking Describing forms of transport and preferences Finding out about experiences of travelling by car
Part 4 SB page 120	Vocabulary Games Extend your vocabulary – words that mean *make* Grammar *Both*, *neither* Pronunciation Sentence stress and intonation	Listening A talk about two classic board games: Scrabble and Monopoly	Speaking Talking about experiences of board games Playing a board game
Function globally	Ending a conversation Students prepare and practise ways of starting and ending conversations		
Global voices	Listening to people expressing opinions about favourite words and expressions in English Guessing words from definitions The uses of *you know*		
Writing	Writing a report on studies Using *a / an* for new information; giving reasons using *because* or *as* Students organise ideas and describe language activities to write a report		
Global review	Grammar and vocabulary review Extra speaking and writing practice		
Study skills	Students learn how to evaluate their pronunciation and strategies for improvement		

Additional resources

eWorkbook	Interactive and printable grammar, vocabulary, listening and pronunciation practice Extra reading and writing practice Additional downloadable listening and audio material
Teacher's Resource CD	Communication activity worksheets to print and photocopy
Go global: ideas for further research	**New** – Ask students to find more new words and their explanations at the *Macmillan Dictionary* site **Old** – Ask students to find images of old things they like (eg cars, toys, traditions) using a web image search. Make a slideshow called "Old but Loved" and present it to the class

Part 1

Lead-in

Draw an ice cream on the board and write up the word. Say / elicit the word 'compound noun'. Bring in a collection of 'compound noun' objects, and display them. Choose compounds that students probably do not know, but may be able to guess from the parts, eg *tea bag, tea spoon, board pen, soap dish, face cloth, wedding ring, pencil case, bottle opener, hot water bottle, address book, cough sweet, sun cream, soft toy*, etc. Students work in pairs to list the compounds. Check open class at the end.

Reading and Listening (SB page 114)

This listening is an interview with a dictionary writer who describes the nature and origin of new words in the English language.

1 Write the first two words of the book title on the board: *Brave New*_____ and see if students can remember the name of Huxley's book 'Brave New World', if necessary referring them to SB Unit 4, page 46. (The title here is a play on words).

Students refer to the cover on page 115 and spot the difference in the headings. Elicit what this book might be about. Let students read the introduction to find out more. Then elicit what the book is about.

Mixed ability

To help **less strong students** understand this extract, hold up your mobile phone, and ask students these three questions: *In what way is this mobile similar to language? Why does language change? Do all words change?* Give students a couple more minutes to re-read the text, if necessary, then take feedback.

2 🔊 **2.73** Before listening, students read the short summary of the author, Kerry Maxwell. Tell them they are going to hear an interview with her and let students first read the list of topics. Check their understanding of these topics via examples, eg *abbreviations (FCE), combining words (sofa-bed)*.

Play the recording. Let students compare their answers before feedback. Students may need to listen again first.

1 combining words
2 combining parts of words
3 abbreviations
4 giving new meanings to words
5 borrowing words

🔊 **2.73**

A So, your book Brave New Words is all about new words in English. How do new words appear?

B One of the most common ways of making new words is simply to combine two words which already exist. So for example in the past we had texts, and we had messages, now with mobile phones we have …

A Text messages.

B Yes. That's right. Another common way of making a new word is to combine parts of words. Consider brunch. Brunch is a meal that people can have at 11 o'clock in the morning, a combination of breakfast and lunch.

A So combinations are how new words are made.

B There are other ways too. Abbreviations, for example, are a common way of making new words. Do you know what a digital versatile disc is?

A Errr …

B A DVD …?

A Of course.

A Yes, the abbreviation becomes the new word. Another way is to give a word a new meaning. We have new meanings for all kinds of words connected to computers – for example mouse and virus.

B Or windows.

A Yes. Finally, we can borrow words from other languages. An example of this would be a tsunami – a Japanese word which became very frequent in English after the natural disaster in Asia in 2004.

B Will all these new words continue to exist?

A Maybe not. Some will continue, others won't. But the way we create these new words … combination, abbreviation, giving old words new meanings or borrowing words … well these are going to be with us for a long time.

3 Give students time to look at the example words in pairs to work out which categories they might fall into. Then they listen to check.

1 combining words – text messages
2 combining parts of words – brunch
3 abbreviations – DVD
4 giving new meanings to words – mouse, virus, windows
5 borrowing words – tsunami

4 Put students together in same language groups if possible. They discuss new words in their own language.

Ask students which category from exercise 3 these words fit into. In whole class feedback, they share any interesting examples.

Vocabulary (SB page 114)

1 Students look at the pictures and deduce the bold words from the context in pairs. If students use these words in their own language, this task will be easy. Elicit from students the word class of the three words, eg *google* (v) /ˈguːgəl/; *carbon footprint* (n); *sudoku* (n) /suˈdəʊkuː/. (Students may already know *google*, but not as a verb).

2 Students find the definitions. Take feedback if you feel it is necessary.

> to Google – to search for something on the internet using the search engine Google
>
> carbon footprint – the amount of greenhouse gases that an activity produces
>
> sudoku – a number game from Japan which is now popular in English newspapers

3 Students ask and answer the four questions in pairs.

Grammar (SB page 115)

Write the following prompts from the three example sentences on the board, with books closed. Monitor as students try to reconstruct them in pairs. This focuses students on the target language and shows you how much they already know:

Tsunami … Japanese word … (be) used frequently in English
Brunch … meal … people (can have) at 11am
Kerry Maxwell … someone … (write) books about new words

Show students how *which* or *that* can substitute each other in the examples. Ask students when *who* is used. Students then read the generalisations under **Grammar**.

1 Students work alone on the exercise, before checking in pairs. For feedback, simply ask students which sentences use *who*.

1		2		3	
a	which	a	who	a	who
b	which	b	which	b	which
c	who	c	who	c	which

2 Students work in pairs to select the right definition. In feedback, students read out the whole sentence, with the relative clause: *We think …*, thus drilling themselves on the target language.

1 a	2 c	3 b

G Grammar focus

Show students the icon. Write page 150 on the board and ask them to find it. Show students the language summary on defining relative clauses.

You can use exercise 1 on page 151 for:

a) extra practice now
b) homework
c) review a couple of lessons from now.

The answers are on page 144 of the Teacher's Book.

Language note

These examples are called 'defining' or 'identifying' relative clauses. They give information about the noun, and are also sometimes called 'adjectival clauses'. At this level, avoid going into issues such as when to omit the relative pronouns, unless asked:

Brunch is a meal (which/that/-) people can have at 11 am.

'Brunch' is the object of the verb in the relative clause so can be omitted.

Students often misuse *what* in relative clauses: ~~that's the shop what I like~~. They might also identify something which has already been defined: ~~My puppy which I bought is sick~~, instead of: *The puppy which I bought is sick.*

Writing (SB page 115)

Do a class example together on the board, if necessary, with a made-up amusing word, such as 'peacher'. Elicit what the meanings of this nonsense word might be, eg *A peacher… a) is a teacher who likes peaches b) is a person who picks peaches c) is someone who knows a lot about fruit and vegetables (peas and peaches).*

Students do the same task, with the real words provided. They write two other definitions for their two words (explain that the real definition is given on SB pages 127 and 129). Monitor as they are writing and assist, ensuring that they use the target language. If they need to, students can write their definitions with a partner.

Re-group students. They then test their new partner by reading out / showing all three definitions and the partner identifies the correct one.

TEACH GLOBAL THINK LOCAL Extra activity

Divide students into pairs, A and B. Give them their respective list of words (see below), ensuring they keep it secret. Students define their words (without saying the word) to their partner, but first let them read their list and check any unknown words with you or a dictionary. Students use relative clauses to define the word: *it's a thing that / which …, it's someone who … .* Give a model to start and ban gestures, realia or drawings. The winning pair is the one who finishes their lists first.

A	B
doorbell	calculator
chimney	dictionary
memory stick	salt
nephew	waiter
landlord	babysitter

Part 2

TEACH GLOBAL
THINK LOCAL
Lead-in

Write up place names on the board from recent news events – local, national and international. Students discuss in threes why these places have been in the news lately. In class feedback, elicit why the places are significant and also where exactly the village / town / country is.

Vocabulary (SB page 116)

1 Students work in pairs to put the words in order. Make dictionaries available. As you elicit the answers in whole class feedback, highlight the main stress (first syllable of all the nouns). Drill if necessary. If you need to check students' understanding, then use your school address or local places (for *city, state, town, village, capital*).

> village, town, city, capital, state / province, country, continent, planet

Language note

In Britain, the equivalent of *state* and *province* is 'county'.

2 Students find the odd one out on their own, before discussing their choices in pairs, giving reasons. This way students will use the target words, eg *capital*.

1	Armenia	4	Canada
2	Italy	5	Liverpool
3	Singapore		

3 Students do the same task as in exercise 2. If necessary, put students in pairs to produce their examples. Then pairs can split and work with another partner to spot the odd one out. Early finishers can write more than one example.

Reading (SB page 116)

This reading describes various states and cities in North America.

1 Show a map of North America, quickly asking one or two questions, eg *Show me where Florida is; Is New York on the east or west coast?*

Students work in pairs to brainstorm the list of places (states or cities). In feedback, hear the longest list.

2 Elicit any American places starting with 'New'. Students then read the text. This initial task will require most students to do more than simply skim. Students will need to read and refer to the map. Allocate between 4–8 minutes, depending on the students and their geographical knowledge.

Paragraph	1	New World	4	New Mexico
	2	New York	5	New Orleans
	3	Newfoundland	6	New Jersey

3 Students complete the sentences with the place names. Ask students to first read through the sentences to see if there are any unknown words, eg *destroy* and *colony*, before reading the text again. Students check their answers in pairs.

1	Newfoundland	4	New Jersey
2	New Mexico	5	New York
3	New Orleans	6	Newfoundland

4 Students read the text to find the words described. These words are likely to be new for students, so they will be deducing words from context. To help students, indicate the location of these words by providing the paragraph numbers: 1 (para 5); 2 (2); 3 (4); 4 (6). Check students' understanding in feedback, eliciting the word class. Highlight the stress on *unique* /juˈniːk/ and *commute* /kəˈmjuːt/.

1	birthplace	3	unique
2	to found	4	to commute

5 Students give suggestions for place names with 'new' as a whole class. Students should also consider places in their first or other languages too, translating the word 'new'.

> New Haven, New Delhi

Background note

North America is the northern continent of the two Americas. These are often considered as one continent, America. The United States of America, otherwise known as America or the US, comprises 50 states which are mainly in the North American sub-continent. Alaska is a separate state in the north-west, bordered by Canada and Russia. The string of islands called Hawaii in the Pacific, is also a US state.

Extend your vocabulary – words that mean *new* (SB page 116)

You could start by allowing students to look up the word 'new' in a mono-lingual dictionary, to show how many uses there are. Students read the nouns and their collocations on SB page 116, then complete the task. Students compare answers and check with you if there are any discrepancies. Remind students that these alternatives are important when writing and speaking English, for variety.

1	brand new
2	innovative
3	latest

Grammar (SB page 117)

1 Slowly read out all the rules in the grammar section. Identify the first two examples (the highlighted words) together, then students complete the matching task, initially independently. Students check in pairs. Take whole class feedback.

a	the Big Apple, the population, the birthplace
b	the province, the state, the city
c	the United States of America
d	the most famous city

2 Do the first example together. Students complete the gap-fill with a partner, using the rules from Grammar to support their choice.

New England:	a	the	the	–		
New Zealand:	a	the	the			
New Guinea:	an	the	the	The	the	the

Ⓖ Grammar focus

Show students the icon. Write page 150 on the board and ask them to find it. Show students the language summary on the definite article.

You can use exercise 1 on page 151 for:

a) extra practice now
b) homework
c) review a couple of lessons from now.

The answers are on page 144 of the Teacher's Book.

Language note

Articles in English can continue to cause problems until higher levels, so keep the focus limited. Articles often work in different ways in other languages and students also tend to forget these small grammar words when producing English as they rarely impede communication. Typical mistakes are: ~~Man was very pleased~~ (missing article); ~~I saw a girl and she spoke to me. A girl's mother then came out~~ (failure to refer back); ~~She wears the glasses~~ and ~~I like to eat the sugar too much~~ (this makes the reference to glasses and sugar specific rather than general).

Speaking (SB page 117)

1 Write up: *I think America …* and elicit possible ways to finish the sentence orally as a whole class. Students work in pairs to read and finish the incomplete quotations, all said by famous people. Students then compare their endings with a partner from a different pair. Hear one or two examples as a whole class.

If students find this difficult, write up the second halves on the board or a hand-out randomly. Students simply match up the halves (you can add one or two extra distractors too).

2 Students could then work with different students, in threes, to compare their suggestions. They then respond to the two questions given.

3 Students read the originals on SB page 130. Be prepared to clarify who the speakers were, if students are interested. Give students the opportunity to ask or comment on the quotations.

Background note

Ronald Reagan (1911–2004) was the 40th US president (1981–89). He was a well-known actor before entering politics. He is generally considered a popular president.

Garrison Keillor (1942–) is an author (of books for adults and children), columnist, humorist and radio host.

George Bernard Shaw (1856–1950) was an Irish playwright, literary critic and political activist for socialist causes. He wrote more than 60 plays, usually dealing with social issues, and with a humorous element.

Sigmund Freud (1856–1939) was a Jewish Austrian who had a tremendous influence on psychology, based on his understanding and research into the human mind.

Barack Obama (1961–) became America's 44th president, sworn in in January 2009, the first ever black man to hold this position.

TEACH GLOBAL THINK LOCAL Homework extra

Students choose a state in the US that they would like to know more about, then do a web search. The following areas could be researched: *size, geography, population, natural resources, industries, famous for ......, any additional information of interest.* Students should prepare to talk for at least three minutes, and use a map / sketch to show its location. Next lesson, students work in threes to exchange information.

Part 3

TEACH GLOBAL
THINK LOCAL
Lead-in

Tell students about your car: make, model, what you like about it, how long you have had it, why you bought it, etc. Ask students to write down a) a car they have (or their parents have) b) a car they'd like to have (money no object!) c) a car they would never buy, for whatever reason. Students discuss and compare their answers in threes.

Vocabulary and Speaking (SB page 118)

1 Students can discuss the different forms of transport pictured, commenting on how they differ from the same forms of transport today. Hear any interesting points in whole class feedback. Note that an underground train is often referred to as *the metro* in other European countries (in Britain it is *the tube*), and *the subway* in the US.

a	plane
b	taxi
c	bicycle (penny farthing)
d	coach / bus (horse drawn carriage)
e	motorbike
f	rowing boat
g	train
h	the underground

2 Elicit the meaning of 'tracks' before students start. Handle this exercise as a quick, whole class activity: ask the four questions out loud and nominate individuals to respond.

1	wheels – a car, a train, a bicycle, a plane, a taxi, an underground train, a bus
2	tracks – a train, an underground train
3	wings – a plane
4	an engine – a car, a train, a motorbike, a plane, a taxi, an underground train, a bus

3 Do the first example together. Students work alone, then compare answers in pairs. When checking together, drill students on the phrasal verbs, to show linking and weak forms:

You get on a /ə/ plane but you get in and /ən/ get out of /əv/ a /ə/ car.

drive: a car, a bus
ride: a motorbike, a bicycle,
get on/off: a plane, a bus, a motorbike, a bicycle
get in/out of: a car

4 Students discuss the four questions in pairs. If students need support, then provide extra questions (see below).

TEACH GLOBAL
THINK LOCAL
Extra activity

If you need extra questions in speaking task Exercise 4, provide these, either on the board or on slips of paper which you can pass quietly to students:

What's the best way to get around in your town / area and the country as a whole?

What's the best / worst time to travel in your country?

Are roads safe in your country? Which aspect of transport would you like the government to spend money on? (services, roads, safety, etc)

If students respond well to some of these, take some whole class feedback.

Pronunciation (SB page 118)

1 🔊 **2.74** Students listen and repeat the consonant clusters.

🔊 **2.74**
/pl/, plane
/tr/, tracks
/st/, stop
/str/, street

2 🔊 **2.75** Before listening, you read out the four sentences yourself, as quickly as possible. Let students read the tongue twisters in their heads before listening to the sentences and repeating them. Students try to say them as fast as possible in pairs. Monitor and assist with individuals' pronunciation problems, where appropriate. Some students will find the task more difficult than others, depending on their first language.

🔊 **2.75** See Student's Book, page 118

Reading (SB page 118)

This reading describes facts relating to the Trabant, including its features, its history and its popularity.

1 Show students the photo of the Trabant (SB page 119). If you would like more pictures, do an image search with the key words: *Trabant*. Elicit from students what they know about this car.

Pre-teach: *communist* (adj); *fan* (n); *nostalgic* (adj) (see glossary); *speed* (n), then students complete exercise 1 in pairs. They circle the words they think will come up.

2 🔊 **2.76** Students read and listen and find out if their predictions were right. If you want students to merely scan the text for the target words, then give a time limit of 4–6 minutes and play the recording in exercise 3.

Ask them to underline any of the words they find from exercise 1 in the text. Be aware that students will probably get little sense of the overall meaning. In feedback, just elicit the eight words mentioned.

> communist, Germany, smoke, pollution, fans, jokes, nostalgic, speed

TEACH GLOBAL THINK LOCAL Mixed ability

Particularly **for less strong students**, provide this comprehension activity at this point, to help them cope with the following task (exercise 3). Ask students to find out what these points refer to and to compare answers in pairs:

more than 3,000,000
fellow traveller
1957
duroplast
Russia
112km
pollution
fan clubs
50th anniversary

3 Give students more time to complete this comprehension task, eg 8–12 minutes. Pairs work together to finish off and compare answers.

Early finishers read the jokes to themselves, and prepare to read them out to the others at the end.

> 1 it needs 20 seconds to go from 0 to 100km; it produces 5 times more carbon monoxide than modern European cars; it makes a lot of noise.
>
> 2 they are collectors' items; there are many fan clubs; the smell of Trabi exhaust smoke has been sold on the internet.

4 If students need some ideas for the second question, give the following prompts: *toys or games which you no longer see; food which you no longer have / buy; clothes; vehicles,* etc. Give personal examples to help.

TEACH GLOBAL THINK LOCAL Homework extra

Students research everyday objects used 100–200 years ago. Show students an example, using a picture of a mangle (US: 'wringer'), explaining to students how it was used to get water out of newly washed, wet clothes. Students similarly think of an object, eg how people used to iron, wash, cook, communicate, write, treat illnesses, etc. They research this on the internet (or use other sources) and also do an image search. Next lesson students come prepared with a visual, and talk about their everyday object for 1–2 minutes in groups.

Grammar (SB page 119)

1 This exercise is consolidation, revising verb structures studied in earlier units.

Students find examples of the verb forms in the Trabant text, working on their own. They then work in pairs to compare their examples and at the same time discuss why that verb form is used in each case. Students could talk in their first language about these points, if they wish.

> regular past tense verbs: *appeared; needed; produced; called; celebrated*
>
> irregular past tense verbs: *was; made; had*
>
> continuous: *They are still driving*
>
> going to future: *there are going to be celebrations*
>
> present perfect: *have/has been; have become*
>
> past simple passive; *were made*
>
> real conditional: *if this kind of popularity continues … will have the last laugh*

2 Let students decide if they want to work alone or in pairs from the start. They compare and discuss answers. Monitor and try to establish which parts are causing difficulties.

If necessary, to help less strong students, provide two possible choices for each answer on the board, for example: 1) *exists* or *has existed*; 2) *was being* or *was*.

In feedback, check students' understanding by asking 'why' questions, eg *Why is the past simple used there? Why is the passive used?*

> has existed
>
> was
>
> was built
>
> wanted
>
> cost
>
> could go / went
>
> had produced
>
> started
>
> are
>
> drive

3 Most of these questions are for drivers. You could adapt this for another form of transport, depending on your students' situations. Students work in pairs to make the questions.

Monitor and assist, asking relevant concept questions. Take whole class feedback. Drill some of the questions, focusing on natural sentence stress and connected speech.

1	did
2	Do
3	was
4	have ever travelled
5	have ever travelled
6	Have, had
7	could have, would you choose
8	Is
9	Is
10	is

Ⓖ Grammar focus

Show students the icon. Write page 150 on the board and ask them to find it. Show students the verb form review.

You can use exercise 1 on page 151 for:

a) extra practice now
b) homework
c) review a couple of lessons from now.

The answers are on page 144 of the Teacher's Book.

Speaking (SB page 119)

Give students a minute to circle their chosen six questions.

Encourage students to ask at least one follow-on question for each one they ask, giving the following example: *When did you get your driver's licence?* → *How old were you? / Did you pass first time?* Monitor as students are talking and note down any areas of language for remedial work afterwards.

Early finishers can ask the other remaining questions from exercise 3, or change partners to re-do the task.

Part 4

Listening (SB page 120)

TEACH GLOBAL THINK LOCAL Lead-in

If possible, bring in some genuine board games, to stimulate interest. Talk about these together (briefly eliciting / explaining how you play, the aim, etc.) Students think of a game they know well – a board game, a card game or even an outdoor game. Students can draw a mini-sketch of the game if appropriate. Assign two minutes for students to consider how to explain their game. Students work in threes to explain their game in turn. Monitor and note down any language areas of relevance to the topic. This activity highlights what games-related language students know already. It also revises modal verbs in context.

This listening is a talk about Scrabble and Monopoly: the origins of these two famous games and the features they share.

1 Students look at the pictures. Discuss the two questions in pairs. When they have finished, elicit three or four things that the two games on the right have in common, if students are familiar with them, eg *they both use a board.* This prepares them for the listening. See if they can spot the spelling mistake in the picture!

2 **2.77** Students listen for similarities and compare answers. Monitor and note if students are using, misusing or avoiding the target language (see later under Grammar: *both, neither*). Do not highlight this yet though.

They have seven things in common according to the talk:

1 invented during the Depression
2 inventors American
3 inventors didn't have a job
4 made the game by hand
5 games were not accepted by the toy companies at first
6 games are played on a board by two or more people
7 games are very popular and very successful around the world

2.77

In 1929 many people in the United States suddenly lost their jobs. This was the beginning of what Americans call the Great Depression, and it lasted for about four years. During the Great Depression, two of the most famous board games in the world were invented: Monopoly and Scrabble. While the games are very different, the story behind each one is similar. Alfred Butts, the inventor of Scrabble, and Charles Durrow, the inventor of Monopoly, were both American.

Neither inventor had a job. Butts had lost his job as an architect in 1929, and Durrow was an unemployed sales representative in 1933.

At the beginning, the inventors made every edition of their game by hand.

Neither game was accepted by toy companies at first. They said that Monopoly was too complicated, and that nobody would be interested in Scrabble.

Both games are played on a board, and can be played by two or more people.

Both games have been extremely popular: according to its makers, more than 750 million people have played Monopoly, and two hundred million copies of Scrabble are sold every year.

Both of them are successful worldwide. They are published in over 25 languages today, and are available in more than 80 countries.

3 Students first look at the words and numbers. With their partner they share any information they already know. Then students listen. Pause the recording or replay it as necessary: students need to listen for specific details here.

Take whole class feedback and give more details/help in particular with *Great Depression* and *by hand* (these are not really explained in the text itself).

Great Depression: a time in the USA when a lot of people suddenly lost their jobs

architect: Alfred Butts was an architect

by hand: the inventors made their games without using machines

two or more: the number of players for each game

750 million +: the number of people who have played Monopoly

200 million: number of copies of Scrabble sold every year

80: number of countries where the games are available

25: number of languages the games are published in

Extend your vocabulary – words that mean *make* (SB page 120)

TEACH GLOBAL THINK LOCAL **Alternative procedure**

For variety, manage this exercise as a wall dictation. Stick the five sentences from the exercise (plus the three below, to make eight) around the room, on eight separate strips of paper:

6 *She made a lovely cake for his birthday.*
7 *The little boy made a sandcastle on the beach.*
8 *Sales of the new computer made a lot of money for the company.*

Students work in pairs. As stand up, find a sentence and dictate four of the sentences to Bs before changing roles to complete the last four sentences. Students underline the verb *make* in each case. They look at the exercise in the SB,

to find an appropriate substitute in each case from the list. Tell students there is one sentence without a synonym in the SB: they need to think of a possible substitute themselves (number 6: *bake*). **Stronger students** think of substitutions before looking at the suggested options in the SB.

Tell students to write down a sentence with *make*. Hear some alternatives and compare the meaning in different cases. Ask: *what does 'make' mean in your sentence?* Write up any different meanings on the board.

Ask students to look at the list of synonyms in the SB, page 120, and then to replace *make* in the sentences. Students compare answers in pairs.

Inform students that this list of synonyms can be found in modern dictionaries (this example is from the *Macmillan Essential Dictionary*).

1 causes / produces
2 building
3 manufactured / produced
4 invented / developed / created
5 designed / developed / created

Grammar (SB page 120)

If possible, use any appropriate student utterances that you noted above (Listening exercise 2) as an initial focus on the target language. Put correct or incorrect example(s) on the board. Ask students to tell you the difference between *both* and *neither*, in terms of meaning and form. Let students read the examples and explanations under **Grammar**.

Language note

After *neither of* it is also possible to use a singular verb, eg *Neither of the bananas is ripe*. The singular verb is considered correct but more formal than a plural verb in this case. In current spoken English, the plural verb is more frequent: *Neither of the bananas are ripe*. Note that students may become confused when using this structure with verbs with negative meanings, eg *we hate cabbage* → *we both hate cabbage*, not *neither of us hates cabbage*.

1 Students work in pairs. Do the first example together. If necessary, elicit which sentences are negative to begin with, and therefore use *neither*. Take whole class feedback.

1 Both games are American.
2 Neither of the inventors had a job.
3 Both games are played on a board.
4 Neither game was accepted by toy companies at first.
5 Both games are published in over 25 languages.

2 Ask students to work in pairs. Elicit different topics that could be discussed, putting these on the board. Give additional prompts, if necessary, eg *family*, *transport you use*, *hobbies*, *education*, *home*, *daily routines*, etc. Start the clock!

Students should read out two or three of their most interesting similarities.

Ⓖ Grammar focus

Show students the icon. Write page 150 on the board and ask them to find it. Show students the language summary on *both* and *neither*.

You can use exercise 1 on page 151 for:

a) extra practice now

b) homework

c) review a couple of lessons from now.

The answers are on page 144 of the Teacher's Book.

Vocabulary (SB page 121)

1 Elicit from students the first steps in the procedure of playing Scrabble. Students complete the two texts, initially on their own, then check in pairs. Use the photos (SB page 120) or a real board game to help clarify meaning.

Take whole class feedback and put any relevant language on the board, eg *the object is to …*, *counter*, etc.

Scrabble:	Monopoly:
points	dice
turn	square
board	money
miss a turn	

2 Students look at the photos on this page. Find out if they are familiar with the three games: give the name of the game and students put their hands up if they know it. Students work in pairs to identify the game from the sentences.

1	Snakes and ladders	4	Trivial Pursuit
2	Trivial Pursuit	5	Snakes and ladders
3	Chess	6	Chess

3 Students discuss the questions in pairs. Take some whole class feedback.

Tell students you are going to ask one 'mystery' student to re-explain Scrabble, and another Monopoly (or preferably a different board game, if they know one) to the class. Do not say which students. Give students two minutes to prepare, then nominate two different students to explain one game each, with books closed.

If students tell you about a new board game, encourage them to use the board during the explanation to clarify visually.

Students then work in pairs and tell each other about one game. If students did the lead-in, ensure they are working with a different partner. Listen and check that students are using games language appropriately.

Pronunciation (SB page 121)

1 Students work in pairs to put the words in order. Challenge them to do it as a race: the fastest pair are the winners.

1	Roll the dice.	5	Go again.
2	It's your turn.	6	Whoever rolls highest goes first.
3	Pick a card.	7	Which is your piece?
4	Miss a turn.	8	No cheating!

2 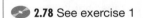 **2.78** Students listen and check, then listen and repeat. These are all spoken phrases so ensure that they sound as natural as possible. Re-drill, as appropriate.

2.78 See exercise 1

Speaking (SB page 121)

Give out a copy of the board game to groups. Let students read the rules on page 131 quietly. This is a useful opportunity for students to read for a purpose, intensively. Clarify 'heads' and 'tails' of a coin. Students play the game.

Try not to intervene too hastily if a procedure-related issue comes up: this forces students to go back to the rules. Monitor and note down any linguistic points of interest, either directly games-related or when they are talking freely, for later feedback.

TEACH GLOBAL THINK LOCAL Extra activity

If you have a game of Scrabble, then experiment with one of the following:

1 Ask one student to select any 10 letters from a bag, without looking: 4 vowels and 6 consonants. Write these chosen letters on the board. Students have 2 minutes in pairs to make as many words as possible. They can re-use the letters in other words.

2 Students work in pairs and receive 10 letters: 4 vowels and 6 consonants. They try and form a word with the highest value, according to the number values on each letter square.

3 Divide up the letters between three groups (of 4–5 students), sharing out the vowels between the groups. Challenge them to form a mini grid of at least three words, with the words intersecting, eg one horizontal and two vertical, as in a crossword.

Function globally: ending a conversation

These lessons in *Global* are designed to provide students with **immediately** useful functional language. They all follow a similar format.

Warm up (SB page 122)

Aim: to introduce the topic via a quick speaking task or picture work.

Tips:

- Do not over-correct here, especially in speaking activities.
- Encourage students to use what language they can at this stage.

Listening (SB page 122)

Aim: to present the functional language in context via a conversation or series of conversations.

Tips:

- Ask students to read the questions first before listening.
- Play the audio all the way through for each task (there are always two tasks).
- For multiple conversations pause the audio after each one.
- If students find it very difficult, play the audio a final time and allow them to read the audioscript at the back of the book.

---

1 🔘 **2.79–2.80**

1 A: Oh, hello, there you are.
   B: Hello.
   A: Listen, I'm afraid there's some bad news.
   B: Oh?
   A: Yes. The thing is, the company is closing.
   B: Really? When?
   A: Tomorrow. The whole thing. It's been sold.
   B: Sold?
   A: Yep.
   B: So … so, what's going to happen to everyone?
   A: There'll be an official announcement. Oh, here's my floor.
   B: Err … I'm still …
   A: Anyway. Sorry to rush off. Talk later, OK?
   B: OK. Bye.
   A: Goodbye. (**situation 4**)

2 A: Phew. Isn't it hot?
   B: Hmm. Sorry?
   A: I said, isn't it hot?
   B: Yes. Yes. Very hot.
   A: I can't remember a summer like this since … since the nineteen seventies.
   B: Yes. It is very hot.
   A: Nineteen seventy-six it was.
   B: I don't really remember, I was quite …young then.
   A: I guess you were. Well, it was so hot that …
   B: Really.
   A: Yes. I was in love then …

   B: Oh look. Here's my floor.
   A: Oh.
   B: Well, I have to go. Nice to talk to you.
   A: Yes, yes.
   B: Goodbye. (**situation 1**)

2
Conversation 1: The boss is very busy. The man feels nervous because the company is closing.
Conversation 2: The woman has good memories of the past. She says she was in love then.

Language focus: ending a conversation (SB page 122)

Aim: to draw students' attention to the items of functional language.

Tips:

- Make sure students have time to understand the form and meaning of the phrases, but you needn't translate them word for word.
- Students should be able to pronounce these phrases intelligibly, so drill them.

---

1 and 2 🔘 **2.81**

1 I'd better be going.
2 I really have to go now.
3 Sorry to rush off.
4 I should be going.

3 🔘 **2.82**

1 I know, I know. It *was* funny. **Anyway** … talk to you tomorrow OK? Yep.
2 … and so that's what we'll do. **Right**, that's it. We'll continue after the break, OK?
3 A: What time does the film start?
   B: Nine o'clock.
   A: Nine o'clock. **OK**, see you then.
   B: OK, bye.
4 **Well**, I think that's it. Yes, I'll send the email. Bye.
5 A: Was there anything else?
   B: No … I don't think so.
   A: **All right**. You can pay over there.
   B: Thanks. Bye
   A: Bye.

Speaking (SB page 122)

Aim: to allow students an opportunity to use this language in a meaningful, real-world context.

Tips:

- There is sometimes a choice of task. Any task involving reading a script will be easier than a task involving making students' own scripts. This gives you flexibility for mixed ability classes.
- Give students time to prepare this activity, and circulate and monitor carefully.
- Correct sensitively, paying particular attention to the target language.
- If time allows, ask students to repeat the task, but with a new partner.

Global voices

These lessons in *Global* are designed to provide students with exposure to authentic speakers of English from both native and non-native English backgrounds. They all follow a similar format.

Warm up (SB page 123)

Aim: to introduce the topic and highlight potentially difficult vocabulary the students will encounter.

Tips:

- Be generous in helping students with the vocabulary here, but let them try and work it out first.
- Circulate and monitor any speaking task, but be careful not to overcorrect.
- Follow up any short discussion pairwork with an open class discussion, asking students to report back what they said.

Listening (SB page 123)

Aim: to expose students to English spoken with a variety of accents.

Tips:

- The first time students listen, tell them you don't expect them to understand every word; some of it will be hard. This is because the text has not been scripted or graded in any way. It's what they would hear in "the real world".
- Pause after each speaker on the second listening, and don't be afraid to replay the whole thing if students appear to need it.
- Students can read the audioscript at the back of the book if you / they wish.
- Try to avoid hunting for specific pronunciation or language errors. In real world communication not everyone speaks perfect English all the time, not even native speakers.

🔊 **2.83–2.89**

Arthur, France: My favourite expression in English is '**Oh my god!**' That's it! Because we heard this expression very often in movie, in television and I think it is a cliché of the English people or American people. Oh my god.

Diego, Italy: There are a lot of very interesting words in English. My favourite word in English is for example '**love**'.

Kristina, Russia: My favourite words in English. I think when I came to England last year everybody said, oh he looks **gorgeous** and it's gorgeous, the weather is gorgeous and so it became my favourite word.

Elodie, Switzerland: My favourite words in English are – I really like the word **perhaps**. I don't know why – because of the sound, because of the pronunciation, I don't know. Perhaps. What else? Well … I don't know.

Semih, Turkey: For me, my favourite words in English are **awesome** and **legendary**. I don't know why because when I say awesome or legendary it makes me feel happy.

Bea, England: My favourite words in English are '**you know**' because they are very useful words. When you are not sure what to say you can use them to fill in a sentence and they are very good words to give you time and so that you can think about, concentrate on what you are thinking, and maybe think of different ideas, you know.

Guy, England: One of my favourite words in English is **harmony**. I think it's a nice word, it's got a nice sound to it. I like the structure of the word. I think the ideas that it represents are very positive whether you are talking about musical harmony or artistic harmony or harmony when people work together well or understand each other well and I think probably there's a similar word in many other languages so it's a word that people understand quite easily.

2 1 movies; 2 are; 3 weather; 4 pronunciation; 5 happy; 6 they give her time to think; 7 it exists in lots of other languages

Language focus: *you know*

Aim: to raise students' awareness of a particular piece of language present in the listening.

Tips:

- This language is not included in tests or reviews, it is here to help students understand international English.
- Don't expect students to produce this language in an exercise or in conversation immediately.

---

1 She talks about use b

2 Suggested possibilities:
1 This is an old card game, you know.
2 I don't feel well, you know, I've got a headache and a sore throat.
3 He won an Olympic medal you know.
4 You know, I had never heard that before.
5 It was a big change in her life, you know. She was never the same again.

Speaking (SB page 123)

Aim: for students to discuss the same or similar questions as the speakers in the listening.

Tips:

- The speaking tasks here are slightly more open to allow for students to explore the subject. Give them time to do this.
- If students are working in pairs, circulate and monitor. Make notes of incorrect language use to correct afterwards (or in a future class).

Writing a report on studies

Reading (SB page 124)

1 Elicit from students where they would like to study if they could have a free 4-week English course anywhere in England. If / when students mention Oxford, ask why. Elicit suggestions such as: *historical, beautiful, university town*, etc. You could bring in pictures of the city to raise interest. Tell student that a young Polish woman called Magdalena studied there, doing a language course. Students read her report for her new English teacher and find out if it was a positive or negative experience for her.

> Yes, because she really liked speaking with her classmates and her teacher was very patient and kind.

2 Tell students that in Oxford the teacher wrote a report on Magdalena about her progress. This exercise checks students' comprehension of the text. Let students compare answers in pairs before whole class feedback.

> Magdalena has completed a <u>one</u>-month course at <u>elementary</u> level. She has worked hard, both in class and after class in the <u>study centre/afternoons</u>. She has made good progress, especially in her <u>speaking</u>. However, she could still improve this, and also needs to work on her <u>grammar</u> and <u>writing</u>.

Language focus: *a/an* for new information (SB page 124)

Tell students there is a missing word in the first sentence of Magdalena's report. Students then find three more places where the indefinite article is missing.

> I stayed with <u>a</u> host family; we studied <u>a</u> book; there was <u>a</u> study centre

Language note

The indefinite article is used with a singular, countable noun when the reference is non-specific; when someone or something is referred to for the <u>first</u> time eg *I studied in <u>a</u> small language school. <u>The</u> school was really good.* The focus is a consolidation of the definite article (SB page 117). Omission of articles when speaking or writing English can sometimes purely be a slip: students may be aware of the rules, but are more concerned with getting the main message across. In addition, indefinite articles are very hard to hear in spoken English.

Writing skills: giving reasons (SB page 124)

Put up the first clause from the example on the board. Elicit possible ways to finish the sentence:
I enrolled on a language course because / as … .

1 Students insert the 'reason clauses' into Magdalena's report. Do the first example together. Allow sufficient time, monitoring to see how much they need. Let them check in pairs. If you have the facilities, project the text onto the board, to facilitate the checking stage in class feedback.

> 1 I stayed with a host family because I wanted to practise speaking outside the class.
> 2 Sometimes I worked there in the afternoons as this is a good way to practise on my own.
> 3 I enjoyed the course very much because the classes were always varied and never boring.
> 4 I should try to speak more as I am quite shy.
> 5 I also need to improve my grammar and writing as I still make a lot of mistakes.

2 Students work alone to complete the two sentences given with a reason. Students write up their reasons on the board, both to check their language and for interest.

> suggested possibilities:
> 1 I need to pass an important exam / it is an important global language
> 2 I don't have enough time / the pronunciation is difficult for me / I have few opportunities to practise it

Preparing to write (SB page 124)

To give authenticity to the task, try to ensure that this report coincides with a term-break, if feasible. Tell students this report will be read and filed by you, as feedback on the course so far; that it may be shown to the course leader / director or their next teacher. This provides students with a genuine reason for writing, as well as justifying the choice of genre: a report. To formalise it further, add this information to the board: *the course code / formal title; the exact dates; tutor(s) full name(s)*, for students to incorporate into the first paragraph. Add this starter sentence, in a different colour: *I have been a student at X (place) for X (length of time).*

Refer students to the **Describing language** section, if necessary highlighting key phrases on the board, with their collocates: *do a lot of X activities; improve X; extend vocabulary; work on X; make progress in X.* Then let students work in pairs but emphasise that this is only the note-taking phase. Some students may prefer to work alone, even at this stage.

Writing (SB page 124)

Students write the first draft of the report in class, individually. Allow them to use dictionaries, and monitor to assist, paying particular attention to articles, where relevant. Given the genre, it would be very appropriate to work the final draft on computer, if possible. This could be assigned as homework.

Global review

These lessons in *Global* are intended to review some of the language and topics covered in the unit. They follow a similar format.

Grammar and Vocabulary (SB page 125)

Aim: to review the main grammar and vocabulary in the unit.

Tips:

- Students can do these exercises alone or in pairs, in class or at home, depending on their learning style and your teaching situation.
- Ask students to read the questions first to establish the grammar and vocabulary areas which are focused on.
- Encourage students to check their own answers by looking back through the unit.

China is *the* largest country in East Asia. *The* Population of China is over 1.3 billion, and *the* capital city is Beijing. One of *the* most famous buildings in Beijing is *the* Forbidden City. This is where *the* last Emperor of China lived, and today it is visited by millions of tourists every year.

Sport is very popular in China, and *the* 2008 Olympic Games were held in Beijing. Every morning many people practise qigong and tai chi chuan in *the* city's parks. Go is another famous game that was invented in China. It is played with counters on a board, and *the* objective is to control *the* largest part of *the* board.

1	brand	5	board
2	underground	6	get
3	cause	7	turn
4	footprint	8	ride

Speaking and Writing

Aim: to provide extra speaking and writing practice that will review and consolidate language presented in the unit.

Tips:

- Before speaking encourage students to think first about what language they need to focus on from the unit, and a good way to start their conversation.
- Before they do the writing practice, ask students to either make notes or discuss ideas with a partner to activate useful language.
- Monitor as students are working and note any points for feedback at the end.

Study skills

Evaluating your pronunciation (SB page 125)

1 Let students read points 1–5 silently. Clarify any words as necessary, eliciting as much as possible from the students themselves, eg *native speaker*, *comprehensible*, *noticeable*, *consonant*, *vowel*, *rhythm*, etc. Students then circle the correct answer for themselves.

After students have discussed the questions in pairs, take whole class feedback. Point out that native speaker pronunciation is unrealistic (question 2).

At the end, point out that being aware of where their problems lie is the first step to improving pronunciation.

2 Students look at the sound chart. After identifying their favourite / least favourite / most difficult English sound, ask students to think of example words containing those sounds.

3 Students as a whole class brainstorm ways of improving their pronunciation onto the board. They compare their ideas with the list given in the book, adding any of their own extra ideas from the board at the end. They tick the ones they have used and underline the ones they'd like to try.

4 Students work in pairs to compare strategies they have used and ones they would like to try. Take whole class feedback: this is a way of raising the profile of both pronunciation and autonomous learning. Help students to make the strategies 'real' and tangible, eg if a student chose 'an area of pronunciation or a sound you want to improve', ask them which sound, etc.

Grammar focus answer key

Unit 1 (SB page 133)
Word order in question forms

1 1 incorrect: Are they from Japan?
  2 correct
  3 incorrect: Did you learn a language at school?
  4 correct
  5 incorrect: Do you like chocolate?
  6 incorrect: How many students are there in the class?

2 1 Where is your family from?
  2 Do you speak any languages?
  3 What is your job? / Do you have a job? / Have you got a job?
  4 Where do you live?
  5 Are you married?
  6 Do you have any children? / Have you got any children?
  7 Do you play any sports?
  8 Who are your favourite writers?
  9 Do you like music? / What music do you like?

What and How questions

1 1 What colour is your car?
  2 How old are you?
  3 What does your teacher look like?
  4 How far is the school from here?
  5 What (sort of / kind of) credit cards have you got? What (sort of / kind of) credit cards do you have?
  6 How often does it rain here?
  7 What's she like?

Present simple, frequency

1 1 They check their email every day.
  2 We hardly ever watch TV in the daytime.
  3 She goes to the cinema once a week.
  4 I sometimes meet colleagues from work at weekends.
  5 He often spends all evening on the internet.
  6 My wife usually gets up before me.
  7 We go out for a meal every Saturday night.

Present continuous

1 1 are you working   2 is living
  3 Do you like   4 prefer   5 works
  6 don't enjoy   7 Do you speak
  8 am taking   9 am learning
  10 aren't planning

Unit 2 (SB page 135)
Countable / uncountable nouns, *some, any*

1 1 any   2 a   3 some   4 some, any
  5 a   6 some   7 some   8 an

a lot of, a little, a few, (not) enough, much, many

1 1 much, little   2 many, A lot
  3 lots of, don't have enough
  4 a few, lots of
2 Students' own answers.

The infinitive with *to*

1 1 to   2 to   3 –   4 to   5 to   6 –   7 to

Infinitives of purpose

1 1 I went to the baker's to buy some bread.
  2 He looked round the café to find a good table.
  3 She smiled at me to show she wasn't angry.
  4 He went into the garden to pick some tomatoes.
  5 We cycled into town to meet our friends.
  6 They organised a party to celebrate her birthday.

Unit 3 (SB page 137)
Past simple and past continuous

1 1 What were people doing in the park at midday yesterday?
  2 Two workers were digging a hole.
  3 A man was reading a newspaper on a bench.
  4 A woman was eating a sandwich – but she wasn't enjoying it.
  5 Two children were playing hide and seek.
  6 An old woman was walking her dog.
  7 Two tourists were taking photos.

2 1 were cleaning, started
  2 she was looking, noticed
  3 was getting, switched
  4 dropped, were carrying
  5 was closing, saw
  6 was painting, fell off

Used to

1 1 used to listen
  2 used to play
  3 didn't use to have
  4 didn't use to go
  5 used to feel
  6 didn't use to like

Unit 4 (SB page 139)
Future hopes and plans

1 1 c   2 f   3 d   4 e   5 b   6 a

Future plans and intentions (*going to*, present continous)

1 1 are going to give
  2 is not going to help
  3 are you going to stop
  4 are we going to feed
  5 are not going to give up
  6 is going to help
  7 am going to fight
  8 are going to destroy

2 1 Where are they holding it?
  2 I'm meeting her (Lisa) after work tomorrow actually.
  3 Where are you going?
  4 He isn't coming round today, I'm afraid.
  5 No, I'm not working at all this weekend.

Prediction and ability (*will, be able to*)

1 1 will   2 will   3 will   4 won't   5 won't
  6 won't   7 will

2 1 are having
  2 will enjoy
  3 are you going to do
  4 will find
  5 's going to be
  6 are you meeting
  7 will happen
  8 'm going to check

Future time clauses

1 1 will start, get   2 do, will cook
  3 will be, read   4 finishes, will go
  5 will be, forgets   6 will send, arrive

Unit 5 (SB page 141)
Have

1 1 had   2 haven't   3 are having
  4 has (got), doesn't have / hasn't got
  5 don't have   6 hasn't
  7 haven't got / don't have / didn't have
  8 Do you have / Have you got

Modal verbs

1 1 a   2 b   3 b   4 a   5 a   6 b

-ing forms

1 1 He can type without looking.
2 We had two weeks of training.
3 She's excited about starting her new job.
4 Looking good is an important part of the job.
5 I hate making tea and coffee at work.
6 She's always reading magazines instead of working.

Present perfect

1 1 Have you ever tried skiing?
Yes, we have been skiing in France twice so far.
2 What have you done with the remote control?
I haven't seen it but your mum has just watched a programme.
3 My son has stopped collecting stamps.
Has he ever thought about collecting coins?
4 Have you been on holiday this year?
I've had a busy year at work so I haven't had any time to relax.
5 She still hasn't finished talking on the phone.
I hope she hasn't called that friend in Brazil.

2 Students' own answers.

3 1 a 2 b 3 b 4 a 5 a 6 b

Unit 6 (SB page 143)
Comparative and superlative adjectives

1

Adjective	Comparative	Superlative
tall	taller	the tallest
hot	hotter	the hottest
safe	safer	the safest
easy	easier	the easiest
expensive	more expensive	the most expensive
good	better	the best
sad	sadder	the saddest
cheap	cheaper	the cheapest
beautiful	more beautiful	the most beautiful
heavy	heavier	the heaviest

Comparative adjectives (*a bit, much, as ... as*)

1 1 He is more patient with the children than her.
2 She is happier now than (she was) last year.
3 Most people get a bit fatter when they get older.
4 I sleep better in my own bed than in a hotel.
5 Money isn't as important as health.
6 This chair is much more comfortable than that one.
7 Some new robots are as intelligent as humans.
8 My home computer starts more slowly than my work computer.

Superlatives

1 1 highest 2 strangest
3 most expensive 4 fastest
5 most popular 6 best

Phrasal verbs and objects

1 1 it down 2 it in 3 them off / out
4 it in 5 it up 6 it down
7 them up 8 it down

Unit 7 (SB page 145)
Present perfect with *for* and *since*

1 1 since 2 for 3 for 4 since 5 for
6 since 7 since 8 for

2 1 have been 2 produced
3 have used 4 cooked
5 have been 6 started
7 has been 8 said

Present perfect with *yet* and *already*

1 1 A: Have you paid the electricity bill yet?
B: No, but I've already paid the water bill.
2 A: We haven't heard about that loan yet.
B: I've already called the bank twice about it.
3 A: We've already spent all our money for this month.
B: Oh dear, have you checked the lottery ticket yet?
4 A: Our railway shares have already made a profit.
B: Good but the water shares haven't improved yet.
5 A: Have you had the letter about your inheritance yet?
B: No, the solicitor hasn't sent anything yet.

2 1 Tom has lived in Germany **since** he was a child.
2 Has Emma (**already**) got married (**already**)?
3 He hasn't done his homework **yet**.
4 They **finished** the book yesterday.
5 She's worked here **for** three months.
6 We haven't done this **yet**.

Unit 8 (SB page 147)
The passive voice

1 1 The Empire State Building in New York was used in the *King Kong* film.
2 The two Emirates Towers in Dubai are connected to a huge shopping centre.
3 30 St Mary Axe in London is called 'the Gherkin' by Londoners.
4 Sydney Opera House was built to look like a ship.
5 The Guggenheim Museum in Bilbao is often compared to a fish or water.
6 The Petronas Towers in Kuala Lumpur are occupied by international companies.
7 The new Jewish museum in Berlin was designed by the architect Daniel Libeskind.
8 The Pompidou Centre in Paris was named after a French president.

2 1 The flats were built in the 1980s.
2 The building is called 'Huntingdon House.'
3 The building is surrounded by restaurants and cafés.
4 The walls in our flat were painted white.
5 A new kitchen was put in last year (by us).

First conditional

1 1 give, will you send
2 will call, see
3 haven't got / don't have, you can't get
4 might take, has
5 is, can go
6 go out, won't have to
7 won't listen, doesn't tell
8 doesn't work, will complain

Second conditional

1 1 if you were 2 I'd go
3 if my boss gave me
4 I'd go walking 5 if I did
6 if you explained

2 1 b 2 e 3 c 4 d 5 a 6 f

Unit 9 (SB page 149)

Modal verbs of advice

1 1 shouldn't worry about it.
 2 should go and see your doctor.
 3 should drink more water.
 4 you should drink so / as much coffee.
 5 should go to bed earlier / shouldn't go to bed so late.

Could / couldn't, had to / didn't have to

1 1 couldn't   **2** had to   **3** had to
 4 didn't have to   **5** could   **6** couldn't
 7 had to   **8** couldn't / didn't have to

Past perfect

1 1 She was tired because she had run 20km.
 2 When I had finished playing tennis, I took a shower.
 3 The swimmer lost his medal because he had failed a drugs test.
 4 Before she won the race, she had been optimistic.
 5 After the referee had sent a player off, the team played with ten men.
 6 She paid a fine because she had hurt another player.

Reported statements

4 1 I had woken up that morning and I had had problems getting out of bed.
 2 I had had that problem before.
 3 I had never experienced that before.
 4 she was just going to take a look.
 5 would feel a pain.
 6 hurt but that my back felt much better.

Unit 10 (SB page 151)

Defining relative clauses

1 1 who / that   **2** where   **3** which / that
 4 which / that   **5** who / that   **6** where

Definite article (*the*)

1 1 a   **2** the   **3** the   **4** the   **5** a
 6 The   **7** -

Verb form review

1 1 could, was invented   **2** flew
 3 were making, became
 4 built, had watched   **5** made
 6 have ordered   **7** is planning
 8 goes, will be

Both, neither

1 1 Both (of the) friends live in a big city.
 2 Neither friend / Neither of the friends / Neither of them is married.
 3 Neither friend / Neither of the friends / Neither of them has a car.
 4 Both (of the) friends own property.
 5 Both (of the) friends enjoy playing chess.
 6 Both (of the) friends have written / They've both written books but neither book / neither of their books has been published.

Global Teacher's Resource CD

The Global Teacher's Resource CD includes a comprehensive range of resources

The Communication activities section contains a number of photocopiable worksheets for classroom use provided as printable PDFs. There are two worksheets directly linked with the content of each of the units in the Coursebook. In addition, there are generic worksheets appropriate for different points of the course (e.g. beginning of the year)

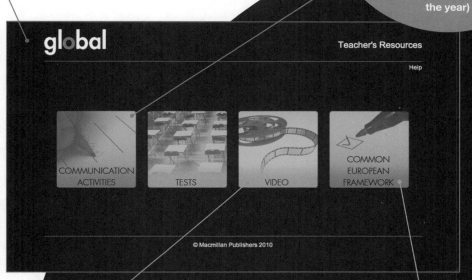

global   Teacher's Resources

                                                              Help

COMMUNICATION
ACTIVITIES   TESTS   VIDEO   COMMON
                                           EUROPEAN
                                           FRAMEWORK

© Macmillan Publishers 2010

Also included are video clips for classroom use, with their corresponding worksheets and teacher's notes provided as printable PDFs.

Each level of Global is mapped against the corresponding level in the Common European Framework

The Teacher's Resource CD also contains numerous Global-related tests for use in class.

global   Tests Menu

home   Help

PLACEMENT &   UNIT TESTS   PROGRESS   END-OF-YEAR
DIAGNOSTIC   TESTS   TESTS
TESTS

© Macmillan Publishers 2010